THE RISE AND FALL OF MC
IN THE UNITED STATES AND CANADA

In *The Rise and Fall of Moral Conflicts in the United States and Canada*, sociologist Mildred A. Schwartz and political scientist Raymond Tatalovich bring their disciplinary insights to the study of moral issues. Beginning with prohibition, Schwartz and Tatalovich trace the phases of its evolution from emergence, establishment, decline and resurgence, to resolution. Prohibition's life history generates a series of hypotheses about how passage through each of the phases affected subsequent developments and how these were shaped by the political institutions and social character of the United States and Canada.

Using the history of prohibition in North America as a point of reference, the authors move on to address the anticipated progression and possible resolution of six contemporary moral issues: abortion, capital punishment, gun control, marijuana, pornography, and same-sex relations. Schwartz and Tatalovich build a new theoretical approach by drawing from scholarship on agenda setting, mass media, social movements, and social problems. *The Rise and Fall of Moral Conflicts in the United States and Canada* provides new insights into how moral conflicts develop and interact with their social and political environment.

MILDRED A. SCHWARTZ is professor emerita in the Department of Sociology at the University of Illinois Chicago and visiting scholar, New York University.

RAYMOND TATALOVICH is a professor in the Department of Political Science at Loyola University Chicago.

The Rise and Fall of Moral Conflicts in the United States and Canada

MILDRED A. SCHWARTZ AND
RAYMOND TATALOVICH

UNIVERSITY OF TORONTO PRESS
Toronto Buffalo London

© University of Toronto Press 2018
Toronto Buffalo London
www.utorontopress.com
Printed in Canada

ISBN 978-1-4426-3726-9 (cloth)   ISBN 978-1-4426-2883-0 (paper)

∞ Printed on acid-free, 100% post-consumer recycled paper with
vegetable-based inks.

Library and Archives Canada Cataloguing in Publication

Schwartz, Mildred A., 1932–, author
The rise and fall of moral conflicts in the United States
and Canada / Mildred A. Schwartz and Raymond Tatalovich.

Includes bibliographical references and index.
ISBN 978-1-4426-3726-9 (cloth). – ISBN 978-1-4426-2883-0 (paper)

1. Canada – Moral conditions – History – 20th century.   2. Canada –
Moral conditions – History – 21st century.   3. United States – Moral
conditions – History – 20th century.   4. United States – Moral
conditions – History – 21st century.   5. Canada – Social conditions –
20th century.   6. Canada – Social conditions – 21st century.   7. United
States – Social conditions – 20th century.   8. United States – Social
conditions – 21st century.   I. Tatalovich, Raymond, author.   II. Title.

HN110.M6S33 2018   306.0971   C2017-906330-8

This book has been published with the help of a grant from the Federation
for the Humanities and Social Sciences, through the Awards to Scholarly
Publications Program, using funds provided by the Social Sciences and
Humanities Research Council of Canada.

University of Toronto Press acknowledges the financial assistance to its
publishing program of the Canada Council for the Arts and the Ontario
Arts Council, an agency of the Government of Ontario.

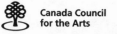

ONTARIO ARTS COUNCIL
CONSEIL DES ARTS DE L'ONTARIO
an Ontario government agency
un organisme du gouvernement de l'Ontario

Contents

Preface

This volume is coauthored by a sociologist who studies politics and organizations and a political scientist who specializes in public policy analysis. Schwartz and Tatalovich first met in the late 1960s, as teacher-student, in a graduate class on electoral politics at the University of Chicago during the period when behavioralism was beginning to become integrated into mainstream political science. At that time the University of Chicago offered doctoral students in political science a choice of being examined in the subfield of political sociology, which shows how much political science was indebted to sociology. And even today, the University of Chicago encourages interdisciplinary work, including a political sociology specialization within the Department of Sociology. This project revisits that kind of close interdisciplinary collaboration.

In 1981 Tatalovich coauthored arguably the first case study of abortion politics in the United States, and in the same year Schwartz published an article comparing three moral conflicts in the United States and Canada. As in most subsequent research on morality policy, their primary concern in each case was the emergence and politicization of moral conflicts. Their limited time perspective, however, did not allow for speculation about the resolution of those volatile controversies. Although more research spanning decades has been dedicated to morality policy, especially on abortion and gay rights in Canada and the United States, no scholarship has yet broached the question of when (if ever) and how moral conflicts are ended without undue social trauma and political turbulence. This volume addresses the missing pieces of the morality policy puzzle by looking within the life histories of evolving moral conflicts to the point where resolution may become possible. Those life histories are viewed, in part, through the lenses provided by the literatures on agenda setting in policy analysis and on social movements and collective action in sociology. But neither the research on policy termination in policy studies nor the sociological work on the evolution of social problems provides much theoretical guidance to unearthing the processes by which intense moral conflicts are settled. Some moral conflicts may "die" because of authoritative decision making by legislatures, courts, or the executive; others may fade for quite different reasons; and some, despite legal resolution, may reappear. Still others may display a formidable resistance to resolution. Why these differences exist should come to light through our analysis of the phases through which issues pass. Those phases reveal the contingent nature of issue life histories, where what occurs at each point in time continues to affect subsequent outcomes.

We are indebted to many individuals on both sides of the border who facilitated our collaboration and helped bring this project to fruition. A special thanks goes to Jennifer Stegen, inter-library loan librarian at Loyola University Chicago, who obtained a seemingly endless number of books and articles, and to Benjamin Aldred, reference and government information librarian, who secured access to the online historical records of the *Globe and Mail*. Our extensive use of US opinion surveys was made possible by accessing the Roper Center for Public Opinion polling archives with the kind and able assistance of Lois E. Timms-Ferrara, associate director, and Marc G. Maynard, director of technical services, when Roper was housed at the University of Connecticut (since then Roper has relocated to Cornell University). Ready access to the election manifestos for the major Canadian political parties was eased by the historical archive maintained by Professor François Petry at Laval University.

Daniel Quinlan, our editor at the University of Toronto Press, was pivotal in moving us toward a successful conclusion. The manuscript was immeasurably improved by the recommendations made by two anonymous reviewers. We are grateful for their insights, suggestions, and encouragement. We wish to express our appreciation to faculty and staff in the Department of Sociology at New York University for providing the ideal environment for scholarship and writing, and particularly to Andrew D'Amico for good-natured technical assistance. Finally, we acknowledge Loyola University Chicago's subvention to partly underwrite the costs of producing this volume, for which we extend a special thanks to Tracy Foxworth of the Office of Research Services.

THE RISE AND FALL OF MORAL CONFLICTS
IN THE UNITED STATES AND CANADA

Chapter One

Why Moral Conflicts Matter

At the most basic level, all societies are normative systems that distinguish right from wrong and good from bad. Although, typically, normative systems are deeply embedded in social life and retain great stability over time, they are rarely unchanging or uniformly embraced by all societal members. As societies respond to their internal dynamics and external pressures, norms change along with them. New norms emerge and old ones fade or disappear; some become more salient, others less so; some generate dissent, others broad compliance; some arouse passionate feelings, others conditional acceptance or indifference; and some become associated with issues that demand a response, whether through institutionalized processes or possibly violent actions. Because a changing normative milieu brings highly charged, conflict-inducing issues into the political arena, those issues call our attention, both as social scientists and as citizens, to the need for identifying when and how political systems are able to resolve moral conflicts. The central concern of this volume is developing a scheme for explaining the fate of moral conflicts.

The political arena, at its most basic level, is where the dominant normative order is enforced. How this happens varies, depending on which moral issues are selected for enforcement, the freedom accorded to dissent and dissenters, the avenues available to express dissent, and the institutional confines in which moral conflicts are played out. The relation between norms of morality, their embodiment in issues, and their potential for becoming politicized leads us to explore two interrelated problems: how moral issues become politicized and how their fate can be explained. We look for answers in their historical trajectory, from the time they emerge and through the various phases they may pass as their life histories unfold. It is within these phases that we find the factors that facilitate or impede eventual resolution. Our analysis is based on a selection of issues that have been, or continue to be, highly contentious in both Canada and the United States.

We begin by assessing what has come to be called morality politics. In the following section we examine how moral issues compare to what is believed to be the more normal set of issues that make up the political agenda of developed societies. Those "normal" issues fit along a left-right dimension that subsumes economic, social welfare, and international policies in ways that do not apply to moral issues. Conversely, it is possible to argue that all policy matters, including those conventionally given a position on a left-right scale, have an essentially moral content because they express normative preferences about what makes a good society and what are that society's rightful pathways. We conclude by summarizing the principal characteristics of morality politics, opening the way to justify selecting specific issues to test our expectations about their life histories.

The section following examines how the life history of moral issues has been approached from different disciplinary perspectives, particularly those of sociology and political science, and what remains missing from them. Five processes are identified, beginning with the origin and emergence of an issue. That process may be followed by any of the following: establishment and legitimation, decline in salience or impact, resurgence, and resolution. None of these subsequent processes are inevitable nor do they imply a linear or cyclical progression.[1] Instead, we propose a contingent theory of issue processes, in which possible outcomes depend, for example, on conditions at the time in which an issue emerges to prominence, how interests are mobilized, what resources are available to proponents and opponents, and the obstacles and opportunities encountered.

Defining Moral Issues

Historians and other scholars have long been interested in political conflicts over moral issues. More recently, what has come to be called morality politics has aroused new interest among social scientists who

---

1 This is analogous to Hilgartner and Bosk's (1988: 54) theory of social problems, which does not assume a "natural history" of issue development.

look at the range of issues that are both moralized and politicized, identify their common characteristics, and debate whether they deserve classification as a special type of policy. Different disciplines tend to use different terminology, with sociology and psychology more inclined to refer to issues, and more specifically, social issues (Wurgler and Brooks 2014), and political scientists to policies. In addition, sociologists who write about social problems also capture elements of our own interest in moral issues (Best 2012). We accommodate disciplinary-specific usages by recognizing their common concerns.

In the United States moral conflicts have been popularized as "culture wars" between "progressive" and "orthodox" worldviews (Hunter 1991), which can pose threats to consensus building, political stability, and even public civility (Hunter 1994). Because religious beliefs often underlie these debates, moral conflicts have occurred more frequently in the United States[2] than in Canada or the more secular countries of Europe (Studlar 2001). Moral conflicts have most usually surfaced in those countries where religious-based and secular political parties oppose each other (Engeli, Green-Pedersen, and Larsen 2012).

Early work by Christoph (1962a; 1962b), on the abolition of capital punishment in Britain, helped define the parameters of morality issues and policies. Along with capital punishment, Cristoph added birth control, prostitution, and homosexuality as "emotional issues that plumb deep-seated moral codes" which "party leaders find uncomfortable to handle" because they are so unpredictable (Christoph 1962a: 173). Anticipating what later voting analysts (Carmines and Stimson 1980) would uncover, Christoph (1962a: 171) observed that "emotional issues are likely to be 'popular' issues in the sense that the layman feels at home with them and competent to pronounce upon them. They evoke widespread public interest of a sort not present when technical or more mundane questions are raised in politics."

Among later work that expands the list of issues and morality policy characteristics is that of Mooney (2001: 3). He includes abortion, capital punishment, gambling, homosexual rights, pornography, physician-assisted suicide, and sex education as morality policies. His selection is premised on the argument that these issues involve debates over "first

---

2 Reimer (1995) shows how the comparatively greater vibrancy of religion in the United States is a cultural attribute that exists apart from religious practices.

principles" that are "no less than legal sanctions of right and wrong, validations of particular sets of fundamental values." Engeli and her associates (2012: 26) limit morality policies to "fundamental decisions about death, marriage and reproduction," and thus restrict their cases studies to abortion, assisted reproductive technologies, embryo and stem-cell research, euthanasia, and same-sex marriage. A more expansive fourfold definition, based on policies, by Heichel, Knill, and Schmitt (2013: 330) is also germane. It moves the boundary lines outward to encompass life-and-death issues (abortion, assisted suicide, stem cell research), sexual behavior (homosexuality, same-sex recognition, prostitution, pornography), "addictive behavior or substances" like gambling and drug use, as well as "all policies defining public limitations on individual self-determination," for example, gun control. In Studlar's (2001: 46) inventory, similarly focused on policies, he lists all morality policies affecting twenty-two North American and Western European nations. He presents thirteen issues: abortion, gambling, alcohol/drugs, religious education/Sunday observance, animal rights, homosexuality, capital punishment, pornography, divorce, euthanasia, women's rights, ethnic/racial minorities, and gun control. According to his accounting, all thirteen issues surfaced in the United States at one time or another, while Canada experienced them all except animal rights and divorce.

Among political scientists, the approach to morality politics has been shaped by concern with the best way to classify policies. They confront Lowi's (1964) influential typology of policy types – distribution, regulation, and redistribution (with constituency added later [Lowi 1972]) – in order to incorporate the apparently distinctive features of moral issues. For example, Smith's (1975) adaptation added attention to "emotive symbolic" policies that

> generate emotional support for deeply held values, but unlike the other [policy] types considered in this work, the values sought are essentially noneconomic. Rather, they are "way of life" issues, and as a result they easily arouse the most intense political passions. This is hardly surprising when the conflict takes place over such issues as the death penalty, prayer in the public schools, abortion legislation, laws relating to homosexuality, and segregation in public schools and commercial establishments. (90)

He concludes that emotive symbolic policies provoke "high levels of intensity and broad scopes of conflict, for they activate large numbers of citizens who feel deeply about the particular issues in question." Moreover, "people may be misinformed" but nonetheless "have strong views regarding the correctness of the issues." Sociologists, as well, recognize that emotions are stimulated through the dramatic presentation of issues (Hilgartner and Bosk 1988: 61–2).

Lowi (1988) himself later acknowledged the need to revise his typology. But in doing so, he rejected the assumption that moral issues are distinctive because they do not involve economic interests. For example, he resisted Tatalovich and Daynes's (1981, 221–8; 1988, 1–4) argument that moral conflicts are a variant of regulatory policy dealing with social regulations rather than economic ones. Instead, Lowi (2011) argued that moralizing can radicalize *any* policy type. In taking this position, Lowi moved morality politics close to recent scholarship in political psychology on "moral convictions" and Moral Foundations Theory (MFT).[3] Political scientists now had a new link with "moral mandates," which are manifested as attitudes held with moral conviction. Such moral convictions "do not require reason or evidence. People at times judge moral and immoral, right and wrong, on the basis of deeply visceral and intuitive, rather than deliberative, cognitive processes that they support with post hoc rather than a priori reasoning" (Skitka and Mullen 2002: 36). Those who hold such feelings have difficulty in working with those who do not (Skitka et al. 2005: 914) and care most about achieving their goals, regardless of the means used (Skitka 2002).

To this point we have identified two characteristics of morality politics: the issues and related policies that embody them involve contested values that provoke strong emotional reactions and those who hold to those values are unwilling to compromise. The assumption is that, when the nature of value conflicts prevents compromise, this leads to political polarization. This connection is fundamental to Lowi's (1988; 2011) contention that the ability to negotiate over economic disputes, a

---

3 MFT is based on five psychological foundations (Harm, Fairness, In-group, Authority, and Purity), and researchers find that liberals and conservatives emphasize different values in making their moral judgments (Clifford and Jerit 2013; Graham et al. 2009; McAdams et al. 2008; Haidt and Graham 2007). These MFT values, and especially Purity, were stronger predictors than political ideology of attitudes toward same-sex relations, same-sex marriage, euthanasia, pornography, animal testing, cloning, and gambling (Koleva et al. 2012: 187).

feature of "mainstream" politics, is transformed by moral rhetoric into a "radical" politics that is immune to compromise.[4]

Another characteristic of morality politics appears to be that issues inspiring conflict are distinctly non-economic in nature. As we noted earlier, this was a position rejected by Lowi. His view that moralizing can radicalize any type of policy finds support in recent scholarship on "moral convictions" by Ryan (2014). He expanded previous research based on putatively moral issues, for example, abortion, capital punishment, marijuana legalization, and building new nuclear power plants (Skitka et al. 2005), to also include purely economic issues. Ryan (2014: 385) found that, although more survey respondents chose stem cell research and gay marriage rather than collective bargaining rights, Social Security reform, or the Afghanistan War as having moral content, in varying degrees all these issues were viewed in moralistic terms by some people. The same applied to such apparently non-moral issues as education and health care (Ryan 2014: 389). He concluded that "characteristically moral responses are more likely on some issues than others, but there is considerable variability even within particular issues, and some issues not widely regarded as moral are moralized for some people" (ibid.: 392–3).

Meier (1994: 246–7) introduced a further characteristic, depending on whether moral arguments are one-sided (the "politics of sin") or two-sided (the redistribution of values). One-sided morality policy issues, like murder, drug abuse, or drunk driving, have no one voicing an opposition position. But two-sided ones can provoke moral arguments for either position. For example, abortion arouses arguments, on one side, about the immorality of destroying innocent life, while the other side is equally passionate about the ethics of self-autonomy and personal choice. This distinction may not be essential to defining morality politics, but the one-sided or two-sided quality of a moral conflict has relevance for its comparative contentiousness and its persistence on the policy agenda.

A further attribute is the ease with which most people feel that they understand the substance of moral issues. That is, moral conflicts are "soft" rather than "hard" issues (Carmines and Stimson 1980) because

---

4 There is, however, disagreement over whether moral conflicts polarize public opinion as much as they do elite attitudes (Fiorina 2010; Williams 1997; Davis and Robinson 1996; DiMaggio, Evans, and Bryson 1996). In addition, in reviewing value positions among the general public, Baker (2005) argues there is considerable consensus.

people do not need much knowledge or expertise in order to express an opinion to which they are committed.

Another basic characteristic of moral issues is their salience. That is, people are aware of and care about them. Wurgler and Brooks (2014) find evidence of salience in the strong effect that social issues have on voter choice and on election outcomes in presidential races between 1992 and 2012. Because saliency implies that ordinary citizens can be readily mobilized around an issue, we can anticipate that there will be a heightened electoral anxiety among political leaders who must make policy decisions. Salience, however, is not easily measured directly, perhaps because salience and importance may not be synonymous. For example, Dearing and Rogers (1996: 8) define salience as "the degree to which an issue on the agenda is perceived as relatively important." Yet, when Mooney and Schuldt (2008) tested the ability of contested values, unwillingness to compromise, technical simplicity, and saliency to distinguish among fourteen issues through polling data, their conflation of saliency with importance proved unproductive. Overall, gay marriage and abortion were unequivocally termed morality policies and, to a lesser degree, so were capital punishment and casino gambling. With the possible exception of crime or race relations (especially during the 1960s), only the smallest fraction of the US public asked its opinion has ever judged issues of morality to be the "most important" problem facing the nation (Smith 1980; Gallup 2014).

When we move from the characteristics of moral issues to their substantive content we find strong agreement among previous researchers. Issues they select come from a narrow family of value positions. For the most part, these deal with life and death, sex and reproduction, and stigmatized individual behaviors (Knill et al. 2015; Studlar et al. 2013). Despite the proposition that any issue can be moralized, we find little attention to economic issues and we will follow that approach.[5]

Guided in our search by the requirements of value conflicts, uncompromising positions, "softness" or relative simplicity, and salience, we have selected for analysis six contemporary issues that have disturbed

5 We recognize that openness to a broader range of issues, especially those relating to social welfare, has the potential to yield additional insights. For example, contested values, unwillingness to compromise, relative simplicity, and great public salience all characterize current healthcare politics in the United States. In Canada, where the issue has been largely resolved, people identify the existence of national healthcare as a positive value characterizing Canadian nationhood.

the social and political fabric in both countries: abortion, capital punishment, gun control, marijuana use, pornography, and same-sex relations. We go back in time to include the case of prohibition because it allows us to survey all phases of the life span of a moral issue, including its final resolution. Prohibition is discussed separately in the next chapter and lays the groundwork for expectations about the development of moral issues more generally. Descriptions of the six issues that represent our sample are found in the chapter following.

Life Histories

Emergence

External and internal societal shocks, instigating challenges to old values and the emergence of new ones, underlie the birth of moral conflicts. Wars, economic upheavals, mass migrations, and other sources of major demographic shifts and the ensuing competition among population groups all bring with them the potential for unsettling social changes reflected in political contention.

The United States and Canada, from the beginning of the twentieth century onward,[6] were disturbed by major wars: the First World War in Europe, the Second World War in Europe and the Far East, the Korean War, and, more central to the United States, wars in Vietnam, Iraq, and Afghanistan. Ramifications from those wars, as well as events leading up to them, included mass migrations into both Canada and the United States and the advent of the Cold War. They also raised new questions about prevailing relations among different ethnic, religious, and racial groups. Economic dislocations occurred at intervals, with especially drastic force at the time of the Great Depression. The shift from rural to urban centers proceeded with the creation of suburban communities and the economic decline of inner cities. From the end of the Second World War onward, scientific advances revolutionized medicine and industry. Mass public education was vastly increased, with great numbers of young people entering institutions of higher education. Women were now a permanent and increasing part of the workforce, changing

---

6 By adopting this timeframe we avoid the issue of slavery, which was, in any case, primarily a US problem, and use that as license to largely sidestep the whole area of civil rights as it applies to African Americans.

the nature of family life. Established centers of authority, whether stemming from the state, religion, or dominant ethnic groups, were more readily challenged.[7] The opportunities, suffering, competition, and grievances that these and related changes brought with them then stimulated new or enhanced concerns with moral problems.

Ongoing social changes in the United States, associated with the civil rights movement and the student movements of the 1960s, began an era of contentious politics and social upheaval that was also manifested in Canada and elsewhere by what have been called "new" movements, like those of students, women, anti-war groups, and environmentalists (Meyer and Tarrow 1998). They were considered new because they were no longer primarily concerned with old issues of class, as had been the case with labor movements. What they did was bring new issues, or new ways of conceiving old ones, into the public domain.

New social movements also brought with them a "rights revolution" (Epp 1998; Scheingold 1974), where the favored method of dealing with moral conflicts became litigation and reliance on judicial activism. This new reliance on the courts for obtaining redress began in the United States but spread to Canada after its adoption of the Charter of Rights and Freedoms in 1982.

Consequences from these varied social and cultural upheavals have been found in value changes in the United States as well as more broadly in the industrialized world. Researchers, led by Ronald Inglehart (1990; 1997; also Inglehart and Welzel 2005), point to the advent of "post-materialist values," manifested as a shift in values dominated by economic and political security to ones emphasizing personal autonomy and self-expression.[8] In Canada, Neil Nevitte (1996) argued that value changes had brought about a decline in public deference and was producing a more permissive society in which individuals desire autonomy from social hierarchies and governmental interference.

Several efforts have been made to conceptualize how new issues, leading to moral conflicts, emerge. Although he addressed the determinants of collective behavior rather than the emergence of new issues,

---

7 For an excellent overview of population changes in the United States see Hout and Fischer (2006) and, for a similar one for Canada, see Edmonston and Fong (2011).

8 Inglehart and Baker (2000), however, caution against generalizing that even vast societal changes totally undermine traditional values.

Smelser's (1962: 15–17) early, and once influential, approach,[9] includes three elements that, in combination, are relevant to moral issues: structural conduciveness, structural strain, and precipitating factors. Conduciveness, in general, defines the boundaries of the possible, that is, it encompasses those features of social structure that allow conflicts to be expressed. In particular, he directs us to ask whether existing structural arrangements encourage overt hostility while restraining other kinds of protest (ibid.: 384). Strain is the result of changes that produce "ambiguities, deprivations, conflicts, and discrepancies" among social groups based on race, class, religion, partisanship, or other animosities that fuel collective outbursts. Precipitants, better known in the policy literature as triggering events, refer to specific events that provide the fuse for conflict to appear.

In their work on agenda setting, Cobb and Elder (1972, 84–5) postulated that there must be a link between some grievance or "triggering event" and social activists that converts a social problem into a political issue. Similarly, John Kingdon (2010: 94–5) points to "focusing events" like "a crisis or disaster that comes along to call attention to the problem, a powerful symbol that catches on, or the personal experience of a policy maker." Triggering events may be so traumatic that they ignite a social movement. During the early stage of mass mobilization, argues Claus Offe (1990, 236), one ingredient "from which a movement emerges is a widely publicized and highly visible event (or anticipation of an event) that triggers expressions of opinion and protest and helps to define the collectivity of those who are actually or potentially affected by it." Among such recognized triggers for the civil rights movement were the refusal by Rosa Parks to move to the back of the bus and the Montgomery bus boycott of 1955 and, for the gay rights movement, the Stonewall Riots in 1969. Similarly, Walsh and Warland (1983: 775) describe how the Three Mile Island accident fueled mobilization against nuclear power.

---

9 Reasons for the decline in Smelser's influence are related to changes in the field of social movements that directed attention away from grievances and toward resource mobilization and opportunity structures. In addition, current researchers do not accord much attention or importance to precipitating events as major factors leading to the emergence of social movements. Whatever the merit of those later approaches, they do not totally detract from the significance of grievances arising from social changes (Smelser's structural strains) or the possible impact of particular events (Smelser's precipitants) for the emergence of contested issues.

With or without such triggering events, the major source of new issues is the disruptions caused by major social changes, the perspective adopted today by most students of social movements. This is compatible with the position taken by Carmines and Stimson (1989: 5–9), who view the political fate of issues through an evolutionary lens. Their concepts of external disruptions, local variations, and internal contradictions are all Darwinian forms of origination that are compatible with our own view that issues originate from the pressures arising from external and internal environmental changes and dislocations. External disruptions include crises, wars, depressions, and terrorism. Local variations, with "diverse specialized settings" (Carmines and Stimson 1989: 8), give rise to new species of issues in the sense of producing a unique issue definition. Internal contradictions are a source of disequilibrium that challenges the dominance of other issues, a fate that often affects party coalitions. In addition, they assign the most important mechanism accounting for issue emergence to the role played by strategic politicians. Specifically, it is out-of-power politicians who deliberately search for the kind of issue that will give them electoral attention. Actions by such politicians enhance the likelihood that the issues they select, regardless of how they otherwise emerged, will continue. That is, the spur to issue continuity is linked to when issues become a component of partisan politics. It is for this reason that they pay so much attention to strategic politicians who guarantee that politicization.[10]

Given that social existence is an ongoing encounter with changing environments and troubling experiences, and hence a world filled with multiple problems, some social scientists have tended to avoid emphasis on issue emergence itself. For example, Downs (1972: 39) draws attention to the "pre-problem stage" of an "issue-attention cycle," where a problem exists and may be recognized by experts or interest groups but does not attract public attention. Hilgartner and Bosk (1988), who deal with social problems in general rather than with moral issues, begin from the position that there are an unlimited number of problems. Out of that universe, only some will come to engage public attention. Their emphasis is then on the process of competitive selection among problems. Baumgartner and Jones (2009), anchored in a policy perspective, also see multiple issues vying for attention and attribute selection to

---

10 For us, this relationship bears more on the establishment rather than the emergent phase of issues and is consequently discussed in the following section.

political competition that ends with placing only some on the policy-making agenda.

The preceding observations suggest that the emergent stage of moral issues may be difficult to define. Yet we persist in looking for signs of emergence because we see the need for some recognition that a problem exists before it can be a source of conflict or subject to remediation. We find evidence for the emergence of moral issues in initial newspaper coverage and early signs of concern in public opinion data. In chapter 5, we ask how emergence is related to larger social changes and to the advent of triggering events. Following Downs (1972), we will also be alert to the statements and activities of those with special interest in particular issues. That will allow us to observe how emergence is tied to existing social movements, interest groups, and/or to specific demographic groups.

Establishment

We understand moral issues to be established when they are widespread topics of political concern. Ultimately this means that they are now part of the policy agenda, forcing partisan actors to take a position. The pathways through which moral issues become established in this fashion involve the public, the media, and government, all interacting with each other.

One of the most influential perspectives on agenda setting is elaborated by Kingdon (2010) through his conception of three streams – problem, policy, and political – that converge in policy windows of relatively short duration. The identification of a problem is most likely to be addressed when it has some policy solution that can be acted on politically. The likelihood and kind of political actions taken will be affected by the partisan makeup of the government, the influence of interest groups, and an otherwise unspecified public mood (ibid.: 152–72). Kingdon goes on to say: "Basically, a window opens because of change in the political stream (e.g., a change of administration, a shift in the partisan or ideological distribution of seats in Congress, or a shift in the national mood); or it opens because a new problem captures the attention of government officials and those close to them" (168).

Missing from Kingdon's formulation is a place for the media and a strong role for public opinion, the two components basic to theories of agenda setting in the field of communications (Dearing and Rogers 1996). Soroka (2002a) overcomes these omissions through a more comprehensive approach, assigning each component – public, media, and policy – its own agenda where relevant actors can develop their specific preferences. Two underlying hypotheses emerge that are directly applicable to our search for the relation between agenda setting and the inclusion of moral issues: "(1) different issues display different agenda-setting dynamics, and (2) this variance in dynamics is linked to issue attributes" (ibid.: 269).

With added issues in further work, Soroka (2002b) divided them into three categories: "prominent" issues (inflation, unemployment), "sensational" ones (AIDS, crime, and environment), and "government" ones (debt/deficit, national unity, and taxes). Although he included none dealing with morality policies, "sensational" issues come closest to embodying some attributes of moral conflict, most notably when AIDS first emerged.[11] Hypothesizing that each type of issue involves a different agenda-setting process, he argues that sensational issues are "media driven" because "they will generally not be obtrusive" and "will probably, but not necessarily, lend themselves to dramatic events" (ibid.: 118).

Our own approach to agenda setting rests on the three domains in Soroka's model but with an expansion of the policy agenda and more nuanced approaches to both the public and the media agendas. By policy, Soroka means the instruments of government that can propose, enact, and enforce policies. He confines these to the executive and legislative branches, their committees, the political parties that operate within them, and the bureaucracy. Our intent is to look at political parties not only in terms of consensual statements of policy preferences but also, in company with Carmines and Stimson (1989), at the actions of strategic politicians who may take more or less independent positions influential to the establishment of an issue. In addition, we give a separate place to the judiciary in agenda setting, thereby acknowledging the historically significant role that the courts in both countries have played by their willingness to accept cases that then establish moral issues as legitimate subjects of public debate.

Our rationale for an expanded model is linked to the identification by Cobb et al. (1976) of three routes for gaining agenda status. One is the "outside-initiative" model whereby public opinion, the

---

11 Because his statistical analyses of AIDS and crime were inconclusive due to data problems (Soroka 2002b: 85–6), Soroka was forced to rely on the environment as the single example of a sensational issue.

media, interest groups, and social movements are critical to lifting an issue from the public agenda to the institutional or policy agenda. We anticipate that this model best explains how, for example, within the gay rights agenda, same-sex relations and same-sex marriage came to be addressed by policymakers in the United States in ways similar to what had occurred with prohibition. A unique route through which the "outside-initiative" model operates is the plebiscite, which was frequently used in Canada on questions of prohibition. Especially in the United States today, referendums offer another venue by which activists can politicize an issue and initiate policy change.

An "inside-access" model, though generally understudied, has direct relevance to moral conflicts. In this case an issue is confined to the institutional agenda of government and the mass public is generally not involved. We open the possibility that "inside-access" activism will account for the trajectory of the abortion issue, with judicial rulings escalating conflict in the United States but less so in Canada. That is, we are alert to how moral conflicts may be the result of social "de-regulations" imposed on the states or provinces by the United States Supreme Court and the Supreme Court of Canada. Such judicial agenda setting is very different from legislative agenda setting (Perry 1991), as we go on to demonstrate.

The third model, a hybrid "mobilization" one, is present when political leaders need public support and rally the electorate, often during political campaigns, to endorse their policy agenda. Unlike social movement theorists, who see mobilization occurring from the bottom up, this policy perspective sees mobilization as the result of top-down initiative. For example, the so-called war on drugs demonstrated how political leaders dramatized the problem during election campaigns even though there was no epidemic of addiction engulfing the United States (Sharp 1992). We anticipate that this hybrid model will be most useful in explaining capital punishment in the United States today as well as pornography (especially child pornography) in both countries.

In the case of the public agenda, we distinguish among interest groups, social movements, and public opinion. Interest groups are the organized representatives of particular population segments whose agenda-setting activities are usually manifested in lobbying activities directed toward government and politicians. Although social movements have been treated as forms of interest groups (e.g., Hojnacki et al. 2012: 380), we separate them and pay most attention to social movements and their impact. This is because, unlike the more usual understanding of interest groups as representing already established groups or factions working within the existing institutional framework of society, social movements imply newness, the mobilization of previously unorganized groups, and the potential for disrupting the normal course of politics. It is just these characteristics that imply an affinity with contentious moral issues.

The role of the mass media in agenda setting presents some ambiguity because of the ways it may affect both the public and policy agendas. When the media covers news about popular attitudes, attentive publics, or the mobilization of activists, it is conveying information about the public agenda. But the media may have its own policy preferences and attempt to shape the public agenda. It may relate to the policy agenda in the same ways, that is, by both reporting on policy developments and trying to influence them. Moreover, its reporting captures the overall saliency of a moral conflict in both the public and policy agendas.

The relation between public opinion and agenda setting is a disputed area of study, ranging from those who see little impact to those who argue that the impact is overwhelming. Page and Shapiro (1992), for example, argue that, at least for the United States and for the issues they considered, public opinion appeared to have a proximate influence on policy. Burstein (2014), in contrast, finds little impact from public opinion on policy outcomes. Equally problematic is the relation between the media and public opinion (Oliver, Hill, and Marion 2011; Hester and Gonzenbach 1995; Gonzenbach 1992; Gonzenbach 1996). Although our findings can be expected to buttress one or other position, it is not our intention to enter into these disputes or to further develop theories of agenda setting. Our objectives are to ascertain in what ways interest groups, social movements, and unorganized public opinion may contribute to agenda setting by bringing moral issues to the forefront of public controversy.

Each agenda-setting domain's role in contributing to the establishment of an issue will be ascertained separately. Media influence will be presumed through newspaper coverage. Public influence will be uncovered through public opinion polls and through the existence and actions of social movements and interest groups that concern themselves with particular moral issues. The government's place in agenda setting will be found in the platforms of political parties, executive and legislative actions promoting policies, output from committees, the willingness of the judiciary to take up specified cases, and the public statements of individual politicians who make claims about their ability to provide issue leadership. In chapter 6, where we concentrate on the establishment phase of life histories, guiding questions are the identity of the most significant agenda setters and the impact they have on particular issues.

Decline

Once emerging, and even once established, some issues may begin to decline. Among the many possible reasons why issues decline in importance or salience is because they are crowded out by other issues with which they compete for attention. Thus, Hilgartner and Bosk (1988: 58–9) argue that competition is affected by the carrying capacity of the arenas, operatives, and publics concerned with particular issues. Decline may then have little to do with the seriousness of the problem itself but more with the resources that advocates or opponents can bring to defend their position. An issue may continue to exist, but it can only count on relatively few diehard supporters to keep it alive.

Downs's (1972: 39–40) "issue-attention" cycle offers three phases that capture some aspects of decline. In the first of these, there is growing realization that any solution to the problem at hand would be very costly, whether in money or in existing privileges. The issue itself then begins to look less pressing, manifested in the next phase by a decline in public interest. Finally, it enters the post-problem stage – "a prolonged limbo." Along the way, some changes or solutions may have been introduced that make the original problem seem less pressing. Conversely, there may not appear to be any solution at hand so that continuing attention would only become a futile exercise for policymakers. Signs of decline, observed in chapter 7, will be found in public opinion polls, media coverage, and party platforms.

But Downs's rationale for issue decline may have limited application to moral conflicts, precisely because the latter do not involve substantial economic costs (unlike the huge costs involved, for example, with any massive environmental clean-up). Moreover, to raise cost considerations would almost trivialize a debate over contested fundamental values. To question the cost of litigation in capital punishment cases versus the cost of lifetime imprisonment would not appease advocates of capital punishment who are thinking in terms of deterrence or retribution. Thus, economic cost-benefit calculations have never been at the heart of the debate over capital punishment, illicit drugs, or pornography, even though the cost to authorities for enforcement can be substantial. Since it is unlikely that purely economic cost considerations would cause a decline in issue saliency for moral issues, we expect other causal factors to impinge upon the level of public awareness or disinterestedness during a period of decline.

Among likely factors affecting decline are successful challenges mounted by interests and movements opposed to the positions advocated in the original formulation of the moral issue. For sociologists, the emergence of such countermovements is often seen as a feature of moral conflicts (Meyer and Staggenborg 1996). As movements and countermovements interact, they produce a "sometimes loosely coupled tango of mobilization and demobilization" (Zald and Useem 1987: 247). The success of the original movement in generating changing conditions opens new opportunities for oppositional interests to mount their own challenges. Countermovements may then diminish the significance of the original movement and its claims to legitimacy by advocating a different and more attractive value position. As Meyer and Staggenborg (1996: 1639) hypothesize, *The likelihood that opposition to a movement will take the form of a sustained countermovement is directly related to the opposition's ability to portray the conflict as one that entails larger value cleavages in society.*"

Although contemporary political science has been less enthusiastic about endorsing the importance of countermovements, recent work by Conger and Djupe (2016), demonstrating their role in the conflict over gay rights, should rekindle interest.

Resurgence

An issue can be said to display resurgence when there is an upturn in interest, whether from the public, the media, or political actors. Resurgence may have many explanations. The problem itself may have become more serious or widespread, as illustrated by the cycle of rising and falling support for gun control laws in Canada (though not in the United States; see Fleming 2013). When there are shooting massacres, media coverage spikes, public concern rises, and Parliament invariably enacts tougher gun laws. Similarly, Petersen (2009) documents how public attention to international terrorism is stimulated by terrorist incidents but then declines when the media coverage decreases. Resurgence could be associated with the appearance of new solutions to the problem. The party out of office, or some of its individual politicians, may find the issue a useful vehicle for rekindling electoral interest.

Resurgence will be traced through similar data sources used for determining decline. In chapter 7, we add our examination of resurgence to that of decline. In the case of resurgence, we look for reasons for its presence and how different issues are affected.

Resolution

The resolution of moral conflicts brings an end to their life histories, the culmination of the phases they have passed through. Yet, despite the critical importance of this last phase, it has received relatively little attention in the policy literature, where it is conceptualized as termination. For example, the "stages" model, popularized by James Anderson (2011), devoted roughly three pages to policy termination, and his examples are all about economic policies. Termination was given no attention in the "streams" of policymaking by John Kingdon (2010). His neglect was addressed by Geva-May (2004: 311; also see Geva-May 2001), who argued that "termination occurs in opportunity windows, which open and close as political, policy, and problem streams converge," though again none of her examples involved morality policies. Child abuse may be considered a one-sided morality policy, but the insights from Nelson's (1984) variation of the stages model offer no hint about its ultimate resolution. The fundamental problem with the scant coverage (e.g., see Bardack 1976; Daniels 1997) given to termination in the policy literature is that virtually every case study involves an existing government policy, program, or agency rather than an ongoing controversy, and none focuses on morality policy.

The sociological literature on social problems has been similarly inattentive to issues of resolution. Early students in the field followed a "natural history" model of problem stages (Fuller and Myers 1941), but this approach has fallen out of favor (Hilgartner and Bosk 1988). Although attention to issue stages did presume an end point, the social constructivist approach that characterizes much of the work on social problems leaves that point open-ended and subject to redefinition and reassessment by political actors (Jensen et al. 1991).

By approaching moral issues from when they first become two-sided and hence contentious and then following them over time, we are able to fill in the gaps to explain their final outcome. The forms that resolution takes may be manifested in several possible ways, depending on whether or not they entail political action or, when political action is taken, whether it is through executive decisions, legislation, or judicial rulings, followed either by acquiescence and approval or by dissent and disapproval.

A de facto conclusion occurs when a moral issue is resolved without any political action, under conditions like those we enumerated when describing decline. In one scenario, changing societal conditions remove the issue's salience. In another, proponents fail to mobilize adequate support in order to bring about political action. More forcefully, opposition forces demonstrate sufficient strength to push aside the issue, with such "veto points" an especially potent force maintaining the policy status quo in the United States. In any of these scenarios, resolution then is the equivalent of failure. For example, Jasper (1988: 372–3), looking at public opinion toward nuclear power in the United States and abroad, argued that Downs's "issue-attention cycle" was predictive of its trajectory, not as the result of media and public boredom but because, without clear government policy, "large majorities of the public and the media … now believe that nuclear energy … doesn't work well in the United States, and no visible group provides alternative interpretations of the facts behind these claims."

An example of acceptance is provided by Mazur and Lee (1993: 688), who documented how media coverage of the dangers from aerosol sprays dropped in May 1977 after plans were announced by several federal agencies to prohibit "nonessential" uses of chlorofluorocarbons (CFCs). This had the effect of banning cosmetic spray cans, the source of nearly half the US consumption of CFCs. Media coverage dropped as did government attention, manifested by the rapid decline in congressional hearings on the subject. Similarly, in her study of media coverage of the pesticide controversy, Gunter (2005: 691) concluded that "there is a substantial decrease in coverage of pesticides following the passage of the FIFRA [Federal Insecticide, Fungicide and Rodenticide Act] amendments …, thus conveying the sense that amendments have 'solved the problem,' and no further action is needed." With respect to the rise and fall of the "Limits to Growth" debate of the late 1960s and early 1970s, Sandbach (1978: 511) similarly observed that "much of the environmental concern was alleviated through legal and administrative developments" such as the National Environmental Protection Act of 1970 and creation of the Environmental Protection Agency in the United States.

Because social movements employing contentious tactics may force issues on to the policy agenda, their subsequent reactions to official actions can be a critical step in issue histories, depending on whether or not they reduce activism and moderate demands. For example, Meyer (1993a; 1993b) links the content of policy on nuclear weapons to the reactions of social movements opposed to their use. He concludes that "movements subsided when an administration institutionalized at least part of its opposition, narrowing the public debate and defusing public concerns and activism. This institutional accommodation entailed symbolic concessions, and sometimes real changes in policy" (Meyer 1993b: 474). Similar shifts in social movement militancy following policy enactments, whether substantive or symbolic, have been traced for the anti-rape movement of the 1970s (Gornick and Meyer 1998) and black insurgency between 1930 and 1970 (McAdam 1982).

The history of the women's movement suggests that decline in issue salience can follow from either supportive legislative actions or from failure to achieve them. So initial success in enacting women's suffrage in 1920 ended the first wave of the women's movement (Freeman 1975), or at least forced its remnants into abeyance (Taylor 1989), whereas second-wave feminism suffered a decline after the failure to gain ratification of the Equal Rights Amendment (ERA). Building on theory developed by McAdam, Costain (1992: 99) argues that, at the outset, US government policies nurtured women's activism in the 1960s, but

> the increasingly single-minded focus on passage of the ERA set the stage for a dramatic decline in movement visibility in the 1980s. The movement lost its main issue when ERA failed to win ratification by the 1982 deadline. At that point, with the first president to hold office in nearly forty years who was openly antagonistic to most key women's issues [Reagan] and with their primary issue (the ERA) dead for the foreseeable future, the national women's movement began to fade rapidly.

Costain's conclusion reminds us how issue resolution can be linked to partisan agendas. In Carmines and Stimson's (1989: 12) evolutionary perspective, although the norm is for issues to change gradually, there can be "cataclysmic adaptation," when dramatic events, including sharply defined partisan platforms, produce dynamic change. Then policies, or their promise, may bring about new partisan alignments linked to particular issues (Carmines and Wagner 2006).

Hurka et al. (2016), working from the perspective of punctuated equilibrium theory, argue that morality policies are strongly punctuated, depending on the intensity of the moral conflicts entailed. Although not all our issues conform to their definition of what constitutes manifest morality politics, we still explore whether any of them result in major changes of the kind that they and Carmines and Stimson predict.

Yet even the most authoritative enactments, as in the case of a constitutional amendment enabling prohibition, do not always put an end to moral controversies. It is for this reason alone that prohibition deserves further consideration. In addition, continuing challenges to abortion after *Roe v. Wade* in the United States and the *Morgentaler* decision in Canada make it clear that what appears to be the resolution of a moral issue at one time may not be the final word. Those examples direct us to search for new or continuing windows of opportunity that allow remobilization to take place.

In summary, resolution may assume active forms through the enactment of new policies or the adaptation of old ones. These can come about either through legislative action, judicial rulings, or a combination of both. The results may put a lasting stamp on attitudes and behavior or they may be of temporary duration, still subject to challenges and reinterpretations. Which of these outcomes prevail will be identified through public opinion, legislation proposed and enacted, and judicial rulings. Research questions addressed in chapter 8 begin with the presence or absence of political actions. If the latter is the case, we search for reasons for that absence and the relation with particular kinds of issues. Where actions are taken, we will examine their nature and content, their partisan links, and their relations with types of issues.

Outline of the Book

Chapter 2 begins by illustrating the meaning of moral issues and the value of comparing Canada and the United States through the exemplary case of prohibition. Most critically, tracing the history of prohibition from its beginning to its end demonstrates how attention to the phases of issue unfolding enhances understanding the outcome of moral conflicts. It is here that we develop a series of hypotheses about how phases develop.

Chapter 3 offers brief descriptions of the moral issues that are the basis for our argument about how such issues develop and are resolved. In a very preliminary way, those descriptions suggest how the content of an issue may have an impact on its outcome.

Chapter 4 justifies our comparison of Canada and the United States. By close attention to differences that arise from demographic factors, civic culture, and political institutions, we are able to generate a series of hypotheses that predict their impact on issue outcomes.

Chapters 5 through 8 are each devoted to the analysis of a singular phase among issue life histories. We rely on thick descriptions of the different issues as we explore similarities and differences among them in their national settings. Data sources, as we have already indicated, include public opinion polls, media coverage (see appendix 1), and party platforms.

Chapter 9 brings us to a conclusion where we assess how the phases through which moral conflicts pass reveal the factors and processes that facilitate or impede their resolution.

REFERENCES

Anderson, James E. 2011. *Public Policymaking*. 7th ed. Boston, MA: Wadsworth Cengage Learning.
Baker, Wayne E. 2005. *America's Crisis of Values: Reality and Perception*. Princeton: Princeton University Press.
Bardack, Eugene, ed. 1976. "Termination of Policies, Programs and Organizations." *Policy Sciences* 7 (2): 123–31.
Baumgartner, Frank R., and Bryan D. Jones. 2009. *Agendas and Instability in American Politics*. 2nd ed. Chicago: University of Chicago Press. https://doi.org/10.7208/chicago/9780226039534.001.0001.
Best, Joel. 2012. *Social Problems*. 2nd ed. New York: W.W. Norton.
Burstein, Paul. 2014. *American Public Opinion, Advocacy, and Policy in Congress: What the Public Wants and What It Gets*. New York: Cambridge University Press.
Carmines, Edward G., and James A. Stimson. 1980. "The Two Faces of Issue Voting." *American Political Science Review* 74 (1): 78–91. https://doi.org/10.2307/1955648.
Carmines, Edward G., and James A. Stimson. 1989. *Issue Evolution: Race and the Transformation of American Politics*. Princeton: Princeton University Press.
Carmines, Edward G., and Michael W. Wagner. 2006. "Political Issues and Party Alignments: Assessing the Issue Evolution Perspective." *Annual Review of Political Science* 9 (1): 67–81. https://doi.org/10.1146/annurev.polisci.9.091905.180706.
Christoph, James B. 1962a. *Capital Punishment and British Politics: The British Movement to Abolish the Death Penalty 1945–57*. Chicago: University of Chicago Press.

Christoph, James B. 1962b. "Capital Punishment and British Party Responsibility." *Political Science Quarterly* 77 (1): 19–35. https://doi.org/10.2307/2146495.

Clifford, Scott, and Jennifer Jerit. 2013. "How Words Do the Work of Politics: Moral Foundations Theory and the Debate over Stem Cell Research." *Journal of Politics* 75 (3): 659–71. https://doi.org/10.1017/S0022381613000492.

Cobb, Roger W., and Charles D. Elder. 1972. *Participation in American Politics: The Dynamics of Agenda-Building*. Baltimore, MD: Johns Hopkins University Press.

Cobb, Roger W., Jeannie-Keith Ross, and Marc Howard Ross. 1976. "Agenda Building as a Comparative Political Process." *American Political Science Review* 70 (1): 126–38. https://doi.org/10.1017/S0003055400264034.

Conger, Kimberly H., and Paul A. Djupe. 2016. "Culture War Counter-Mobilization: Gay Rights and Religious Right Groups in the States." *Interest Groups and Advocacy* 5 (3): 278–300. https://doi.org/10.1057/s41309-016-0004-7.

Costain, Anne N. 1992. *Inviting Women's Rebellion: A Political Process Interpretation of the Women's Movement*. Baltimore, MD: Johns Hopkins University Press.

Daniels, Mark R. 1997. *Terminating Public Programs*. Armonk, NY: M.E. Sharpe Publishers.

Davis, Nancy J., and Robert V. Robinson. 1996. "Are the Rumors of War Exaggerated? Religious Orthodoxy and Moral Progressivism in America." *American Journal of Sociology* 102 (3): 756–87. https://doi.org/10.1086/230996.

Dearing, James W., and Everett M. Rogers. 1996. *Agenda Setting*. Thousand Oaks, CA: Sage.

DiMaggio, Paul, John Evans, and Bethany Bryson. 1996. "Have American's Social Attitudes Become More Polarized?" *American Journal of Sociology* 102 (3): 690–755. https://doi.org/10.1086/230995.

Downs, Anthony. 1972. "Up and Down with Ecology – the 'Issue-Attention Cycle.'" *Public Interest* 28 (Summer): 38–50.

Edmonston, Barry, and Eric Fong, eds. 2011. *The Changing Canadian Population*. Montreal, Kingston: McGill-Queen's University Press.

Engeli, Isabelle, Christoffer Green-Pedersen, and Lars Thorup Larsen, eds. 2012. *Morality Politics in Western Europe: Parties, Agendas and Policy Choices*. New York: Palgrave Macmillan. https://doi.org/10.1057/9781137016690.

Epp, Charles R. 1998. *The Rights Revolution: Lawyers, Activists, and Supreme Courts in Comparative Perspective*. Chicago: University of Chicago Press.

Fiorina, Morris P. 2010. *Culture War? The Myth of a Polarized America*. 3rd ed. New York: Longman.

Fleming, Anthony K. 2013. *Gun Policy in the United States and Canada: The Impact of Mass Murders and Assassinations on Gun Control*. New York: Bloomsbury Publishing.

Freeman, Jo. 1975. *The Politics of Women's Liberation*. New York: David McKay.

Fuller, Richard C., and Richard R. Myers. 1941. "The Natural History of a Social Problem." *American Sociological Review* 6 (3): 320–9. https://doi.org/10.2307/2086189.

Gallup. 2014. "Most Important Problem." www.gallup.com/poll/1675/most.important.problem.aspx.

Geva-May, Iris. 2001. "When the Motto Is 'Till Death Do Us Part': The Conceptualization and the Craft of Termination in the Public Policy Cycle." *International Journal of Public Administration* 24 (3): 263–88. https://doi.org/10.1081/PAD-100000448.

Geva-May, Iris. 2004. "Riding the Wave of Opportunity: Termination in Public Policy." *Journal of Public Administration: Research and Theory* 14 (3): 309–33. https://doi.org/10.1093/jopart/muh020.

Gonzenbach, William J. 1992. "A Time-Series Analysis of the Drug Issue, 1985–1990: The Press, the President, and Public Opinion." *International Journal of Public Opinion Research* 4 (2): 126–47. https://doi.org/10.1093/ijpor/4.2.126.

Gonzenbach, William J. 1996. *The Media, the President, and Public Opinion: A Longitudinal Analysis of the Drug Issue, 1984–1991*. Mahwah, NJ: Lawrence Erlbaum.

Gornick, Janet C., and David S. Meyer. 1998. "Changing Political Opportunity: The Anti-Rape Movement and Public Policy." *Journal of Policy History* 10 (4): 367–98. https://doi.org/10.1017/S0898030600007132.

Graham, Jesse, Jonathan Haidt, and Brian A. Nosek. 2009. "Liberals and Conservatives Rely on Different Sets of Moral Foundations." *Journal of Personality and Social Psychology* 96 (5): 1029–46.

Gunter, Valerie J. 2005. "News Media and Technological Risks: The Case of Pesticides after 'Silent Spring.'" *Sociological Quarterly* 46 (Autumn): 671–98.

Haidt, Jonathan, and Jesse Graham. 2007. "When Morality Opposes Justice: Conservatives Have Moral Intuitions That Liberals May Not Recognize." *Social Justice Research* 20 (1): 98–116. https://doi.org/10.1007/s11211-007-0034-z.

Heichel, Stephan, Christoph Knill, and Sophie Schmitt. 2013. "Public Policy Meets Morality: Conceptual and Theoretical Challenges in the Analysis of Morality Policy Change." *Journal of European Public Policy* 20 (3): 318–34. https://doi.org/10.1080/13501763.2013.761497.

Hester, J.B., and W.J. Gonzenbach. 1995. "The Environment: TV News, Real-World Cues, and Public Opinion over Time." *Mass Communication Review* 22: 5–20.

Hilgartner, Stephen, and Charles L. Bosk. 1988. "The Rise and Fall of Social Problems: A Public Arenas Model." *American Journal of Sociology* 94 (1): 53–78. https://doi.org/10.1086/228951.

Hojnacki, Marie, David C. Kimball, Frank R. Baumgartner, Jeffrey M. Berry, and Beth L. Leech. 2012. "Studying Organizational Advocacy and Influence: Reexamining Interest Group Research." *Annual Review of Political Science* 15 (1): 379–99. https://doi.org/10.1146/annurev-polisci-070910-104051.

Hout, Michael, and Claude Fischer. 2006. *Century of Difference: How America Changed in the Last Hundred Years*. New York: Russell Sage Foundation.

Hunter, James Davison. 1991. *Culture Wars: The Struggle to Define America*. New York: Basic Books.

Hunter, James Davison. 1994. *Before the Shooting Begins*. New York: The Free Press.

Hurka, Steffen, Christian Adam, and Christoph Knill. 2016. "Is Morality Policy Different? Testing Sectoral and Institutional Explanations of Policy Change." *Policy Studies Journal: The Journal of the Policy Studies Organization* n/a. https://doi.org/10.1111/psj.12153.

Inglehart, Ronald. 1990. *Culture Shift in Advanced Industrial Society*. Princeton, NJ: Princeton University Press.

Inglehart, Ronald. 1997. *Modernization and Postmodernization: Cultural, Economic, and Political Change in 43 Societies*. Princeton, NJ: Princeton University Press.

Inglehart, Ronald, and Wayne E. Baker. 2000. "Modernization, Cultural Change and the Persistence of Traditional Values." *American Sociological Review* 65 (1): 19–51. https://doi.org/10.2307/2657288.

Inglehart, Ronald, and Christian Welzel. 2005. *Modernization, Cultural Change and Democracy: The Human Development Sequence*. New York: Cambridge University Press. https://doi.org/10.1017/CBO9780511790881.

Jasper, James M. 1988. "The Political Life Cycle of Technology Controversies." *Social Forces* 67 (2): 357–77. https://doi.org/10.2307/2579186.

Jensen, Eric L., Jurg Gerber, and Ginna M. Babcock. 1991. "The New War on Drugs: Grass Roots Movement or Political Construction?" *Journal of Drug Issues* 21 (3): 651–67. https://doi.org/10.1177/002204269102100312.

Kingdon, John W. 2010. *Agendas, Alternatives, and Public Policies. Updated.* 2nd ed. New York: HarperCollins.

Knill, Christoph, Christian Adam, and Steffen Hurka. 2015. *On the Road to Permissiveness? Change and Convergence of Moral Regulation in Europe*. Oxford, UK: Oxford University Press.

Koleva, Spassena P., Jesse Graham, Ravi Iyer, Peter H. Ditto, and Jonathan Haidt. 2012. "Tracing the Threads: How Five Moral Concerns (especially Purity) Help

Explain Culture War Attitudes." *Journal of Research in Personality* 46 (2): 184–94. https://doi.org/10.1016/j.jrp.2012.01.006.

Lowi, Theodore J. 1964. "American Business, Public Policy, Case Studies, and Political Theory." *World Politics* 16 (4): 677–715. https://doi.org/10.2307/2009452.

Lowi, Theodore J. 1972. "Four Systems of Policy, Politics, and Choice." *Public Administration Review* 32 (4): 298–310. https://doi.org/10.2307/974990.

Lowi, Theodore J. 1988. "New Dimensions in Policy and Politics." In *Social Regulatory Policy: Moral Controversies in American Politics*, ed. Raymond Tatalovich and Byron W. Daynes, x–xxi. Boulder, CO: Westview Press.

Lowi, Theodore J. 2011. "New Dimensions in Policy and Politics." In *Moral Controversies in American Politics*, ed. Raymond Tatalovich and Byron W. Daynes, xi–xxvii. 4th ed. Armonk, NY: M.E. Sharpe.

Mazur, Allan, and Jinling Lee. 1993. "Sounding the Global Alarm: Environmental Issues in the US National News." *Social Studies of Science* 23 (4): 681–720. https://doi.org/10.1177/030631293023004003.

McAdam, Doug. 1982. *Political Process and the Development of Black Insurgency, 1930–1970*. Chicago: University of Chicago Press.

McAdams, Dan P., Michelle Albaugh, Emily Farber, Jennifer Daniels, Regina Logan, and Brad Olson. 2008. "Family Metaphors and Moral Intuitions: How Conservatives and Liberals Narrate Their Lives." *Journal of Personality and Social Psychology* 95 (4): 978–90. https://doi.org/10.1037/a0012650.

Meier, Kenneth J. 1994. *The Politics of Sin: Drugs, Alcohol, and Public Policy*. Armonk, NY: M.E. Sharpe.

Meyer, David S. 1993a. "Peace Protest and Policy: Explaining the Rise and Decline of Antinuclear Movements in Postwar America." *Policy Studies Journal: The Journal of the Policy Studies Organization* 21 (1): 35–51. https://doi.org/10.1111/j.1541-0072.1993.tb01452.x.

Meyer, David S. 1993b. "Protest Cycles and Political Process: American Peace Movements in the Nuclear Age." *Political Research Quarterly* 46 (3): 451–79. https://doi.org/10.1177/106591299304600302.

Meyer, David S., and Suzanne Staggenborg. 1996. "Movements, Countermovements, and the Structure of Political Opportunity." *American Journal of Sociology* 101 (6): 1628–60. https://doi.org/10.1086/230869.

Meyer, David S., and Sidney Tarrow, eds. 1998. *The Social Movement Society: Contentious Politics for a New Society*. Lanham, MD: Rowman and Littlefield.

Mooney, Christopher Z. 2001. "The Public Clash of Private Values." In *The Public Clash of Private Values: The Politics of Morality Policy*, ed. Christopher Z. Mooney, 3–18. New York: Chatham House Publishers.

Mooney, Christopher Z., and Richard G. Schuldt. 2008. "Does Morality Policy
   Exist? Testing a Basic Assumption." *Policy Studies Journal: The Journal of the
   Policy Studies Organization* 36 (2): 199–218. https://doi.org/10.1111/j.1541-
   0072.2008.00262.x.
Nelson, Barbara J. 1984. *Making an Issue of Child Abuse*. New York: Basic Books.
Nevitte, Neil. 1996. *The Decline of Deference: Canadian Value Change in Cross-
   National Perspective*. Peterborough, ON: Broadview Press.
Offe, Claus. 1990. "Reflections on the Institutional Self-transformation of
   Movement Politics: A Tentative Stage Model." In *Challenging the Political
   Order: New Social and Political Movements in Western Democracies*, ed. Russell
   J. Dalton and Manfred Kuechler, 232–50. New York: Oxford University
   Press.
Oliver, Willard M., Joshua Hill, and Nancy E. Marion. 2011. "When the
   President Speaks ... An Analysis of Presidential Influence over Public
   Opinion Concerning the War on Drugs." *Criminal Justice Review* 39 (4):
   456–69.
Page, Benjamin I., and Robert Y. Shapiro. 1992. *The Rational Public: Fifty Years of
   Trends in Americans' Policy Preferences*. Chicago: University of Chicago Press.
   https://doi.org/10.7208/chicago/9780226644806.001.0001.
Perry, H.W. 1991. *Deciding to Decide: Agenda Setting in the United States Supreme
   Court*. Cambridge, MA: Harvard University Press.
Petersen, Karen K. 2009. "Revisiting Downs' Issue-Attention Cycle:
   International Terrorism and U.S. Public Opinion." *Journal of Strategic
   Security* 2 (4): 1–16. https://doi.org/10.5038/1944-0472.2.4.1.
Reimer, Samuel H. 1995. "A Look at Cultural Effects on Religiosity: A
   Comparison between the United States and Canada." *Journal for the Scientific
   Study of Religion* 34 (4): 445–57. https://doi.org/10.2307/1387338.
Ryan, Timothy J. 2014. "Reconsidering Moral Issues in Politics." *Journal of
   Politics* 76 (2): 380–97. https://doi.org/10.1017/S0022381613001357.
Sandbach, Francis. 1978. "The Rise and Fall of the Limits to Growth Debate."
   Social Studies of Science 8 (4): 495–520. https://doi.org/10.1177/
   030631277800800404.
Scheingold, Stuart A. 1974. *The Politics of Rights: Lawyers, Public Policy, and
   Political Change*. New Haven, CT: Yale University Press.
Sharp, Elaine B. 1992. "Agenda-Setting and Policy Results: Lessons from Three
   Drug Policy Episodes." *Policy Studies Journal: The Journal of the Policy Studies
   Organization* 20 (4): 538–51. https://doi.org/10.1111/j.1541-0072.1992.
   tb00182.x.
Skitka, Linda J. 2002. "Do the Means Always Justify the Ends, or Do the
   Ends Sometimes Justify the Means? A Value Protection Model of Justice

Reasoning." *Personality and Social Psychology Bulletin* 28 (5): 588–97. https://doi.org/10.1177/0146167202288003.

Skitka, Linda J., Christopher W. Bauman, and Edward G. Sargis. 2005. "Moral Conviction: Another Contributor to Attitude Strength or Something More?" *Journal of Personality and Social Psychology* 88 (6): 895–917. https://doi.org/10.1037/0022-3514.88.6.895.

Skitka, Linda J., and Elizabeth Mullen. 2002. "The Dark Side of Moral Conviction." *Analyses of Social Issues and Public Policy* 2 (1): 35–41. https://doi.org/10.1111/j.1530-2415.2002.00024.x.

Smelser, Neil J. 1962. *Theory of Collective Behavior*. Glencoe, IL: Free Press.

Smith, Tom. 1980. "America's Most Important Problems – A Trend Analysis: 1946–1976." *Public Opinion Quarterly* 44 (2): 164–80. https://doi.org/10.1086/268582.

Smith, T. Alexander. 1975. *The Comparative Policy Process*. Santa Barbara, CA: ABC-Clio Books.

Soroka, Stuart N. 2002a. "Issue Attributes and Agenda-Setting by Media, the Public, and Policymakers in Canada." *International Journal of Public Opinion Research* 14 (3): 264–85. https://doi.org/10.1093/ijpor/14.3.264.

Soroka, Stuart N. 2002b. *Agenda-Setting Dynamics in Canada*. Vancouver: UBC Press.

Studlar, Donley T. 2001. "What Constitutes Morality Policy? A Cross-National Analysis." In *The Public Clash of Private Values: The Politics of Morality Policy*, ed. Christopher Z. Mooney, 37–54. New York: Chatham House Publishers.

Studlar, Donley T., Alessandro Cagossi, and Robert D. Duval. 2013. "Is Morality Policy Different? Institutional Explanations for Post-War Western Europe." *Journal of European Public Policy* 20 (3): 353–71.

Tatalovich, Raymond, and Byron W. Daynes. 1981. *The Politics of Abortion*. New York: Praeger.

Tatalovich, Raymond, and Byron W. Daynes. 1988. "Introduction: What is Social Regulatory Policy?" In *Social Regulatory Policy: Moral Controversies in American Politics*, ed. Raymond Tatalovich and Byron W. Daynes, 1–4. Boulder, CO: Westview Press.

Taylor, Verta. 1989. "Social Movement Continuity: The Women's Movement in Abeyance." *American Sociological Review* 54 (5): 761–75. https://doi.org/10.2307/2117752.

Walsh, Edward T., and Rex H. Warland. 1983. "Social Movement Involvement in the Wake of a Nuclear Accident: Activists and Free Riders in the TMI Area." *American Sociological Review* 48 (6): 764–80. https://doi.org/10.2307/2095324.

Williams, Rhys H. ed. 1997. *Cultural Wars in American Politics: Critical Reviews of a Popular Myth*. New York: Aldine de Gruyter.

Wurgler, Emily, and Clem Brooks. 2014. "Out of Step? Voters and Social Issues in U.S. Presidential Elections." *Sociological Quarterly* 55 (4): 683–704. https://doi.org/10.1111/tsq.12070.

Zald, Meyer N., and Bert Useem. 1987. "Movement and Countermovement Interaction: Mobilization, Tactics, and State Interaction." In *Social Movements in an Organizational Society*, ed. Mayer N. Zald and John D. McCarthy, 147–71. New Brunswick, NJ: Transaction.

Chapter Two

The Example of Prohibition

Meaning

Chapter 1 laid out our rationale for focusing on the phases through which moral conflicts evolve, to be tested using a sample of contemporary issues that became problems in Canada and the United States early in the twentieth century. As a prelude to that analysis, this chapter uses the case of prohibition, prominent in both countries from the early nineteenth century until its resolution in the early 1930s, with roots in the experiences of the first white settlers in British North America and their efforts to build new lives and new nations. Because it has a beginning and an ending, prohibition is an exemplar of the varied phases through which moral issues may cycle and a prototype for how each of the phases may be expressed.

What are prohibited under prohibition are the manufacturer, sale, and consumption of alcoholic beverages. The rationale for banning alcohol from entire communities is normally rooted in religion, specifically as advocated by Islam, Mormonism, and pietistic Protestant sects. Alcohol use is moralized as the pathway to sin because it presumably removes self-conscious barriers to engaging in licentious behavior. Even without invoking the label of sin, advocates of restraint have pointed to how drunkenness, particularly public drunkenness, leads to family breakdown and the loss of an orderly society. Only relatively recently has alcohol abuse been recognized as a medical problem.

Prohibition and temperance are often linked as part of a common movement, although the actual meaning of each concept is quite different. Gusfield (1986: 5) notes that temperance was the term adopted in the 1820s, reflecting a time when efforts were aimed at moderating alcohol consumption, not prohibiting it entirely. As prohibition became the goal, temperance changed its meaning and came to stand for total abstention. Temperance movements emerged in Western Europe in the early nineteenth century and, in both Canada and the United States, prohibition became a theme in nineteenth- and early-twentieth-century politics through the efforts of evangelical Protestants.

Emergence

Moral conflicts emerge from major societal changes out of which new normative standards arise and old ones are challenged. In the prelude to prohibition, old political arrangements would be overturned in the American Revolutionary War and, more peaceably, in the change from Canada's colonial to dominion status. Political challenges would continue with the War of 1812, the Civil War in the United States, the effects of the Boer War on Canada, and the First World War. Those who left the old country for religious reasons would continue to challenge the established churches, found new religions, and help provide a hospitable setting for the Great Awakenings within Protestantism. The First Great Awakening, between the 1730s and 1740s, emphasized individual spiritual experience and gave new legitimacy to American individualism. Pushing westward, settlers came into conflict with indigenous peoples and with harsh environments. Mass migration would bring new ethnic and religious groups and, from east to west, would lead to new cities and new industries. Because the population had an imbalance of men, the need to create stable family life would become a problem for both civic and religious authorities.

Alcohol was an inexpensive anodyne to the chaotic environment that accompanied so many changes. Colonial America began a pattern, continued in the United States, of high levels of alcohol consumption and many drunkards, encouraged by cheap rum that came from trade with the West Indies (Bern 2004). Although Blocker (1989: 5) alleges that drunken behavior was not perceived as a social problem because drunks were "not concentrated visibly on the streets or cities and towns," there is contrary evidence of early concern. For example, the *Falmouth Gazette* in 1785 became the first Maine newspaper to advocate temperance, which then meant moderation (AffordableAcadia 2010). In pre-Confederation Canada, heavy drinking was similarly common among all ages and classes of people, beginning with breakfast, during work, and continuing long into the night (Noel 1995: 13–14).

Even though heavy drinking and its attendant problems on both sides of the border did not assume the character of a triggering event, they can still be regarded as a major stimulus to the emergence of prohibition.

Within an environment of unsettling change, the Second Great Awakening, from the 1790s to the 1830s, found eager converts to a theology that offered individuals the freedom to choose salvation and also opened new roles for women. Protestant clergy and other religious leaders now began to preach against drinking alcoholic beverages, first by advocating moderation and then, by the early 1830s, "teetotalism," where they asked for pledges of total abstention. From their efforts came a new social movement that would then become differentiated along geographic, tactical, and demographic lines. Both countries were similar in that leadership and direction came from evangelical Protestant clergy and their flocks. The objects of their opprobrium were drunkards, who were often immigrants. In the United States, that meant they were also mainly Irish and German Catholics. As Wuthnow (2017) points out, the nineteenth century was characterized by efforts to achieve middle-class respectability through a process that involved maligning those whose religion and ethnicity could be defined as inferior. In Canada, the association of drunkenness with Catholicism would have been more troublesome to the political authorities, eager to ensure the acquiescence of French-speaking Catholics to the new regime. In this regard, they were helped by Catholic clergy, who took a leading role in furthering temperance in rural French Canada during the 1840s (Noel 1995).

The earliest temperance organizations were local. They included the Massachusetts Society for the Suppression of Intemperance, founded in 1813, and the Total Abstinence Society, founded in 1815 in Portland, Maine. The American Society for the Promotion of Temperance, better known as the American Temperance Society (ATS), and founded in 1826, made a more significant mark as it targeted the larger public through revivals and missionary activities. The Washingtonian Movement was a self-help group typically made up of ex-alcoholics who publicly confessed their personal failings and signed a pledge of total abstinence. Along with moral suasion, the Washingtonians also provided material support to the afflicted and that practice was inherited by temperance fraternal societies, of which the largest was the Sons of Temperance, founded in New York City in 1842.

Just as in the United States and its colonial precursors, sustained agitation for prohibition in Canada began with the activism of temperance organizations during the pre-Confederation era. The early temperance movement was made up of self-help groups that relied on evangelical appeals and moral suasion through lectures and appeals for pledges to abstain from alcoholic beverages. Fraternal societies, like the Sons of Temperance, founded in 1842, provided material benefits of insurance and sickness funds as added incentives to membership. And, as in the United States, the movement evolved "from a vision of moderation in the consumption of alcohol in the early 1800s to teetotalism by mid-century, and then to complete prohibition by the latter decades of the nineteenth century" (Ferry 2003: 137).

Disagreements grew within the prohibition movement between those committed to achieving their goals by persuading drinkers to abandon alcohol and those who felt that prohibition could only be achieved through legal means. That is, the latter were beginning a move away from the emergent phase of the movement into the establishment one. The state of Maine was a critical battleground in this tactical shift under the leadership of Portland's mayor, Neal Dow. Dow was instrumental in shepherding through the Maine legislature what became known as the Maine Law of 1851, which prohibited the sale and manufacture of alcohol. That law inspired other states to campaign for prohibition between 1851 and 1856 (Cherrington 1969: 136), and twelve passed similar legislation. The push for legislative solutions became strongly identified with women's activism, of which the Women's Christian Temperance Union (WCTU), founded in 1874, was "the largest women's organization to that point in American history" (Blocker 1989: 64). The WCTU's goal was the achievement of prohibition through statewide referendums. The WCTU was followed by an even more successful movement, the Anti-Saloon League, founded in 1893. Its strong organizational makeup was rooted in local chapters and aimed at curtailing commerce in alcohol through local legislation (Kerr 1985; Odegard 1928; Szymanski 2003).

Like their counterparts in the United States, the northern British colonies also began to divide over strategies, with those who felt that "the sale of alcohol created problems faster than temperance workers could correct them" moving to take up "prohibitive legislation designed to outlaw the liquor traffic entirely" (Birrell 1977). Among the leading advocates of legislative action was the Canadian Temperance League, founded in 1853, soon to change its name to the unequivocal Canada Prohibitory Liquor Law League. In the leading prohibitionist city of Montreal, the United Canadian Alliance for the Suppression of the

Liquor Trade (UCASLT) was established in 1863. Following Confederation, the Grand Lodge of Canada of the Independent Order of Good
Templars and the Grand Division of the Sons of Temperance agreed to
merge into the Canada Temperance Union (Spence 1919: 105). Shortly
after, the new umbrella organization resolved to focus its efforts in
Ontario (renaming itself the Ontario Temperance and Prohibitory
League), but also forming branches in Quebec and New Brunswick.

Under pressure from the new direction in movement tactics, and
influenced as well by its neighboring state, New Brunswick enacted a
measure like the Maine Law in 1855, but enforcement was controversial,
leading to its repeal in 1856.[1] In conjunction with pressure from the new
movements, the Maine Law also influenced the province of Canada.
According to temperance advocate Ruth Spence (1919: 92), the "legislature was inundated with a flood of petitions from congregations,
Sunday schools, temperance organizations, municipal corporations,
and individual citizens. In 1864 Mr. Christopher Dunkin introduced a
bill, 'To amend the laws in force respecting the sale of intoxicating liquors and issue of licenses therefor, and otherwise for the repression of
abuses resulting from such sale.'" The Dunkin Act, officially the Canada
Temperance Act, allowed counties and municipalities in the province of
Canada to ban the sale of liquor by majority vote.[2]

One aid in tracking phases in moral causes, used in later chapters,
relies on evidence of media attention, described in appendix 1. For this
chapter we attempted to do this by looking for articles mentioning
"National Prohibition" in the *New York Times* and "Temperance" in the
Toronto *Globe* (later the *Globe and Mail*) from 1880 to 1950 (see figures 2.1
and 2.2).[3] However, because the initial emergence of prohibition as an
issue that would inspire moral conflict took place locally, with even the
pressure for legislation locally based, the kind of newspaper coverage
available is an uncertain measure of public concern. The considerably

---

1 New Brunswick was, like the New England states, a major locus for the prohibition
movement as well as an area of heavy drinking. With respect to the latter, the city of
Saint John averaged one tavern for every 50 people (Heron 2003: 27).
2 The law permitted the sale of alcohol for medical or sacramental uses.
3 The term "National Prohibition" had a precise meaning in the United States but not in
Canada, which only experienced "national" prohibition briefly during the First World
War. In the Canadian context, the more accurate term was "Temperance," which
denoted not only its social movement opposing alcoholic consumption but also the
"local option" laws of 1864 and 1878.

Figure 2.1 Media coverage of prohibition in the United States, 1880–1960

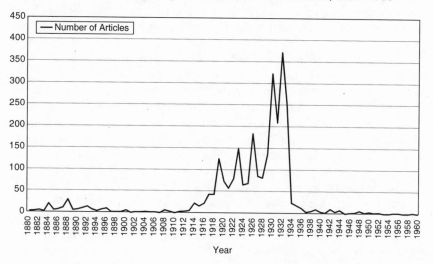

Figure 2.2 Media coverage of prohibition in Canada, 1880–1950

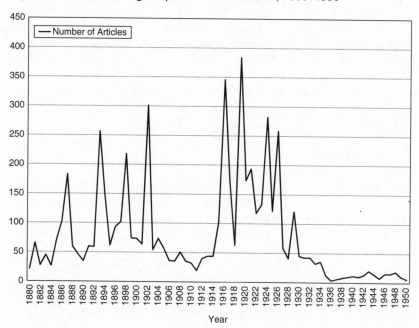

greater coverage in Canada during the initial appearance of prohibition likely reflects the concentration of prohibition-related activities in
eastern Canada compared to their greater geographic dispersion in the
United States.

There should be little surprise that the emergence of alcohol as a
source of moral contention had similar origins on both sides of the
border. All the British North American colonies, regardless of their
later political division, began facing the same kind of socially disruptive changes and found solace in the same kind of uninhibited alcohol use. They were also alike in their openness to religious revival in
which, initially, restraint in how alcohol was used could be an individual moral choice. But impatience with relying on individual choice to
solve the social ills attributed to alcohol led pro-dry forces to a different
approach, where legal authority was advocated to prohibit the manufacture, sale, and consumption of alcohol. Social movements, whether
on the side of moral choices by individuals or legal constraints, were
similarly led by Protestant clergy and served to mobilize women into
social activism.

One notable difference in the emergent phase of prohibition in
what would become two distinct nations was the more overt hostility directed by the movement in the United States against Irish and
German Catholic immigrants. This difference can be attributed to the
deliberate efforts of the British authorities to cultivate the loyalty of
its francophone population by working through the Catholic clergy
who remained to tend their parishioners. Moreover, ultramontanism,
an ascetically conservative perspective in Catholicism, dominated in
Canada (Noll 1992: 251–3) and made prohibition congenial despite its
connections with Protestantism (Noel 1995: 176).

Establishment

The establishment phase of prohibition that moved it on to the national
policy agenda in both countries came about through the continued
efforts of social movements, the responses of political parties, and
leading roles taken by individual politicians. Establishment culminated through legislative action although that action was much more
far-reaching in the United States than it was in Canada. Still, in both
countries, the enactment of prohibition had precedent not only in local
legislative efforts but also in prior national legislation permitting the
regulation of alcohol. In both countries, taxes on alcohol, whether on

its importation or manufacture, were a manifestation of early efforts at nation building (Skowronek 1982) by assigning new and often contested authority to the central government. In other words, there was already a window of opportunity to treating alcohol as a problem amenable to a regulatory solution (Kingdon 2010). In order to take advantage of that window, we need to take into account the longer history of the United States as an independent polity. We do this by beginning with that country, moving to Canada once it acquired dominion status, and then dealing with them contemporaneously as they both responded to the First World War.

Agenda Setting in the United States

The US Treasury Department (n.d.) website proudly recounts its history, beginning in 1791, when the first federal taxes imposed were those on distilled spirits. Those taxes paid off the debt incurred from the Revolutionary War and later levies were used to finance the Civil War. The 1791 tax provoked the Whiskey Rebellion, a protest against the fledgling federal government by small-scale distillers on the frontier. Suppression of the rebellion legitimated the authority of the central government and the right of Congress to make nationally binding laws with respect to taxation (Hoover 2014).

The establishment phase of prohibition was more directly aided by initiatives coming from the public and the partisan climate of government. In the United States, one avenue of influence was the continuing efforts of organized social movements.[4] Szymanski (2003) argues that greatest success was displayed by movements like the Anti-Saloon League that engaged supporters in local efforts against drinking before taking up state and national constitutional amendments in favor of prohibition. The WCTU, in contrast, soon became entangled in party politics, aiding in the formation of the Prohibition Party, founded in 1869, and influenced by Republican backers within its ranks. The latter helped to push the WCTU to work for state prohibition through referendums. Blocker (1989: 88) alleges that "the principal force behind the launching of these [statewide] campaigns was the desire of major-party

---

4 Schrad (2007) disputes any emphasis on the impact of social movements, but we conclude that they were one vital component of issue mobilization and contention that affected the policy agenda.

politicians, most of them Republicans, to find a means of blunting prohibitionist demands for a party commitment to the cause, demands backed implicitly or explicitly by the threat of shifting to the Prohibition party."

For those committed to nationwide prohibition, the Prohibition Party was an important instrument for its achievement, appealing to rural and small-town Evangelicals and displaying its strongest electoral performance in 1888 and 1892. Local leaders in the prohibition movement would transfer their support to the Prohibition Party, for which Neal Dow of Maine ran as a presidential candidate. Yet even though the Prohibition Party posed no serious threat to the dominance of the two major parties, it did raise troubling issues affecting their supporters. Banning drink was abhorrent to the foreign-born constituents of the Democratic Party although it was supported by "dry" Democrats across the southern Bible belt. The Republicans, who feared that endorsing national prohibition would help the Democrats as well as alienating their own German-American supporters, tried to keep the wet-dry debate confined to the states. Toward that end, the Wilson Act of 1890, authored by Senator James Wilson (R-Iowa), was intended to defend state prohibition laws by banning inter-state shipments of alcoholic beverages (Hamm 1995: 79–88). What prompted Senator Wilson was the Supreme Court ruling in *Leisy v. Harden* (1890), which essentially argued that the states could not regulate the transportation of alcohol even if the national government refused to do so. The Wilson Act plugged that constitutional loophole. But this legislation was too weak to earn much enthusiasm from prohibitionists, though they generally favored the bill.

The first major federal law advancing prohibition was the Webb-Kenyon Act of 1913, co-sponsored by Senator William S. Kenyon (R-Iowa) and Congressman E. Yates Webb (D-NC). "From its first committee hearing to its final passage, the Anti-Saloon League and the WCTU organized an unrivaled campaign of political pressure for the Webb-Kenyon bill" (Hamm 1995: 216). The law, which banned shipment of intoxicating liquors from a state or foreign country into another state in violation of the laws of that state, was supported by bipartisan votes in the House of Representatives (63 percent of Republicans and 68 percent of Democrats) and in the Senate (60 percent of Republicans and 71 percent of Democrats), but both chambers had to override President Taft's veto before enactment was finalized (Hamm 1995: 218).

Agenda Setting in Canada

Just as in the United States, and using experiences in the neighboring country as part of their repertoire of strategies, social movements
in Canada pressed for federal legislative action. In 1873 the Temperance Prohibitory League orchestrated "an active petitioning campaign
to secure the enactment of a law of total prohibition" (Spence 1919:
107). Sir John A. Macdonald, the Conservative prime minister, moved
that a Select Committee on Prohibition receive those petitions, which
numbered 384 signed by 39,223 individuals as well as others from
82 municipalities and the Ontario legislature. Once Macdonald had to
step down and the Liberals under Alexander Mackenzie formed a new
government, the latter too had to deal with the temperance agenda. In
1874 a conference of the Ontario, Quebec, and New Brunswick Prohibitory Leagues urged Parliament to establish a royal commission to study
alcohol abuse and the impact of prohibitory laws. Liberal MP George
W. Ross, the leading temperance advocate in the house, reported that
petition signatures now totaled 100,687 individuals, including the
majority of the New Brunswick legislature and all members of the
Legislative Assembly of Ontario. A royal commission was created on
1 August 1874 and its members began traveling throughout the Mid-
west and northeastern United States, examining the effects of prohibition. Its report in favor of national prohibition, issued in 1875, was
adopted by the Senate (25–17), but the Commons took no action.

In light of this legislative inaction, a general convention of temperance activists was held in Montreal in 1876 in order to form a national
organization – the Dominion Alliance for the Total Suppression of
the Liquor Traffic – that would coordinate the efforts of all provincial
organizations. After adopting a resolution in favor of a local option law,
a deputation met with Prime Minister Alexander Mackenzie. However, he raised concerns about whether public sentiment was strongly
enough in favor of prohibition, the constitutionality of a plebiscite on
prohibition, and conflicting jurisdiction between federal and provincial
levels (Spence 1919: 117).

Parliament extended provisions of the local option contained in
the pre-Confederation Dunkin Act to all provinces and territories in
the Canada Temperance Act of 1878, known as the Scott Act after its
sponsor, Senator Richard William Scott. As a Liberal Party measure,
it appeared to align that party's policies with the views of its social
base in the Maritimes, Ontario, and the West. Waite (1971: 89) observes

that, "in the heartland of Mackenzie liberalism – Southwest Ontario – Methodists, Baptists, Congregationalists, Free Kirk and Presbyterians were strongly prohibitionist; the great bulk of this vote was Liberal."

Yet, with neither political party prepared to take an unequivocal position in support of prohibition, a division developed within the ranks of the prohibition movement, separating the dominant Dominion Alliance faction, which favored lobbying individual legislators and allying with pro-prohibition MPs of either party, from an emerging minority faction that wanted to establish a "New Party" along the lines of the Prohibition Party in the United States (Spence 1919: 141). With a slate of MPs elected in the general election of 1891 now committed to the Dominion Alliance agenda, a resolution was offered "that in the opinion of this House the time has arrived when it is expedient to prohibit the manufacture and sale of intoxicating liquor for beverage purposes."[5] The response of the Conservative government was to appoint another royal commission, whose report in 1895 again failed to recommend prohibition.

When the Liberals returned to power in 1896, they did so with a pledge by their leader, Wilfrid Laurier, that, once in power, the government would hold a nationwide plebiscite on prohibition. By then, the provinces of Manitoba, Prince Edward Island, Ontario, and Nova Scotia had all held referendums with majorities in favor of prohibition. But when a national plebiscite was held in 1898, prohibition won favor with only 51 percent of those eligible voting. At the same time, the vote in Quebec was 71 percent opposed. The results were sufficient for the prime minister to refuse to enact legislation enabling prohibition. As he wrote in justifying his position to the Dominion Alliance, "The electorate of Canada, to which the question was submitted, comprised 1,233,849 voters, and of that number less than twenty-three per cent, or a trifle over one-fifth, affirmed their conviction of the principles of prohibition." Moreover, he continued, "no good purpose would be served by forcing upon the people a measure which is shown by the vote to have the support of less than twenty-three per cent of the electorate" (Spence 1919: 252).

---

5 According to Spence (1919: 161–3), the resolution was supported by representatives from the Methodist General Conference, the Presbyterian General Assembly, the Disciples of Christ, the Congregationalist Union, Salvation Army, W.C.T.U., Sons of Temperance, Royal Templars of Temperance, and Independent Order of Good Templars.

The nation-building implications of alcohol regulation became evident after Confederation with the passage of the Canada Temperance Act of 1878. That law was challenged in Fredericton, New Brunswick, the first municipality to vote itself dry under its provisions. There, a local public-house owner, Charles Russell, argued that Parliament could not delegate its powers to another authority. The case went before the judicial committee of the Privy Council of Great Britain, then the highest appeals court. The judges decided that Parliament was within its full legal authority to pass such laws, based on the provision of the new constitution, the British North America Act of 1867, that allowed it to legislate over matters that affected "peace, order and good government" (*Russell v. the Queen*, 1882). Although subsequent Privy Council decisions, including that of *Hodge v. the Queen* (1883),[6] contributed to some diminishment of federal authority, alcohol-related issues remained in the forefront of nation building. Those issues were a major source of court decisions over the constitutionality of the division of powers between the federal and provincial governments (Fish 2011).

Opportunities in Wartime

The First World War began in 1914 and immediately enlisted the support of Canada; the United States did not join in until 1917. In each country, the occasion of war focused attention on alcohol regulation and encouraged the mobilization of prohibitionists. There were, however, some different motivating factors and different post-war repercussions. These differences were reflected in media coverage (see figures 2.1 and 2.2 above). In Canada, the greatest media attention came first in 1916 and was at its highest in 1918. In the United States, coverage slowly rose in 1914 and reached a modest peak in 1919, but never to the level achieved in Canada. Using the *Readers' Guide to Periodical Literature* as his data source and, unlike our narrower focus, Schrad (2007: 446–7) includes all mentions of prohibition and alcohol control and traces a fivefold increase in coverage between 1915 and 1919 compared to the preceding five years, with the majority of articles taking a positive stance toward prohibition.

In the United States, Congress reconvened in April 1917 to declare war, after which the Lever Food and Fuel Control Act of 1917 was

6 This case also involved the conditions under which alcohol could be sold.

enacted, banning the production of distilled spirits for the duration of the war. That policy was strengthened by the War Prohibition Act of 1918, which forbade the manufacture and sale of all intoxicating beverages of more than 2.75 percent alcohol content (including beer and wine as well as spirts) until demobilization was completed. Kyvig (1979: 10) summarizes how war brought together all the factors promoting prohibition.

> The need to sacrifice individual pleasure for the defense and improvement of society became a constant theme. The war centralized authority in Washington, loosening restraints on activity by the federal government. The importance of conserving food resources became apparent, and drys seized the opportunity to emphasize the waste of grain in the production of alcoholic beverages. Finally, the war created an atmosphere of hostility toward all things German, not the least of which was beer.

Wartime legislation in the United States was part of a continuing momentum to ensure that prohibition would become national policy. It was with only brief debate that Congress considered the Eighteenth Amendment, prohibiting the manufacture, sale, and consumption of alcoholic beverages throughout the country. "By 1917 so many congressmen were prepared to vote for a constitutional amendment that the doubters found themselves brushed aside" (Kyvig 1979: 11). The Eighteenth Amendment was proposed by two-thirds of the House of Representatives (282–128) and the Senate (65–20) and took effect on 17 January 1920 following ratification by three-fourths of the states. It had virtually equal partisan support in the House (69 percent of Republicans and Democrats) and the Senate (78 percent of Republicans and 75 percent of Democrats) in the Republican-controlled 65th Congress. Schrad (2007: 449) attributes the rapid passage of prohibition to shifting feedback mechanisms – increased public attention to the issue, a focus from "one set of underlying views on the issue to another," the anticipated prospects for success of policy change, a shifting institutional venue from states to the national government, and a shortened time horizon for the political debate that emphasized the most obvious policy options, notably prohibition.

In Canada, many of the same wartime experiences as in the United States were present and initially produced similar responses. A request to Parliament in March 1917 by the Dominion Prohibition Committee (the latest umbrella organization of temperance activists) for wartime prohibition of the importation, manufacture, and interprovincial trade in intoxicating liquors preceded Prime Minister Robert Borden's order-in-council on November 1917 providing that "after the first of December no grain of any kind, and no substances that can be used for food shall be used in Canada for the distillation of potable liquors." Immediately following the December 1917 general election that legitimated Borden's Unionist pro-conscription government, another order-in-council was issued, mandating that "the importation of intoxicating liquors be prohibited during the continuance of the war, and for one year thereafter," and the various prohibitory measures were consolidated in a March 1918 order-in-council. Yet, despite the urging of the Dominion Prohibition Committee and an abortive legislative effort, once the war ended and the relevant order-in-council was no longer operative, prohibition disappeared from the national agenda.

Evaluating Establishment

There are several common features in how prohibition became established on the policy agenda in the two countries. Most notably, agenda setting was primarily the result of the mobilization of similar kinds of people associated with Protestant evangelism who took political action under the leadership of clergy and activist women. The social movement in the United States emerged earlier and provided models for the Canadian movement. The anti-Catholic underpinnings of the movement were more overt in the United States, while a more restrained approach by the Canadian government was tied to ensuring the loyalty of French-speaking Catholics. Even though the Dominion Alliance discouraged participation by francophones and Catholics, for whom total prohibition was undesirable, a French-language counterpart, La Ligue Anti-alcoölique, was formed in 1906 to advocate legal restriction on the use of alcohol.

Both countries experienced the drive to prohibition as highly politicized and contentious. They were initially similar in the reluctance shown by the established political parties to take up the issue of prohibition. But roused by a perceived threat from the single-minded Prohibition Party and extreme displays of nationalism accompanying the First World War, both US parties became advocates for prohibition. The establishment phase then culminated in a constitutional amendment embraced by Republicans and Democrats. In Canada, both parties remained relatively unenthusiastic supporters of prohibition. When the stimulus of war ended, and despite continu-ing pressure, both countries were prepared to retreat from upholding prohibition as national policy.

Once alcohol regulation was established, it relevance to nation building continued, though differently in the two countries. In the United States, questions about which level of government had author-ity to impose taxes or regulate commerce were answered early in its history, and alcohol declined as subject to such constitutional debate even when amendments to the constitution were involved. But histo-rian Lisa McGirr (2015) argues persuasively that prohibition laid the groundwork for the expansion of the federal government and the basis of the penal state that exists today. In Canada, contention over federal versus provincial authority was often focused on alcohol and would continue to occupy the courts into the twentieth century. More than 20 percent of the first 125 cases involving constitutional questions about the division of powers involved alcohol (Risk 1990: 689), and such cases continued to come before the courts at least until 1980 (Fish 2011: 206). The regulation of alcohol, of which prohibition was one possibility, thus played a crucial role in defining the contours of Canadian government and nationhood.

Decline and Resurgence

By the late 1920s there were signs that prohibition was losing its mass appeal in the United States. A *Literary Digest* survey, though imperfect by today's standards, found that 40 percent of its respondents favored repeal in 1930, compared to 21 percent in 1922 (Kyvig 1979: 117). A *New York Herald-Tribune* survey of 110 daily newspapers in 36 states found that "dry" papers outnumbered "wet" papers by two-to-one in 1919, but were evenly divided by 1930 (ibid.: 117). Schrad's (2007: 447) data show a sharp drop in the positive to negative tone in media coverage beginning in 1919. In 1926, eight state referendums were held and, though the questions posed differed, various prohibitory regulations were defeated in New York, Illinois, Wisconsin, Montana, and Nevada, compared to victories by pro-prohibition forces in California, Colorado, and Missouri. Kyvig (1979: 68–9) attributes this decline to the grow-ing strength of countermovements, concluding that "the contemporary appraisal of these returns – that opponents of prohibition had gained considerable popular backing although they had little support in state and federal legislatures – appears accurate."

The underpinnings of these countermovements stemmed from several factors involved in the declining appeal of prohibition. One was the criminalization of ordinary citizens for continuing what had been the common practice of social drinking. Difficulties of enforcement grew as the profits from illegal commerce in alcohol increased exponentially and greatly enhanced the power of large criminal organizations. Those organizations, in turn, used their resources to severely damage the integrity of enforcement agencies (Nelli 1985). The law itself contributed to its own undermining by the loopholes it left for those producing near-beer or alcohol for industrial purposes and the light sanctions imposed on them when they were apprehended (Evan and Schwartz 1964: 274). Moreover, as one prohibition supporter complained, "Dry laws are being administered by wet officials. When Mr. Harding became President he appointed as head of the department responsible for enforcement one who for nearly forty years had been heavily interested in distilling" (Colvin 1926: 496).

As these conditions could not be ignored, President Hoover appointed a National Commission on Law Observance and Enforcement in 1929. Although the commission did not recommend repeal of prohibition, it concluded that its enforcement was unworkable (Wickersham 1931). In chapter 1, we were inclined to be dismissive of Downs's (1972) argument that issue decline could be attributed to the excessively high costs of administration or enforcement, since we did not expect it to be relevant to moral conflicts. However, in the case of prohibition, his position assumes new credibility.

During the height of social movement pressure for prohibition there had been those opposed, for example, the Association against the Prohibition Amendment, founded in 1918, but with little effect. Most opposition came from the brewing and distilling industry, but it did not engage in any coordinated efforts and showed little appreciation of how effective the movement for prohibition had already become (Munger and Schaller 1997: 149). But as the unanticipated effects of prohibition became more troublesome, a new and more effective countermovement emerged. Among its most significant components was the Women's Organization for National Prohibition Reform (WONPR), founded in 1929, with a membership of one million. Because women were such a powerful force within the prohibition movement, WONPR was significant in demonstrating through its opposition that no single position could capture women's interests.[7] The countermovement, "abetted by labor unions, trade and bar associations, medical societies, and veterans groups, retrieved the idea of repeal from the realm of assumed impossibility and made it a serious matter of public discussion" (Kyvig 1979: xv). Legal expertise came from the Voluntary Committee of Lawyers (VCL), founded in 1927, and mobilized by what it saw as the Eighteenth Amendment's violation of individual and state rights (Evan and Schwartz 1964: 273). Once it overcame internal skepticism about the prospects for repeal, it "fashioned the means for ratification of a repeal amendment, through special conventions in the states" (Hamm 1995: 270). Through such organizations existing community leaders were enlisted in support of basic values congruent with constitutional rights (Merz 1931: 296; Root 1934: 17). By emphasizing values every bit as potent as those that prohibitionists had advocated, anti-prohibitionists' success supports a general proposition formulated by Meyer and Staggenborg (1996: 1639). *"The likelihood that opposition to a movement will take the form of a sustained countermovement is directly related to the opposition's ability to portray the conflict as one that entails larger value cleavages in society"* [emphasis in original]. In the end, the effectiveness of the anti-prohibition movement could be measured by the absence of any notable resurgence in support for prohibition.

In Canada, the loss of persuasive power on the part of those who wanted national prohibition came earlier and required much less in the way of policy intervention. Although the Dominion Prohibition Committee, on 2 December 1919, urged that the Government of Canada "take the steps necessary to continue in effect the provisions of the orders-in-council of March 11, 1918 (P.C. 5879), by having the same embodied in legislation to be enacted by the Parliament of Canada," such action failed because of disagreements between the House of Commons and the Senate. The interprovincial importation restriction was repealed, effective 31 December 1920. Even subsequent provincial plebiscites, held in all provinces except Quebec and British Columbia, in which majorities voted to ban the importation of alcoholic beverages, were ineffective in preventing such interprovincial commerce. If those

---

7 With the passage of the Nineteenth Amendment, enfranchising women, women's energies could now be redirected to other causes, or even to lessened political involvement (Munger and Schaller 1997: 150).

plebiscites showed that there were still reservoirs of prohibition sentiment, they could not overcome the unwillingness of the federal government to take up the cause.

Resurgence of a moral conflict is one possible phase in issue life
histories. But in the case of national prohibition, once it declined as a
viable issue, it had no resurgence. Whatever potential that existed for
prohibition to rise again was reshaped by concern directed to alcohol
as a product to be excluded from use to one that could be more lightly
controlled through regulation. Another kind of reframing might have
occurred, in which abuse of alcohol was at the center and alcohol addiction was defined as a psychomedical problem, but the time for this perspective was still in the future.

Resolution

The resolution of the conflict in the United States entailed by prohibition took an unprecedented form – the repeal of an amendment to
the constitution and its replacement by another. The countermovement
supporting repeal was aided by a changed political opportunity structure resulting from the Great Depression. According to Kyvig (1979:
116): "The growing malaise of the Great Depression introduced new
political and social as well as economic circumstances, greatly acceler-
ating the revolt against prohibition and causing the prospect of repeal
to be taken seriously for the first time."

Social movement discourse shifted from the sinfulness of alcohol
consumption to the pauperization of ordinary citizens who could not
find work. The economic collapse, moreover, occurred at a time when
pressure for repeal polarized the major parties. Earlier in the controversy over prohibition, both political parties had tried to avoid taking
a stand on the issue. When prohibition was enacted in 1920, neither
party platform mentioned it. But, by 1924, the issue had become troublesome to both parties, especially the Republicans. This was because
the Republicans "had become its custodians by virtue of their holding
office since 1920" (Kyvig 1979: 63). In contrast, the Democrats became
identified with the "wet" forces, especially after nominating Alfred E.
Smith, a New York Catholic, as their 1928 presidential candidate. In
1932, the Democratic Party platform openly endorsed repeal and the
subsequent election of Franklin Roosevelt was "'widely interpreted as
a voter directive for repeal'" (Hamm 1995: 271). Repeal would remove
the enormous costs of failed enforcement and provide new tax revenues

to support the promises of the New Deal.[8] For the Republicans, its 1932 "platform fight marked a new peak in anti-prohibitionist strength within Republican ranks, but it demonstrated, to a nationwide radio audience among others, that wets remained a minority at odds with party leaders" (Kyvig 1979: 155).

In the end, majorities of both Republican and Democratic congressional delegations voted for the Twenty-first Amendment, though Democrats gave more support to repeal than Republicans during the "lame-duck" session of the 72nd Congress. The partisan divide was 79 to 67 percent in the Senate and even sharper in the House – 85 to 55 percent. Repealing a constitutional amendment was unprecedented and many critics of prohibition thought it virtually impossible, but ratification of the Twenty-first Amendment came about even more quickly than the Eighteenth, though with more (8) dissenting states. Repeal was the only amendment of the twenty-seven added to the US Constitution that utilized the option of special ratifying conventions, intended to insulate the political process from "dry" forces and neutralize the influence of rural state legislatures that more likely favored continuing the ban. The two-thirds margin in the House (289–121) and the Senate (63–23) in February of 1933 led to ratification by the required 36 states on 5 December 1933, with Maine and Montana ratifying later. According to Schrad (2007), the speed with which repeal (as well as prohibition) was instituted was due to a kind of "error correction," arising from the feedback mechanisms inherent in the US policymaking process. Although, like us, he gives credit to the drastic environmental changes that preceded those policies – the First World War in the case of prohibition and the Great Depression in the case of repeal – to him those remain no more than stimuli. And, unlike us, he is dismissive of the impact of social movements and countermovements as among the engines of change.

In assembling evidence for each of the phases, it would have been possible to assign passage of the Eighteenth Amendment to the resolution phase on the presumption that no political act could be more decisive and secure than a constitutional amendment. Certainly, to those who worked toward that goal, it was a victory that legitimated their

---

8 Munger and Schaller (1997: 159) argue that the "most powerful force in the Repeal movement may well have been the desire of New Deal reformers to finance their programs."

actions. Could the Twenty-first Amendment be yet another tenuous victory? The answer is very unlikely, given the solid evidence of lack of enthusiasm for prohibition that grew from the time of its existence until after repeal. Almost three-quarters of the voters in 37 states electing delegates to state ratifying conventions by November 1933 favored repeal (Kyvig 1979: 152). A spring 1932 *Literary Digest* poll showed a similar percentage favoring repeal, though it may have exaggerated majority opinion. From 1936 through 1939 Gallup asked its national sample two related questions: "If the question of national prohibition should come up again, would you vote to make the country dry?" or "Would you vote for prohibition or against it?" In a total of eight polls, about two-thirds opposed prohibition.[9]

After 1933, the US population under statewide prohibitory laws shrank markedly (Schrad 2007: 446). Economists Strumpf and Oberholzer-Gee (2002: 4–5) report that, in 1935, approximately 38 percent of the population still lived in areas that prohibited the sale of distilled spirits, but this declined to about 18 percent by 1940 and further dropped and stabilized at 6 percent in 1970. Protestant churches, especially the pietistic or evangelical denominations, had always been in the forefront of the temperance movement (Hamm 1995: 36; Gusfield 1986: 117–18), but newer research on the further decrease of "dry" counties between 1970 and 2008 (when they numbered only 263) showed that the key factor was the "decline in a religious atmosphere dominated by Evangelical Christians" (Frendreis and Tatalovich 2013: 387).

Media coverage of national prohibition plunged from its highest peak in 1932 to virtually nothing by 1937 (see figure 2.1). Another indicator of the death of prohibition was the complete absence of any opinion polling on the subject by 1950, although the issue was important enough during the 1930s and 1940s to warrant regular scrutiny by pollsters. Between 1935 and 1949, sixty surveys were conducted, but after there were only four polls on prohibition-related subjects through 2010. In 1950 Gallup found that "if the question of national prohibition should come up again," 72 percent would vote against prohibition and 23 percent would vote in favor. In December 1954 Gallup, without reference to prohibition, asked, "Would you vote to outlaw the sale of

9 Polls are archived at the Roper Center for Public Opinion Research, using the iPOLL search engine and keyword "prohibition," at http://www.ropercenter.uconn.edu.
flagship.luc.edu/CFIDE/cf/action/ipoll/iPollResult.cfm?keyword=prohibition.

alcoholic beverages, or not?" and 63 percent answered in the negative. A May 1985 ABC News/*Washington Post* poll found 81 percent opposed when asked: "Would you favor a total prohibition of all alcoholic beverages, including beer, wine and liquor, like we had during the 1920s or not?" And more recently, a Drinking and Driving Survey by the Harvard School of Public Health in 2001 reported 78 percent opposed when asked: "If the question of national prohibition should come up again, would you vote to outlaw the sale of alcoholic beverages, or not?" The "dry" minority now represents roughly 20 percent of the US public.

One measure of the policy or governmental agenda is the number of congressional hearings on a subject (Baumgartner and Jones 1993). Using that variable as a third indicator of issue salience, over 1900–33, there were forty-five congressional hearings on subjects related to prohibition, but following repeal in 1933, there were only four each during the 1930s and 1940s and eight between 1950 and 1970. Typically, these were concerned with federal administrative details like prohibiting or regulating alcoholic beverages in the military and in the District of Columbia or advertising alcoholic beverages on television.[10]

The evidence is clear: prohibition had ended its sojourn on the US national agenda and, despite continuing pockets of support, its potential for re-emergence is extremely limited.

The Canadian story finds resolution even earlier than in the United States. In Canada, prohibition as national policy had a much less stable legal basis – as a limited order-in-council – compared to the force of a constitutional amendment. Prohibition, if it were to continue, would be a matter of provincial policy and, except for Quebec, was, in fact, initially adopted by all other provinces once they were free to do so. But many of the same ills that accompanied enforcement in the United States spilled over into Canada, where "rum-running" became a lucrative pursuit and a threat to law enforcement (Steinke 2004).

British Columbia was the first to abandon prohibition in 1920, followed by Manitoba in 1923 and the two other western provinces the following year. Ontario and New Brunswick continued with prohibition until 1927 and Nova Scotia was the last holdout until 1930. Instead of prohibition, and with popular support demonstrated through

---

10 Congressional hearings from 1900 to 1970 were identified from the "congressional. proquest.com" search engine using the terms "Prohibition" and "alcoholic beverages."

referendums in several provinces, all provinces enacted government-controlled sale of alcoholic beverages that continues to the present. British Columbia first demonstrated how beneficial to provincial finances this arrangement could be and stimulated other provinces to follow (Forbes 1971: 31). Those financial benefits, in themselves, make it highly unlikely that pressure for national prohibition will re-emerge.

Prohibition and Its Phases

As moral conflicts pass through different phases, those phases are affected by their social and political environments, the nature of the issues themselves, and the national setting in which they occur. In this chapter we selected the case of prohibition primarily to demonstrate environmental effects on phases. Although we examined the experience of prohibition in both Canada and the United States, we deliberately made little comment on why the two countries differed because we are waiting until chapter 4 to systematically spell out which differences are relevant and our expectations about their impact. Given that we deal here with a single issue, it would appear there is little that can be said with confidence about how the character of an issue might affect its life history. Yet even from this one case, we begin to see prospects for the unique qualities of an issue to have an impact on its history. In the case of prohibition, it is the regulation of alcohol that occupies a special place in the course of nation building. We wait for chapter 3, where we present basic information about the six other issues that make up our sample of moral conflicts, to speculate more fully about what it is about issues themselves that may affect their fate. The focus here is solely on how prohibition illuminates issue phases, from which we generalize a set of testable hypotheses.

From the case of prohibition we generalize to five hypotheses about *emergence*. The first proposes that periods of rapid and major change create conditions that challenge established institutions and values and allow morally ambiguous behavior to flourish. As a result,

H_{p1}: moral conflicts are likely to emerge from large-scale social and political changes.

In a turbulent environment, specific events can act to symbolize the conflict surrounding a moral issue. Students of public policy assign great weight to the role of such events in encouraging conflicts to become a focus of controversy. It was difficult to isolate such events in the case of prohibition, which suggests that, while specific events may be a stimulus to moral conflicts, they are not an essential ingredient for emergence. The latter position is now dominant among students of social movements. We therefore hypothesize that

H_{P2}: while the emergence of moral conflicts may be stimulated by triggering events, the latter are not critical to that emergence.

Groups organized either into interest groups or new social movements are critical to issue emergence because these

H_{P3}: groups openly confront what they view as challenges to important values and aim to limit morally undesirable behavior.

Groups, distinctive because of demographic or social characteristics, are often differentially recruited into moralistic social movements. Such particularistic recruitment is also common in interest groups. Actions taken by either kind of group can benefit from their association with the identity of collective actors who, as Wuthnow (2017) argues,

H_{P4}: highlight their own social status and contrast it with other population groups associated with morally undesirable behavior.

The tactics social movements and interest groups select to achieve their goals are tied to their organizational resources. Resources include money, prestige, effective leadership, and committed members. The latter represent the organization on the ground and include those with local attachments. In general,

H_{P5}: more effective group tactics are tied to the ability to draw on rich resources.

Prohibition also provides insights about how issues are established. The *establishment* of moral issues on the policy agenda is affected by existing political procedures and outside pressures as well as by new environmental opportunities and the use of relatively unusual political avenues. Prohibition experiences suggest five hypotheses. Carrying over from groups' effectiveness in channeling the emergence of moral issues, prohibition demonstrated how they also reveal the power of

Cobb et al.'s (1976) model of outside-access in establishing moral issues on the policy agenda. From this we anticipate that

H_{p6}: active groups, by continuing their pressure, using both more or less institutionalized means, can bring about establishment of moral issues.

The search for establishment takes place in an environment that is set to either repel the entry of moral issues or enhance the likelihood of their acceptance onto the policy agenda. For example, because the regulation of alcohol was already the subject of national governmental actions, calls for increased regulation became easier to accept. We generalize from this that,

H_{p7}: the entry of moral issues will be eased when prior laws and procedures have acknowledged their legitimacy as subjects of policy.

Political parties, for the most part, prefer to avoid involvement in contentious issues that could alienate critical segments of the electorate. When this no longer becomes possible, one party will assume ownership of the issue by staking a claim to that side of the controversy that appears most appealing to its constituents. In the case of prohibition, although the Republicans were more "dry," the Democrats also came to embrace a similar stand that then led to passage of the Eighteenth Amendment. Yet, in accounting for the initial stages,

H_{p8}: the establishment of moral issues proceeds when at least one major party takes a position.

Establishment of moral issues takes place in a continually changing environment and such change can augment opportunities for establishment. In the case of prohibition, opportunities were opened by the advent of the First World War that gave new justification to proponents. Opportunities for establishment can most readily be grasped by authoritative actors whose decisions are binding on the polity. They may be based in executive, legislative, or judicial settings. The judiciary is included among our enlarged set of institutional agenda setters, as discussed in chapter 1, who can make policy in Cobb et al.'s (1976) model of inside-access agenda setting. That is,

H_{p9}: authoritative leaders use new conditions and events to contribute to establishment.

The case of prohibition suggests that normal political procedures may not be sufficient for moral issues to become fully established. In the United States, establishment came through the unusual route of a constitutional amendment. In Canada, there was an equally unusual use of referendums, both federally and provincially. This alerts us to the likelihood that

H_{P10}: moral issues will become established through atypical political procedures.

Moral issues encounter trying times when they *decline* in the attention they receive. Yet not all issues will experience decline, at least not until they are fully resolved. When they do decline, reasons and signs are subsumed under three hypotheses. Prohibition, for one, illustrated the inability to regain support once decline had set in. That suggests decline may be insurmountable when

H_{P11}: changing environmental conditions make the original moral objectives outmoded or untenable.

Decline may be manifested through the loss of popular appeal and the unwillingness of political authorities to engage with the issue. Prohibition offered the likelihood that

H_{P12}: declining support for an issue will follow when it becomes evident that the costs of administration or enforcement are unacceptably high.

Decline may also come about when opposing interests organize into countermovements. The tension between movements and countermovements rests on the ability of each to frame their objectives in moral terms.

H_{P13}: Countermovement effectiveness is associated with the ability to mobilize support through appeals to core values.

Although prohibition failed to overcome its decline and regain its centrality, nevertheless, its experiences suggest two possible ways for moral issues to make a comeback from decline. One possibility for *resurgence* is tied to the unfolding history of the issue in question, the second to the relative success of tactical responses.

H_{P14}: Resurgence occurs when the problems initially addressed become more acute.

H_{P15}: Resurgence occurs when either a participating social movement or a countermovement is able to assert or reassert the legitimacy of its arguments.

The final phase of issue life histories is the *resolution* of the problems raised, allowing them to be dropped from the policy agenda. The principal way this comes about is through some authoritative action with force of law. Yet prohibition provided an unusual case where two apparent resolutions appeared at different times – the first when prohibition became US law and the second when a new constitutional amendment undid the first and gave back authority to the states. If we ask when authoritative actions signify the true end to conflict and when they can be reopened to challenge, prohibition presents an answer. Because major social and economic changes alter the political climate and open new opportunities for contenders,

H_{P16}: the end-state resolution will favor the side challenging the original presentation of the moral issue.

Prohibition also demonstrated the importance of the values that are affirmed through resolution. Initially, prohibition was legitimated through sectarian values divisive of the national society. But its final resolution took place through the legitimation of a set of values more in keeping with the national culture, ones that favored individual and locally based decision making about personal behavior. From this we predict that

H_{P17}: resolution will be effective when it symbolizes commitment to inclusive and fundamental values representative of the larger national interest.

Because of the conflict engendered by moral issues, we have already noted that established political parties will generally try to avoid entanglement. But, once the conflict is well underway, partisan stakes alter and political parties become polarized. But, as conflict continues and pressure for resolution mounts, however tepid it may be,

H_{P18}: bipartisan consensus comes to define the final policy outcome.

This analysis points to how the life history of prohibition is a rich source for guiding subsequent exploration of the phases through which moral conflicts may pass. Because prohibition took place in a very different world from the contemporary one and was resolved in an unusual way, we can understand skepticism about its applicability to predicting the life histories of current moral conflicts. While taking full account of how the institutional fabric of both countries has changed, the ensuing analysis will demonstrate to what extent the model we have presented offers an adequate explanation for how moral issues live and sometimes die.

Before testing the hypotheses we first look, in the following chapter, at the full set of the moral conflicts to be examined, searching for clues as to how aspects of moral issues may affect their phases. Chapter 4 brings us to an examination of the differences between Canada and the United States and their likely effect on phases.

REFERENCES

AffordableAcadia. 2010. "Maine: First Dry State in 1851." http://www.affordableacadia.com/2010/maine-first-dry-state-in-1851/.

Baumgartner, Frank R., and Bryan D. Jones. 1993. *Agendas and Instability in American Politics*. Chicago: University of Chicago Press.

Bern, Eric. 2004. *Spirits of America: A Social History of Alcohol*. Philadelphia: Temple University Press.

Birrell, A.J. 1977. "D.I.K. Rine and the Gospel Temperance Movement in Canada." *Canadian Historical Review* 58 (1): 23–44. https://doi.org/10.3138/CHR-058-01-03.

Blocker, Jack S., Jr. 1989. *American Temperance Movements: Cycles of Reform*. Boston: Twayne Publishers.

Cherrington, Ernest H. (1920) 1969. *The Evolution of Prohibition in the United States of America*. Montclair, NJ: Patterson Smith.

Cobb, Roger W., Jeannie-Keith Ross, and Marc Howard Ross. 1976. "Agenda Building as a Comparative Political Process." *American Political Science Review* 70 (1): 126–38. https://doi.org/10.1017/S0003055400264034.

Colvin, D. Leigh. 1926. *Prohibition in the United States*. New York: George H. Doran.

Downs, Anthony. 1972. "Up and Down with Ecology – the 'Issue-Attention Cycle.'" *Public Interest* 28 (Summer): 38–50.

Evan, William M., and Mildred A. Schwartz. 1964. "Law and the Emergence of Formal Organization." *Sociology and Social Research* 48: 270–80.

Ferry, Darren. 2003. "'To the Interests and Conscience of the Great Mass of the Community': The Evolution of Temperance Societies in Nineteenth-Century Central Canada." *Journal of the Canadian Historical Association* 14 (1): 137–63. https://doi.org/10.7202/010323ar.

Fish, Morris J. 2011. "The Effect of Alcohol on the Canadian Constitution … Seriously." *McGill Law Journal / Revue de Droit de McGill* 57 (1): 189–209. https://doi.org/10.7202/1006421ar.

Forbes, E.R. 1971. "Prohibition and the Social Gospel in Nova Scotia." *Acadiensis* (Fredericton) 1 (Autumn): 11–36.

Frendreis, John, and Raymond Tatalovich. 2013. "Secularization, Modernization, or Population Change: Explaining the Decline of Prohibition in the United States." *Social Science Quarterly* 94 (2): 379–94. https://doi.org/10.1111/j.1540-6237.2012.00878.x.

Gusfield, Joseph R. 1986. *Symbolic Crusade: Status Politics and the American Temperance Movement*. 2nd ed. Urbana: University of Illinois Press.

Hamm, Richard F. 1995. *Shaping the Eighteenth Amendment: Temperance Reform, Legal Culture, and the Polity, 1880–1920*. Chapel Hill: University of North Carolina Press.

Heron, Craig. 2003. *Booze: A Distilled History*. Toronto: Between the Lines.

Hoover, Michael. 2014. "The Whiskey Rebellion." http://www.ttb.gov/public_info/whisky_rebellion.shtml.

Kerr, K. Austin. 1985. *Organized for Prohibition: A New History of the Anti-Saloon League*. New Haven, CT: Yale University Press.

Kingdon, John W. 2010. *Agendas, Alternatives, and Public Policy. Updated*. 2nd ed. New York: Longman.

Kyvig, David E. 1979. *Repealing National Prohibition*. Chicago: University of Chicago Press.

McGirr, Lisa. 2015. *The War on Alcohol: Prohibition and the Rise of the American State*. New York: W.W. Norton.

Merz, Charles. 1931. *The Dry Decade*. Garden City, NY: Doubleday Doran.

Meyer, David S., and Suzanne Staggenborg. 1996. "Movements, Countermovements, and the Structure of Political Opportunity." *American Journal of Sociology* 101 (6): 1628–60. https://doi.org/10.1086/230869.

Munger, Michael, and Thomas Schaller. 1997. "The Prohibition-Repeal Amendments: A Natural Experiment in Interest Group Influence." *Public Choice* 90 (1–4): 139–63. https://doi.org/10.1023/A:1004921405015.

Nelli, H. 1985. "American Syndicate Crime." In *Law, Alcohol, and Order*, ed. David E. Kyvik, 123–38. Westport, CT: Greenwood Press.

Noel, Jan. 1995. *Canada Dry: Temperance Crusades before Confederation*. Toronto: University of Toronto Press.

Noll, Mark A. 1992. *A History of Christianity in the United States and Canada*. Grand Rapids, MI: Wm. B. Eerdmans.

Odegard, Peter. 1928. *Pressure Politics: The Story of the Anti-Saloon League*. New York: Columbia University Press.

Risk, R.C.B. 1990. "Canadian Courts Under the Influence." *University of Toronto Law Journal* 40 (4): 687–737. https://doi.org/10.2307/825682.

Root, Grace C. 1934. *Women and Repeal*. New York, London: Harper and Brothers.

Schrad, Mark Lawrence. 2007. "Constitutional Blemishes: American Alcohol Prohibition and Repeal as Policy Punctuation." *Policy Studies Journal: The Journal of the Policy Studies Organization* 35 (3): 437–63. https://doi.org/10.1111/j.1541-0072.2007.00232.x.

Skowronek, Stephen. 1982. *Building a New American State: The Expansion of National Administrative Capacities, 1877–1920*. New York: Cambridge University Press. https://doi.org/10.1017/CBO9780511665080.

Spence, Ruth Elizabeth. 1919. *Prohibition in Canada: A Memorial to Francis Stephens Spence*. Toronto: Ontario Branch of the Dominion Alliance.

Steinke, Gord. 2004. *Mobsters and Rumrunners of Canada: Crossing the Line*. Vancouver, BC: Lone Pine Publishing.

Strumpf, Koleman S., and Felix Oberholzer-Gee. 2002. "Endogenous Policy Decentralization: Testing the Central Tenet of Economic Federalism." *Journal of Political Economy* 110 (1): 1–36. https://doi.org/10.1086/324393.

Szymanski, Ann-Marie E. 2003. *Pathways to Prohibition: Radicals, Moderates, and Social Movement Outcomes*. Durham, NC: Duke University Press. https://doi.org/10.1215/9780822385301.

US Treasury Department. n.d. "The TTB Story." http://www.ttb.gov/about/history.shtml.

Waite, Peter B. 1971. *Canada 1874–1896: Arduous Destiny*. Toronto: McClelland and Stewart.

Wickersham, George W. 1931. *Enforcement of the Prohibition Laws. Official Records on the National Commission on Law Observance and Enforcement Pertaining to Its Investigation of the Facts as to the Enforcement, the Benefits and Abuses under the Prohibition Laws both before and since the Adoption of the Eighteenth Amendment to the Constitution*. Washington, DC: US Government Printing Office.

Wuthnow, Robert. 2017. *American Misfits and the Making of Middle-Class Respectability*. Princeton, NJ: Princeton University Press.

Chapter Three

Issue Portraits

Shared Meanings, National Stories

All the moral issues we consider share a more or less common meaning in Canada and the United States. This shared meaning is an indicator of the relative ease with which these issues are understood and one of their defining characteristics. Whether talking about abortion, capital punishment, gun control, marijuana, pornography, or same-sex relations, publics in both countries immediately understand their content and do so in similar ways. This does not mean that they necessarily feel the same way about an issue or draw the same conclusions about how it should be handled. It is, instead, the shared understandings of what the issues mean that are at the foundation of our comparisons between the two countries.

The purpose of this volume is to understand the phases of moral issues, from their first appearance to their final outcome. To accomplish this goal, each of the chapters, beginning with chapter 5, will address a single phase and examine how all the selected issues manifest similarities and variations within that phase. In order to avoid continually repeating basic information about the issues, we use this chapter to present brief portraits. Readers can then return to it whenever they need to be refreshed about factual material.

A concise template for each issue answers the following questions:

1. How is the issue commonly understood?
2. When did it first appear as a source of contention on the national political horizon?
3. What is its current political status?
4. In what ways do Canada and the United States differ in regard to any of these questions?

Abortion

Abortion is understood as the termination of a pregnancy through the removal of an embryo or fetus from the womb. Unlike a miscarriage, when the embryo's expulsion is unintended, an abortion occurs through some intentional action. Whether legal or not, abortions have always been performed, either through the initiative of the one pregnant, a midwife, or a physician. When treated as a political issue, the moral content of abortion derives from two opposing positions. On one side are those who argue that abortion, in ending a burgeoning life, is akin to murder. The opposition gives primacy to the pregnant woman and argues she is the one with the right to choose whether she should continue to carry the fetus. Although today, in the United States as well as elsewhere, the conservative position is pro-life, earlier in the history of the United States the opposite was the case. Historian Daniel K. Williams (2016) demonstrates that it was Progressives, concerned for the poor and the powerless, who were the major advocates of criminalizing abortion.

In the United States, inducing abortions was practiced quite freely until well into the nineteenth century, when individual states began to make it illegal.[1] The medical profession took the lead in pressing for illegality and the latter was achieved nationally in 1880 (Mohr 1978). At the same time, room was left to allow terminating pregnancies when the mother's life was at stake. Other abortions were performed surreptitiously, often using dangerous methods, by midwives, physicians, or the affected women. Not until the middle of the twentieth century were new legal questions raised about the conditions under which abortions could be performed. At that point, the legal profession began to press for changes in the law, joining a medical profession that had long abandoned its opposition to narrow definitions of therapeutic abortion.

Changes came about gradually, with a few states allowing abortion under special circumstances, such as pregnancies resulting from rape or incest, with decisions about appropriateness made by physicians and hospitals. In 1970, New York, Washington, Alaska, and Hawaii passed

---

1 For an historical overview, see the chapter on abortion in Boston Women's Health Collective (2005). For political and sociological analyses, drawn on later in this volume, see Brodie et al. 1992; Halfmann 2011; Haussman 2005; Luker 1984; Tatalovich 1997.

laws that made abortion possible virtually on demand if performed by a physician in a medical facility. Then, in 1973, the Supreme Court ruled in *Roe v. Wade* that "the right of privacy ... founded in the Fourteenth Amendment's concept of personal liberty ... is broad enough to encompass a woman's decision whether or not to terminate her pregnancy." The court's legalization of abortion was qualified by its application only to the first trimester of pregnancy. Decisions made after that time could be subject to state restrictions as long as the mother's life was not endangered.

In present-day United States, abortion is legal but increasingly hedged in by legal, financial, and extra-legal means. For example, individual states have introduced restrictive measures ranging from requirements of parental involvement in the case of minors, to counseling for all requesting an abortion, to mandatory waiting periods, with parental involvement most common (Keller and Yarrow 2013). For the most part, abortion services are available only in urban centers. Training in providing abortions is provided in a small minority of residency programs in obstetrics/gynecology. Meanwhile, forces opposed to abortion under any circumstances have grown in strength and visibility and hold out the potential for successfully undoing *Roe v. Wade*.

With Confederation, Canada inherited criminal law from Britain, where the first anti-abortion laws were passed in 1803. The Canadian criminal code was altered in 1929 to permit abortion when needed to save the life of the mother. But in a revision of the Criminal Code in 1955, the term "unlawfully" was dropped, raising new questions about whether abortion was legal under most circumstances. By the mid-1960s, the topic was prominent in both legal and medical circles. Clear change came in 1969 with passage of an omnibus bill in Parliament that redefined several restrictions on personal behavior, including abortion. The new law permitted only therapeutic abortions, performed by a physician, and approval by a hospital-appointed therapeutic abortion committee. Grounds for permitting abortion were based on the mental or physical health of the mother.

Just as in the United States, there were soon challenges to the law, both from those opposed to abortion and from those testing its limits in order to broaden availability. The most dramatic case involved Dr Henry Morgentaler, who came to trial four times for performing abortions without consultation and in his own clinic. Each time he was tried, a jury found him innocent. The Crown (i.e., the government in office) appealed, a practice that had been eliminated in Britain and the United States more than one hundred years ago, and the jury verdict was overturned (Farkas 1976). But in *R. v. Morgentaler* (1988), the Supreme Court ruled that the abortion provisions in the Criminal Code were unconstitutional (Richer 2008). That ruling left Canada in the unusual position of having no law governing abortions. However, just as in the United States, access to abortions remains unevenly distributed by province and, within provinces, between urban and rural settings (Palley 2006; Haussman 2005: 1).

Public attention to abortion, measured by media coverage, has varied over time.[2] In the United States, over a sixty-year period, the highest level of coverage was in 1989, with progressively less coverage following (see figure 3.1). In the new millennium, coverage has averaged fewer than fifty articles per year. Before the peak in 1989, there was a relatively small one in 1967 and an increased one in 1973, with subsequent coverage fluctuating downward until 1989. Events that heightened media attention were, in the case of the first peaks, a combination of concern about the rise of problematic pregnancies due to thalidomide, an unapproved drug used to treat morning sickness (Winerip 2013), and an epidemic of rubella (Stencil 1976); changing roles for women that allowed abortion to be seen as part of women's rights (Rossi 1969: 338–46); and, most notably, the Supreme Court's ruling permitting legal abortion. The second peak chronicled the growing contention over abortion, including incidents of violence against doctors and clinics performing abortions. It was also the year when the Supreme Court, in *Webster v. Reproductive Health Services* (1989), delivered a blow to pro-abortion advocates by upholding a Missouri law banning the use of public employees and facilities to perform abortions and requiring physicians to test for viability at twenty-four weeks of gestation.

Canadian media coverage in the same period shows a more uneven trajectory, with four peaks along with signs of increasing interest from about 1962 through 1975 (see figure 3.2). The rise in coverage that began in the early period can be attributed to similar stimuli that affected US coverage – the effects of rubella, thalidomide,[3] and the mobilization of women – plus the advent of the 1969 legislation affecting abortion. The first noticeable peak occurred in 1985; the next, and highest, between

2 See appendix 1 for a description of data sources and methods of coding.
3 Thalidomide became available in Canada in 1959 in sample form and was licensed for prescriptions from 1961–2 (Thalidomide Victims Association of Canada n.d.).

Figure 3.1 Media coverage of abortion in the United States, 1950–2010

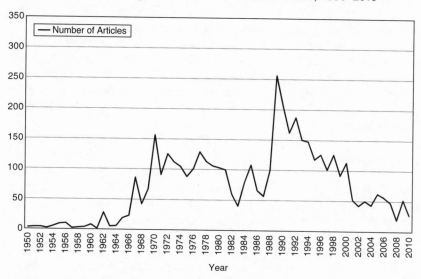

Figure 3.2 Media coverage of abortion in Canada, 1950–2010

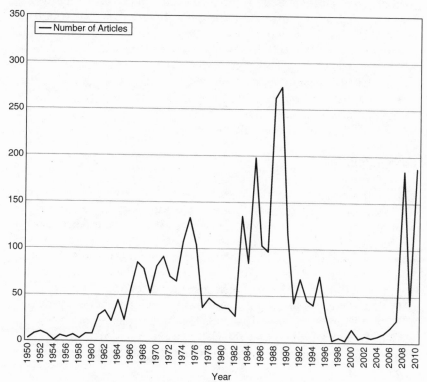

1988 and 1990; and then one each in 2008 and 2010. The earliest peak, along with some prior smaller ones, is associated with efforts to keep Dr Morgentaler from performing abortions in an unauthorized fashion. The last two peaks again have some association with Dr Morgentaler, who, after all his legal battles, was appointed a Member of the Order of Canada in recognition of his contributions to the complete decriminalization of abortion.

Public opinion polls in both countries indicate that a majority of voters accept the right of a woman to have an abortion along with reservations about how freely abortion should be available (Schwartz and Tatalovich 2009: 86–7). Total opposition to abortion remains a minority position, even among groups like evangelical Protestants (Wald and Calhoun-Brown 2007: 191) or supporters of what had been the socially conservative Reform Party in Canada (Harrison 1995: 206).

The issue of abortion demonstrates several similarities between Canada and the United States. It began as an illegal act in both countries along with some place for medical procedures. It changed into a politically contentious issue through the movement to decriminalize. This occurred at approximately the same time in the two countries. In Canada, the Supreme Court was the critical actor in full decriminalization and Parliament has not moved to create an alternate law. Although opposition to abortion remains in both countries, only in the United States is the anti-abortion movement strong enough to seriously threaten abortion's legality. Both countries remain similar in the limited access available to women, the responsiveness of the media to abortion-related events, and the views of the public.

Capital Punishment

Capital punishment is understood as the application of the death penalty for serious (i.e., capital) offenses. The authority to take the life of a sinner or criminal rests with those entrusted to take responsibility for the moral regulation of the community. Today, opposition to capital punishment puts it among the repertoire of moral issues. Abolition takes its place among those issues by questioning the morality of taking the life of a human, regardless of what that person may have done.

In Canada, capital offenses were always defined nationally, as part of its single criminal code. Until 1859, capital offenses numbered 230 under prevailing British law. By 1865, only murder, treason, and rape were considered capital offenses. Several attempts over the years to do away with the death penalty finally achieved success in 1967, when a bill was passed in Parliament to apply mandatory life imprisonment for murder except when the victim was a police officer or prison guard. The legislation went along with an understanding that its consequences would be monitored for a five-year trial period. Parliament abolished the death penalty with Bill C-84 in 1976 although it remained possible in the military for acts of treason or mutiny. The Canadian National Defense Act was changed in 1998 to put military law in step with civil law. An effort in Parliament to reintroduce the death penalty in 1987 was defeated on a free vote.

The clarity of Canada's present stance on capital punishment stands in contrast to the situation in the United States. There, both the federal government and some states currently permit the death penalty. There are currently forty-one federal capital offices which, in addition to treason and espionage, are tied to various conditions when murder may occur. Both the war on drugs and threats from global terrorism have been an incentive for expanding the death penalty, first under the Violent Crime Control and Law Enforcement Act of 1994 and then in the Anti-Terrorism and Effective Death Penalty Act of 1996 (Koch et al. 2012).

At present, there are thirty-one states with the death penalty. Among them, there is a decline in the numbers sentenced to death (Williams 2015). Nineteen other states, plus the District of Columbia, have abolished the death penalty, one-third of them in the last decade. Abolitionist states are, except for West Virginia and Hawaii, all in the northern half of the country. There appears to be some trend toward abolition at the state level, but not at the federal, and distinct differences among states are shaped by their regional experiences. However, in 2016, Nebraska voted to repeal the abolition of capital punishment and Oklahoma added the death penalty to its constitution.

In contrast to Canada, where both the death penalty and its abolition have followed from the actions of Parliament, in the United States, Congress and state legislatures each play critical roles, with additional impact from the courts. Challenges to the death penalty that come to the US Supreme Court are presented as violating the Eighth Amendment's protections against "cruel and unusual punishment" (Cruel and Unusual 1973). Yet the pivotal case of *Furman v. Georgia, Jackson v. Georgia,* and *Branch v. Texas* (1972) was a fractured opinion which set aside the death penalty on grounds that it was not being consistently applied. That ruling, however, did no more than put a temporary halt to executions. When the Supreme Court of California, in *People v. Anderson* (1972),

ruled that the death penalty violated the state's constitution, this insti-
gated an initiative-led move to amend the constitution with a statement,
contrary to the court's opinion, that the death penalty was neither cruel
nor unusual.

Media coverage of capital punishment in Canada was closely tied to
events (see figure 3.3). Attention peaked in 1976 at the time of abolition.
Smaller peaks can be observed in 1967, when sentencing for murder
was reduced to life imprisonment; in 1972, when the effects of that law
had its mandatory review; and in 1987, when a parliamentary challenge was raised. Since then, coverage has been minimal, suggesting
that the issue has come to rest. Yet, contrary to media signs, the public
is increasingly in favor of restoring the death penalty, with 63 percent
in favor as of 2013 (Angus Reid Public Opinion 2013).

Figure 3.4 presents media coverage that indicates a more volatile
environment in the United States. Over the course of sixty years, greatest attention to capital punishment was concentrated between 1977

Figure 3.3 Media coverage of capital punishment in Canada, 1950–2010

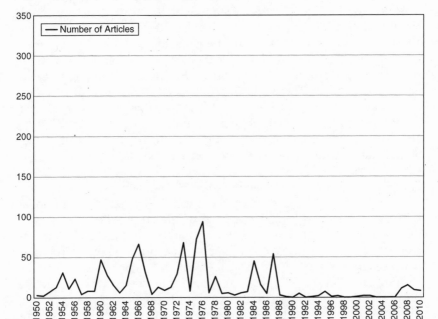

Figure 3.4 Media coverage of capital punishment in the United States, 1950–2010

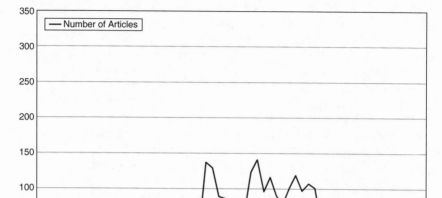

and 1990. Not even the terrorist bombing of the federal building in Oklahoma City in 1995 or the subsequent execution of its perpetrator, Timothy McVeigh, in 2001, evoked the same level of attention. Among the public surveyed in *Washington Post*-ABC polls, 60 percent favored the death penalty in 2014, a decline of 20 percent from a high in 1982 (Somashekhar 2014).

Although both countries appear to have declining media interest in the topic of capital punishment, that decline exists under quite different conditions. In Canada, abolition of the death penalty is now an established part of the legal system. As such, it would appear unlikely to be challenged. Yet public opinion suggests otherwise, paralleling views in the United States. The legal status of the death penalty in the United States remains unsettled and a nationwide solution appears unlikely in the near future.

Gun Control

The concept of gun control is vague beyond referring to some form of regulation of firearms. It can range from completely prohibiting private ownership of firearms of all types to regulations restricting the kind of weapons civilians may own or the kind of people permitted ownership. Concern with such regulation is associated with population concentrations where the safety of the community is delegated to specific agents. Gun control then assumes a moral position by considering how both individual and group safety depend on restrictions over unregulated gun ownership. In the United States, however, morality is also linked to fundamental rights of citizenship, in this case, to the Second Amendment to the Constitution, which states: "A well regulated Militia, being necessary to the security of a free State, the right of the people to keep and bear Arms, shall not be infringed." Whether it is the need for a militia or the right to bear arms that is at its core, interpretations of the amendment continue to keep gun control among the highly contentious issues on the US political agenda (Cook and Goss 2014).

The history of settlement patterns and emerging statehood has left indelible markers on how gun control has evolved. Expansion westward, distant from settled areas and authority, argued for the value of guns to hunt for food and as protection against animals and indigenous peoples. In the United States, the then recent experience with the need for militias to fight for freedom from British colonial rule was the basis of the Second Amendment and a continuing reminder of how guns could protect the new nation. Just as the power of guns in the newly settled western territories could be used to establish authority, so too was their role in enforcing slavery. But there were also limits to total lack of regulation. When gun control laws were passed in the nineteenth century, they were directed against ownership by African Americans, immigrants, and former Confederate soldiers (Mohun 2013).

Canada, though similar to the United States in the role played by guns in western expansion, quickly moved to extend central authority. It established a national police force six years after Confederation that would later become the Royal Canadian Mounted Police, explicitly charged with enforcing the law in the western territories. Today, regulation of guns remains a responsibility of the federal government under the Criminal Code (RCMP 2012a). At the same time, other jurisdictions may have additional regulations, as provinces do over guns used in hunting (RCMP 2012b).

Despite the highly charged nature of the gun control debate, media attention has been quite muted compared to what was found for abortion and capital punishment (see figures 3.5 and 3.6). In the sixty-year time span we review, there was no coverage in the United States, until

Figure 3.5 Media coverage of gun control in the United States, 1950–2010

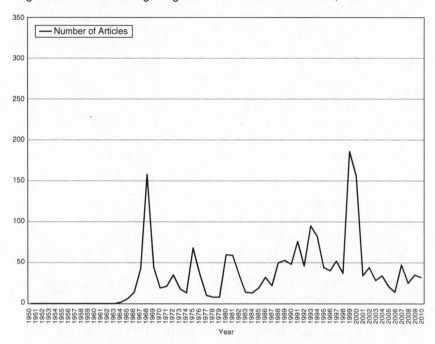

Figure 3.6 Media coverage of gun control in Canada, 1950–2010

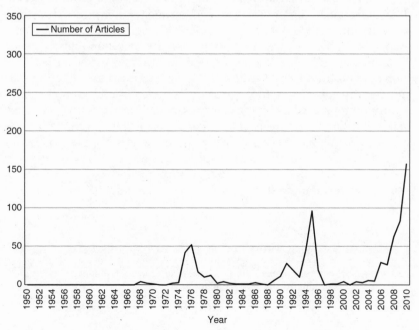

1968, a year that marked the second highest peak. Attention then subsided until the highest peak in 2000, to once again drop sharply. The
first peak occurred when the Gun Control Act of 1968[4] was passed;
the second after the Columbine school shootings and strong support
for gun control from Democratic candidates in the 2000 election. Most
opinion polls find that a large majority favor some form of gun control,
primarily with respect to requirements for registration and background
checks (Semet and Ansolabehere 2011).

Canada displayed an even flatter pattern in media attention, with a
modest peak in 1976, a steeper one in 1996, and then a sharp increase in
attention in 2010. The first peak is associated with Bill C-83, intended to
introduce new firearms offenses with new penalties and new licensing
requirements. That bill died, but new legislation was passed the following year that required, among other features, certificates for firearms
acquisition and ammunition business permits. During 1996, mandatory
sentences for serious firearms offenses came into effect and new control
mechanisms were tabled for discussion. New administrative practices
and legislation under the Firearms Act were phased in beginning at the
end of 1998 (RCMP 2012a). Since then, the focus of greatest attention has
been on long-gun registration. Owners of rifles and shotguns, used for
hunting or other sports and considered "non-restricted firearms" under
the law, were required to register their guns and to have a license for
their possession. The Conservative government attempted to do away
with the gun registry, initially by offering amnesty to non-compliant
owners and then by legislation to abolish the long-gun registry itself.
Two bills aimed at the latter goal, one in 2006 and the other in 2007,
both died on the order table. In 2012, the government passed Bill C-19,
successfully eliminating the registry requirement for long-gun owners.

Support for some kind of gun control is widely accepted in the United
States as much as it is in Canada. What differs is the much greater cen-
tralized control that exists in Canada and the tenor of opposition in the
United States. Only in the latter is opposition rooted in the Constitution
and supported by powerful cultural symbols of western expansion and
equally powerful interest groups (McLean 2015; Kopel 1991).

---

4 That law revised and expanded on gun control laws passed in the 1930s. Among its
provisions were prohibitions on the importation of firearms without sporting uses,
establishment of a minimum age for purchases, expansion of prohibited persons, and
requirements that all firearms have serial numbers.

Marijuana

Marijuana is a psychoactive drug derived from the hemp plant *Cannabis sativa*. Over time, it has undergone distinct changes in popularly understood meanings. The moral content of those meanings resembles that applied to alcohol. On one side are those who argue that freedom to use marijuana should be a matter of personal choice as a decision appropriate to free people. If there are negative consequences, they can be treated individually and with sensitivity to their medical implications. On the other side, marijuana is seen as part of a dissolute lifestyle and associated with crime and criminals. Moreover, it has serious consequences for health and long-term well-being.

Up until early in the twentieth century, marijuana, like other drugs, was unregulated, and abuses or addiction were treated as personal problems. In Lindesmith's (1947: 183) assessment, "The habit was not approved but neither was it regarded as criminal or monstrous. It was usually looked upon as a vice or personal misfortune, or much as alcoholism is viewed today." Not until 1937, with the passage of the Marijuana Tax Act, did its use become a federal crime in the United States. Prior to this, between 1932 and 1936, all states had laws criminalizing the sale or possession of marijuana. In Canada, criminalization occurred even earlier, apparently influenced by the writings of Emily Murphy, a police magistrate and judge in the Juvenile Court in Edmonton.

> It is thought that Mrs. Murphy's writings were probably responsible for the inclusion of marijuana in the Schedule to *The Opium and Narcotic Drug Act* in 1923. There was only passing reference to the subject in the debate and no discussion of the reasons for its inclusion. In any event, a decision was made in 1923, without any apparent scientific bases nor even any real sense of social urgency, to place cannabis on the same bases in the legislation as the opiate narcotics, such as heroin, and is the way it has remained on the statute books ever since. (Report of the Commission of Inquiry into the Non-Medical Uses of Drugs 1972: 230)

As part of the cultural revolution of the 1960s, a change occurred in the number and identity of users in both countries, although possibly a little later in Canada (Schwartz 1981: 78). Now marijuana became the favored recreational drug of middle-class students. Arrests for possession and use increased exponentially. Initially, criminal penalties were harsh but, given a new class of offenders, pressure led to some loosening of how punishments were administered. But the major transformation in how marijuana is perceived did not come until more recently. Reframing the issue came about from recognition that decriminalizing possession would free young and often first-time offenders of a stigma that adversely affected their future. Decriminalization typically means no prison term or criminal record for first-time offenders caught with a small amount of marijuana for personal use. By 2016, twenty-eight US states plus the District of Columbia had passed decriminalization laws. These developments are taking place alongside claims for the medicinal properties of marijuana, especially in helping alleviate pain and other symptoms for cancer patients. The result is that several states now permit marijuana use with a medical permit. At the same time, the official government position remains skeptical of medical claims and generally negative about the effects of marijuana (National Institute on Drug Abuse 2014). But even with this opposition, the latest stage in the history of marijuana also includes a nascent movement to completely legalize the drug, whether for medical or recreational use.

In Canada, as well, marijuana is now understood through the lenses of decriminalization, legalization, and medicalization. In terms of government policy, however, only medical usage is permitted. In 2002 committees of the Canadian Senate and the House of Commons recommended decriminalization, and the Liberal Party under its leader Justin Trudeau endorsed total legalization during the 2015 national elections. The Conservatives have not voiced support for that reform, but the newly elected Trudeau Government proceeded to table legislation in April of 2017 to legalize the recreational use of marijuana, to be effective some time in 2018.

Media attention to marijuana in the United States peaked and was concentrated over a decade from 1967 to 1978 (see figure 3.7). Coverage mainly concerned drug arrests and coincided with an era of cultural protest that was often symbolized by marijuana use. Attention to drug policies was also highest during the same period, though always of lesser magnitude. Since 2004, policy debates have come to engage notice from the media in parallel with police actions. Public views about what those policies should be demonstrate dramatic shifts. In 1969, when the Gallup Organization first asked whether marijuana should be legalized, only 12 percent were in favor, with 84 percent opposed. In 2014, legalization was the choice of 52 percent; 45 percent preferred the status quo. Support for legalization has been on the rise during the last decade. When asked about decriminalization,

Figure 3.7 Media coverage of marijuana in the United States, 1950–2010

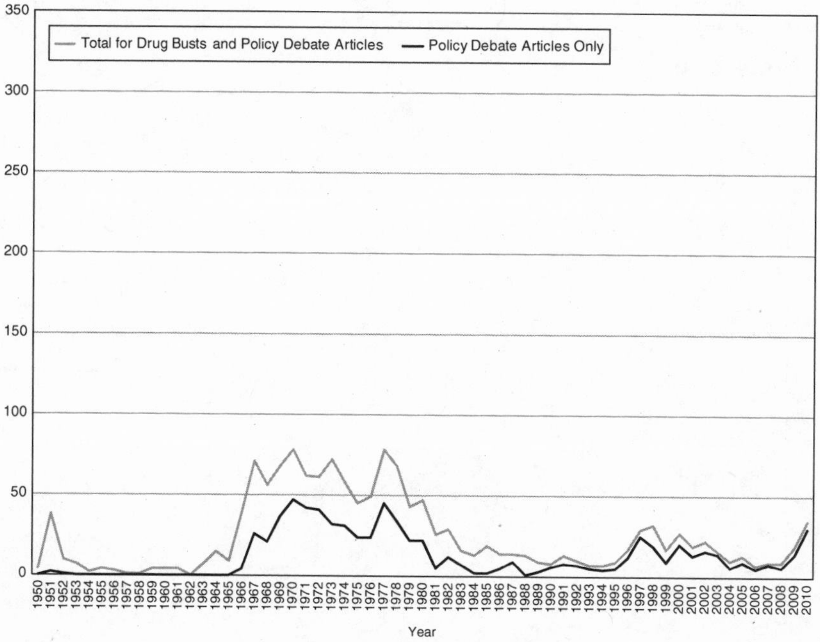

an impressive 76 percent agreed that possession of a small amount of marijuana should not result in jail time (Motel 2015).

Canadian media coverage, although like that in the United States insofar as both were more concerned with drug arrests than with policy, is still distinctly different (see figure 3.8). There was a similar, though considerably smaller and shorter-lived, peak from the 1960s until the early 1970s, followed by relative inattention. Suddenly, between 2008 and 2010, there was a dramatic increase in attention to drug arrests, accompanying a sharp rise in the number of those arrests. Around the same time, the media gave the greatest coverage to policy debates. IPSOS Reid surveys found increasing support for decriminalization, growing from 39 percent in 1987, to 55 percent in 2003, to 66 percent in 2012 (Kennedy 2012).

In both countries policies and perspectives on marijuana have undergone transformations, evolving from lack of regulation, to criminalization, to movements to decriminalize recreational use and legalize medical use. Use of marijuana during the 1960s and 1970s was more

Figure 3.8 Media coverage of marijuana in Canada, 1950–2010

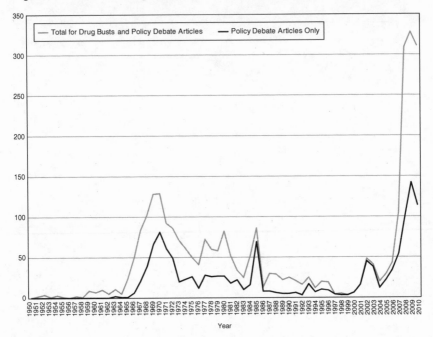

Year

disruptive of the culture of the United States than it was of that in Canada. At the same time as policies of decriminalization take hold and spread in the United States, opposition to those policies during the recent tenure of the Conservative government resulted in more constrained responses in Canada. The 2015 election of a Liberal government portends a national resolution through decriminalization.

Pornography

> Historically, pornography has been understood to be descriptions, in literature or in art, of the life and manners of prostitutes and their patrons. This is consistent with the origins of the word in Greek, the word *porne* meaning "harlot" and *grapho* meaning "to write." (Mahoney 2006)

In Judeo-Christian beliefs, it was abhorrence for the portrayed lifestyle that provided the initial moral basis of opposition to pornography. Pornography and obscenity are closely related and may be used interchangeably. Legal prohibitions and regulations have their origins in the common law and were established in Britain in 1868 as the Hicklin Rule, when the court upheld the definition of obscenity as material that tended "to deprave and corrupt those whose minds are open to such influences," giving obscenity laws similar roots in Canada and the United States. Legal definitions of obscenity are of behaviors and their depictions that are offensive to community standards. But it is this reference to community standards, implying a moral consensus, which has made obscenity or pornography the most elusive of moral issues. That pornography was of only modest concern in the early history of both countries can be attributed to both the homogeneity of dominant groups able to define standards and the limited circulation of pornographic materials. For example, only one of the thirteen colonies had criminalized obscene material.

New legal attention did not occur until about the middle of the twentieth century, when content changed to more explicit material, often linking sex with violence, and marketing was aimed at a much larger audience. The defining legal case in the United States was *Roth v. United States* (1957) in which Samuel Roth, who ran a literary business in New York, was sentenced to five years for distributing obscene material. Ruling in the case, Supreme Court Justice Brennan found that the material was "utterly without redeeming social importance" and, most significantly, was not protected under the First Amendment (Strub 2013). Around the same time in Canada, new concerns surfaced with an amendment to the Criminal Code in 1959 that included a statutory definition of obscenity based on "undue exploitation" instead of the common law assessment of whether material would "deprave" or "corrupt."

As pornographic material became more widespread and more violent, it raised new concerns about the exploitation of women and children. Pornography was reframed as child pornography, a movement that took place in both countries in the late 1970s and into the 1980s. A strong impetus for that reframing came with the surge of materials disseminated through the computer. At present, in both countries, legislation has added new definitions of child pornography and attempted new ways to curtail computer-based circulation (Wortley and Smallbone 2006; Casavant and Robertson 2007). Although all the moral weight would appear to be entirely on the side of those opposed to child pornography, there remain opposing voices concerned about the severity of punishments and the curtailment of free speech (e.g., Extein 2014; Purdy 2013).

In figures 3.9 and 3.10 we have separated media attention to pornography in general (labeled "adult") from that specific to child pornography. In the United States, adult pornography continues to be
the major concern (see figure 3.9). Coverage had its first and relatively
minor peak in 1960, but a notable upsurge did not occur until the 1970s,
with the highest peak of over 160 articles displayed in 1977. There has
been a sharp decline in attention since then, moving in an irregular
path and never reaching more than 70 articles, the situation in 1990.
In contrast, child pornography did not come to even modest attention
by the media until 1976, with just over 20 articles. The highest peak in
coverage occurred in 2007, with over 40 articles.

Media attention in Canada has been sharply different from that in the
United States (see figure 3.10). There was virtually no coverage of adult
pornography until the late 1970s, with a peak of fewer than 100 articles in 1983. Then interest subsided until peaking with over 200 articles

Figure 3.9 Media coverage of pornography in the United States, 1950–2010

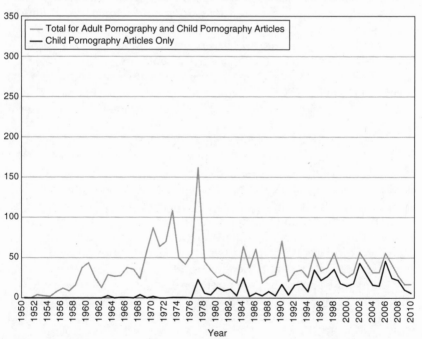

Figure 3.10 Media coverage of pornography in Canada, 1950–2010

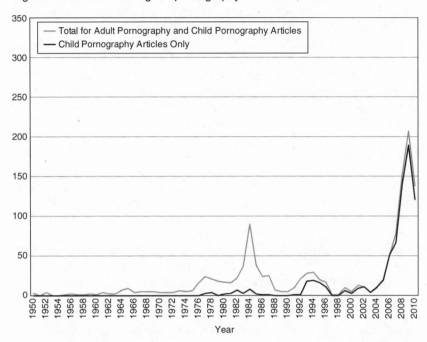

in 2008. Child pornography began to generate attention in the 2000s, when it followed the trajectory of articles about adult pornography, peaking at the same time.

In both countries, neither media coverage nor legislative and judicial actions have prompted polling agencies to survey the public regarding child pornography. One possible indicator of such public opinion may come from Wirthlin Worldwide, which asked whether federal laws against pornography should be vigorously enforced. In 2004, those who said that they both agreed to vigorous enforcement and held their views strongly made up 72 percent of the sample, among whom gender was the strongest demographic divider, with women most concerned (Catholic Online 2004).

Legislative efforts to control child pornography in the United States may clash with freedom of expression. Although the Supreme Court has repeatedly said that pornography is not "protected speech" under the First Amendment, the criteria for determining what is obscene are so complex that much material that would be objectionable for the average American can pass constitutional scrutiny. It does appear, though, that the Protect Act (2003), making it a crime to offer or solicit sexually explicit images of children, is most resilient against challenges (Greenhouse 2008). Canada, too, had difficulty in formulating appropriate legislation to protect children against sexual exploitation, but, under both Liberal and Conservative governments, has succeeded in establishing strong legal protections. Both countries now have resolved the issue of child pornography through legislation.

Same-Sex Relations

Sexual relations between members of the same sex, particularly when they involve males, have been strongly condemned in the Abrahamic religions and, under the common law, punished by civil authority. At the same time, it is now recognized that a minority in every society is only or mainly attracted to members of one's own sex and seeks to act on that attraction. There have always been social settings or special circumstances where same-sex relations were accepted as the norm but the prevailing views were disapproving. Up until recently, homosexuality was regarded as a mental disorder and there is still no agreement about whether or not it is an innate characteristic (Heffner 2003), although efforts to change sexual orientations have been largely discredited.

Canada's position on homosexuality was underscored by a 1967 Supreme Court ruling that upheld the conviction of Everett George Klippert on four counts of gross indecency and his sentence to indefinite imprisonment. Yet, shortly thereafter, under amendments to the Criminal Code in 1969, homosexuality was partially decriminalized (the same time as abortion). The Charter of Rights and Freedoms, which came into effect in 1985, did not explicitly cover sexual orientation. However, by the 1990s, Court decisions effectively extended the Charter provision by outlawing discrimination against homosexuals. Then same-sex relations came to be viewed as the equivalent of heterosexual marriage, first in the 2003 Court ruling in *Halpern v. Canada*, followed by federal legislation in 2005 that extended civil marriage to same-sex couples (Schwartz and Tatalovich 2009: 81).

The United States, with its mix of federal and state laws, has been slower than Canada in extending full rights to homosexuals. The

Supreme Court has yet to apply the Fourteenth Amendment "equal protection" clause to sexual orientation. Anti-sodomy laws were not struck down until 2003 in the Supreme Court ruling on *Lawrence v. Texas*. By 2010, twenty-one states plus the District of Columbia banned discrimination on the basis of sexual orientation. Same-sex marriage continues to be most contentious, emerging as a reframing of the broader issue of same-sex rights during the 2004 presidential election (Green 2011). As of 2014, voters in thirty-four states had approved bans on same-sex marriage. However, those enactments are now moot given the high-court ruling in *Obergefell v. Hodges* (2015), which constitutionalized a right to same-sex marriage in the United States.

Both countries demonstrate major attitudinal shifts in recent years. Using data from the General Social Survey, Smith (2011) plots the move from 70 percent characterizing same-sex relations as "always wrong" in 1970 to 43.3 percent in 2010. Using different measures derived from the World Values Surveys, Andersen and Fetner (2008) document similarly increasing tolerance and note how Canadians have become even more accepting of same-sex relations than those in the United States.

Newspaper coverage of same-sex relations is a further measure of how the issue differs in contentiousness when comparing the United States with Canada. Figure 3.11 demonstrates that US coverage peaked in 1974, earlier than in Canada, where the even higher peak was in 1978 (see figure 3.12). Between 1978 and 1982, Canadian media attention remained high, reflecting new discussions of human rights and anti-discrimination measures. Since then, coverage declined sharply. In the United States, in contrast, at first there was only modest media coverage, even after the 1969 raid by the New York City police on Stonewall, a gay bar in Greenwich Village, that brought the discussion of homosexual rights into the open. Afterwards media attention shot up and continues to manifest steep peaks and lesser valleys up to the end of our data collection. Divergence between the two countries is even more marked when one looks only at same-sex marriage. In Canada, coverage remained low between 2000 and 2010, although this coincided with parliamentary debates on the subject and the Supreme Court's ruling. Attention to same-sex marriage dominated in the United States, beginning with the period leading up to the 2004 election and continuing, though to a lesser extent, since.

For the most part, controversy over same-sex relations, including marriage, has been resolved in Canada. In the United States, issues related to sexual orientation still arouse controversy.

Figure 3.11 Media coverage of same-sex relations/marriage in the United States, 1950–2010

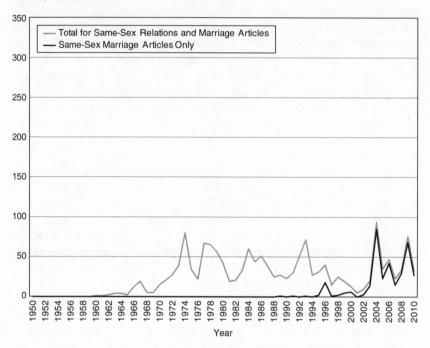

Figure 3.12 Media coverage of same-sex relations/marriage in Canada, 1950–2010

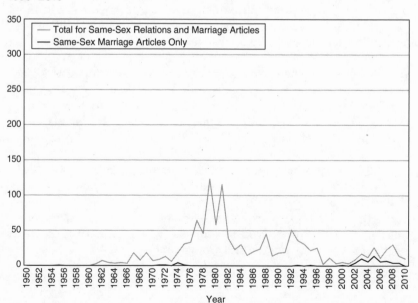

Classifying Issues

Except for gun control, all the issues we consider began with restrictive approaches to behavior and their moral claims were all on one side (Meier 1994: 246–7). Gun control differs only by initially arguing for the absence of regulation. At some point, a shift occurs and all the issues become two-sided, although probably least so in the case of child pornography. That is, opposition begins to press its case by calling on alternative values that buttress its position. The onset of this two-sidedness is the marker for the kind of moral conflicts that concern this work.

Some issues are reframed to capture greater support through new emphases on benefits to health and well-being, with those benefits conceived of as adjuncts of a human-centered moral philosophy. This can happen with issues that begin from a restrictive position, as we find in two cases. With abortion, some of those on the pro-life side now argue that an abortion is detrimental to a woman's health, making later pregnancies unsafe and often being the root of clinical depression (Thevathasan 2012). Although Ruth Bader Ginsburg, before her appointment to the Supreme Court, argued that if abortion had been couched in terms of health rather than rights, it would have avoided its evolution into a division between uncompromising sides (Strickland 2005: 3–4), these recent developments indicate that medical-based viewpoints can find a place on both sides of an issue. A more far-reaching change occurred in the case of pornography when it was reframed as concern with child pornography and the harmful effects on those children who had been exploited in its production.

Two additional issues were reframed into advocacy based on health effects by opponents of what was initially the dominant and lawful position. The strongest argument in favor of decriminalizing marijuana rests on the purported medical benefits for those experiencing the pain of cancer treatments. Those arguing for gun control make their strongest case when they formulate it as a public-health issue. They do so when they equate the widespread availability of guns with rates of suicide and domestic violence (Kellermann et al. 1998).

A framework that rests on health or medical benefits is arguably not the same as one that rests on moral values of right and wrong, but it does have the advantage of sidestepping moral values' ties with particular religious communities and emphasizing what are becoming more broadly based values. Clearly, it is a framework with broad appeal, given its appearance in the arguments of either proponents or opponents of four of the six issues we consider.

It is just such additional concerns that Hurka et al. (2016) argue detract from the manifest quality of what would otherwise be purely moral issues. They see such expanded interests as likely to ease the degree of contention and to enable resolution. Yet, at present, the introduction of health and medical benefits has had only limited consequences for the termination of conflict.

A different kind of reframing has taken place in contention over same-sex relations. There the move has been to expand on the legal rights available to those who are not exclusively heterosexual by arguing for the right to marriage among same-sex couples. The rationale for enlarging the scope of basic rights follows a trajectory set in motion by the prevailing "rights revolution" (Epp 1998; Scheingold 1974).

Two clear findings emerge from this chapter: with the possible exceptions of child pornography and same-sex relations, none of the issues we survey has yet found a policy outcome in the United States that cannot be breached; all but one of them have been resolved, one way or another, in Canada. The sources for these opposing national outcomes are examined in the following chapter and their specific impact on issue phases is developed in the remaining chapters.

REFERENCES

Andersen, Robert, and Tina Fetner. 2008. "Cohort Differences in Tolerance of Homosexuality: Attitudinal Change in Canada and the United States, 1981-2000." *Public Opinion Quarterly* 72 (2): 311–30.

Angus Reid Public Opinion. 2013. "Three in Five Canadians Would Bring Back Death Penalty." 20 May.

Boston Women's Health Collective. 2005. *Our Bodies, Ourselves for the New Century*. 4th ed. Cambridge, MA: Touchstone.

Brodie, Janine, Shelley A.M. Gavigan, and Jane Jenson. 1992. *The Politics of Abortion*. Toronto: Oxford University Press.

Casavant, Lyne, and James R. Robertson. 2007. *The Evolution of Pornography Law in Canada*. Ottawa: Parliamentary Information and Research Service; www.parl.gc.ca/content/LOP/researchpublication/843.

Catholic Online. 2004. "Americans Still Want Federal Obscenity Laws Enforced against Hardcore Internet Pornography." http://www.catholic.org/prwire/headline.php?ID=886.

Cook, Philip J., and Kristin A. Goss. 2014. *The Gun Debate: What Everyone Needs to Know*. New York: Oxford University Press.

Cruel and Unusual. 1973. "Cruel and Unusual Punishment. The Death Penalty Cases: Furman v. Georgia, Jackson v. Georgia, Branch v. Texas, 408 U.S. 238 (1972)." *Journal of Criminal Law & Criminology* 63 (4): 484–92.

Epp, Charles R. 1998. *The Rights Revolution: Lawyers, Activists, and Supreme Courts in Comparative Perspective*. Chicago: University of Chicago Press.

Extein, Andrew. 2014. "Capital Punishment: The Troubling Consequences of Federal Child Pornography Laws." *Huffington Post*, 21 April.

Farkas, Edie. 1976. "Abortion: How Many Trials Will Morgentaler Face?" *Last Post* 5: 13–14.

Green, John C. 2011. "The Politics of Marriage and American Party Politics: Evidence from the 2004 US Election." In *Faith, Politics, and Sexual Diversity in Canada and the United States*, ed. David Rayside and Clyde Wilcox., 300–15. Vancouver: UBC Press.

Greenhouse, Linda. 2008. "Supreme Court Upholds Child Pornography Law." *New York Times*, 20 May.

Halfmann, Drew. 2011. *Doctors and Demonstrators: How Political Institutions Shape Abortion Law in the United States, Britain, and Canada*. Chicago: University of Chicago Press. https://doi.org/10.7208/chicago/9780226313443.001.0001.

Harrison, Trevor. 1995. *Right Wing Populism and the Reform Party in Canada*. Toronto: University of Toronto Press.

Haussman, Melissa. 2005. *Abortion Politics in North America*. Boulder, CO: Lynne Rienner Publishers.

Heffner, Christopher L. 2003. "Homosexuality: Nature or Nurture." *AllPsych*. www.allpsych.com/journal/homosexuality/#.VSvdGpOumXA.

Hurka, Steffen, Christian Adam, and Christopher Knill. 2016. "Is Morality Policy Different? Testing Sectoral and Institutional Explanations of Policy Change." *Policy Studies Journal* online version. https://doi.org/10.1111/psj.12153.

Keller, Michael, and Allison Yarrow. 2013. "Interactive: The Geography of Abortion Access." *The Daily Beast*, 22 April. http://www.thedailybeast.com/the-geography-of-abortion-access.

Kellermann, Arthur L., Grant Somes, Fred Rivara, Roberta K. Lee, and Joyce G. Banton. 1998. "Injuries and Deaths Due to Firearms in the Home." *Journal of Trauma and Acute Care Surgery* 45 (2): 263–7.

Kennedy, Mark. 2012. "Most Canadians Firmly in Favor of Decriminalizing Marijuana: Poll." *Postmedia News*, 2 July. http://news.nationalpost.com/2012/07/02/most-canadians-firmly-in.

Koch, Larry W., Colin Wark, and John F. Galliher. 2012. *The Death of the American Death Penalty: States Still Lead the Way*. Boston: Northeastern University Press.

Kopel, David B. 1991. "Canadian Gun Control: Should the United States Look North for a Solution to Its Firearms Problem?" *Temple International and Comparative Law Journal* 5: 1–50.

Lindesmith, Alfred R. 1947. *Opiate Addiction*. Bloomington, IN: Principia.

Luker, Kristin. 1984. *Abortion and the Politics of Motherhood*. Berkeley: University of California Press.

Mahoney, Kathleen. 2006. "Pornography." In *The Canadian Encyclopedia*. www.thecanadianencyclopedia.ca/en/article/pornography.

McLean, Dylan S. 2015. "Guns in the Anglo-American Democracies: Explaining an American Exception." *Commonwealth & Comparative Politics* 53 (3): 233–52.

Meier, Kenneth J. 1994. *The Politics of Sin: Drugs, Alcohol, and Public Policy*. Armonk, NY: M.E. Sharpe.

Mohr, James C. 1978. *Abortion in America: The Origins and Evolution of National Policy*. New York: Oxford University Press.

Mohun, Arwen P. 2013. *Risk: Negotiating Safety in American Society*. Baltimore, MD: Johns Hopkins University Press.

Motel, Seth. 2015. "6 Facts about Marijuana." Pew Research, 14 April. www.pewresearch.org/fact-tank/2015/04/14/6-facts-about-marijuana/.

National Institute on Drug Abuse. 2014. "Marijuana." *Drug Facts*, January: 1–4. Washington: U.S. Department of Health and Human Services. www.drugabuse.gov.

Palley, Howard A. 2006. "Canadian Abortion Policy: National Policy and the Impact of Federalism and Political Implementation on Access to Services." *Publius* 36 (4): 565–86. https://doi.org/10.1093/publius/pjl002.

Purdy, Chris. 2013. "Professors Defend Tom Flanagan's Right to Express Views on Child Porn." *Globe and Mail*. 1 March.

RCMP. 2012a. *History of Firearms Control in Canada: Up to and Including the Firearms Act*. http://www.rcmp-grc.gc.ca/cfp-pcaf/pol-leg/hist/con-eng.htm.

RCMP. 2012b. *Canadian Firearms Program: Frequently Asked Questions – General*. http://www.rcmp-grc.gc.ca/cfp-pcaf/faq/index-eng.htm#a1.

Report of the Commission of Inquiry into the Non-Medical Uses of Drugs. 1972. *Cannabis*. Ottawa: Information Canada.

Richer, Karine. 2008. "Abortion in Canada: Twenty Years after *R. v. Morgentaler*." In *Parliamentary Information and Research Service*. Ottawa: Library of Parliament.

Rossi, Alice S. 1969. "Abortion and Social Change." *Dissent* 16: 338–46.

Scheingold, Stuart A. 1974. *The Politics of Rights: Lawyers, Public Policy, and Political Change*. New Haven, CT: Yale University Press.

Schwartz, Mildred A. 1981. "Politics and Moral Causes in Canada and the United States." *Comparative Social Research* 4: 65–90.

Schwartz, Mildred A., and Raymond Tatalovich. 2009. "Cultural and Institutional Factors Affecting Political Contention over Moral Issues." *Comparative Sociology* 8 (1): 76–104. https://doi.org/10.1163/156913308X375559.

Semet, Amy, and Steven Ansolabehere. 2011. "Profiling and Predicting Opinions on Gun Control: A Comparative Perspective on the Factors Underlying Opinion on Different Gun Control Measures." Paper presented at the Conference of Empirical Legal Studies. Evanston, IL: Northwestern University. https://doi.org/10.2139/ssrn.1884661.

Smith, Tom W. 2011. *Public Attitudes toward Homosexuality*. Chicago: National Opinion Research Center.

Somashekhar, Sandhya. 2014. "Can the Death Penalty Be Abolished?" *The Washington Post*, 9 December.

Stencil, Sandra. 1976. "Abortion Politics." *Editorial Research Reports* 2: 767–84.

Strickland, Ruth Ann. 2005. "Abortion: Pro-Choice vs. Pro-Life." In *Moral Controversies in American Politics*, ed. Raymond Tatalovich and Byron W. Daynes., 3–35. 3rd ed. Armonk, NY: M.E. Sharpe.

Strub, Whitney. 2013. *Obscenity Rules: Roth v. United States and the Long Struggle over Sexual Expression*. Lawrence: University Press of Kansas.

Tatalovich, Raymond. 1997. *The Politics of Abortion in the United States and Canada: A Comparative Study*. Armonk, NY: M.E. Sharpe Publishers.

Thalidomide Victims Association of Canada. n.d. "Thalidomide: The Canadian Tragedy." www.thalidomide.ca/the-canadian-tragedy/.

Thevathasan, Prevan. 2012. "Shutting Down the Debate: Abortion and Mental Health." *Crises Magazine*, 16 April.

Wald, Kenneth D., and Allison Calhoun-Brown. 2007. *Religion and Politics in the United States*. 5th ed. Lanham, MD: Roman and Littlefield.

Williams, Daniel K. 2016. *Defenders of the Unborn: The Pro-Life Movement before Roe v. Wade*. New York: Oxford University Press.

Williams, Timothy. 2015. "Executions by States Fell in 2015, Report Says." *New York Times*, 16 December.

Winerip, Michael. 2013. "The Death and Afterlife of Thalidomide." *New York Times*, 23 September. www.nytimes.com/2013/09/23/booming/the-death-and-afterlife-of-thalidomide.html.

Wortley, Richard, and Stephen Smallbone. 2006. "Child Pornography on the Internet." Washington, DC: US Department of Justice, Office of Community Oriented Policing Services.

Chapter Four

The Context of Moral Conflicts

Comparing Canada and the United States

We began in chapter 1 by noting the popular appeal and political contentiousness of the same moral issues in Canada and the United States. Although the shared moral space is, in itself, intrinsically interesting, the rationale for comparing issues across the two countries serves a broader purpose – to explain why issues experience a particular life history. By viewing issues in two adjacent countries with many known similarities and differences, it should become possible to isolate those causal mechanisms that affect issue trajectories. That is, when outcomes are the same in both countries, there is a high probability that this is due to the character of the issue itself, to the similar environments that each country provides, or to some combination of the two. When outcomes differ, we look for national characteristics that produce them. This chapter isolates those characteristics that differentiate one country from the other and that prior research has shown to affect policy outcomes.[1]

In all the significant markers of each country's nationhood it is possible to find formative similarities, including national origins through conquest and colonization by the British. In addition, other colonizers left their mark – the French in Canada and the Spanish in the United States – with the French having greater and more lasting impact within Canada.

---

1 Hurka et al. (2016), in their comparative analysis of morality policy change, divided countries into majoritarian and consensus democracies and hypothesized that policy change would be more punctuated in the latter. However, they found that characteristics of states did not have an effect. Our distinctions between Canada and the United States are more fine-grained and we do expect differences.

Geography is another source of parallel, with both nations spanning the same continent and sharing the same topography and many of the same natural resources. Along with similarity in some climatic conditions, there is also a greater expanse of Arctic and Arctic-influenced conditions in Canada and tropical and semi-tropical ones unique to the United States.

Populations in both countries are similarly heterogeneous. Both have indigenous peoples, though proportionately more in Canada. Both reflect their British origins and are predominately English speaking. At the same time, there is one significant difference – Canada has a second official language concentrated in Quebec. Beyond the formative influences from their original European settlers, both continue to be immigrant receivers. However, the national origins of that immigration have changed, shifting away from Europe and, in the case of the United States, to Latin America, and for Canada, to Asia.

Demography

Similarities, like the ones already mentioned, contribute to making the Canada-US comparison historically appealing because they simultaneously limit the number of variables that need to be taken into account and allow segregating the effects of population differences. Of the latter, we examine age, education, religion, and ethnic and racial composition. These demographic characteristics have been selected because previous research has confirmed that they are associated with differences in how moral issues are evaluated. That is, particular demographic groupings are associated with a varying likelihood of opposing perspectives that are able to be mobilized and acted on. To the extent that Canada and the United States differ in the composition of religious, generational, racial/ethnic, and educational groups to whom moral issues are particularly salient and who are prepared to translate that salience into political action, we have a basis for accounting for differences in issue life histories.

Age

Age is relevant for two quite different reasons. On the one hand, and this is virtually a universal finding, younger age is associated with more permissive attitudes (e.g., Fischer and Hout 2006: 235–6). However, young people are much less likely than older ones to vote or to otherwise engage politically (Martinez 2014: 154). Compared to other long-industrialized countries, both Canada and the United States have relatively young populations. At the same time, since the 1940s, the populations have been getting older, the results of lower birth rates and greater longevity (Statistics Canada 2006; Shrestha and Heisler 2011: 13–18). Currently, of the two, Canadians are relatively older (Torrey 2014: 16–18). Recent census data estimate those sixty-five and older to be 14.0 percent of the total in the United States and 15.3 percent in Canada (Statistics Canada 2013). Although we anticipate that younger age will be associated with more permissive attitudes, given the magnitude of comparative differences, we do not expect that age will be a major factor accounting for national differences in the outcome of moral conflicts. These generational differences in permissive attitudes lead us to expect that differences between older and younger age cohorts will be relevant only to those moral issues that recently emerged in society rather than those long-standing on the policy agenda.

Education

The effects of education are similar to those of age in that, like the young, those with higher levels of education also tend to be more liberal and permissive in their attitudes (Fischer and Hout 2006: 235–6). But unlike with the young, more education is associated with greater political participation in all its forms (Schlozman et al. 2012). Both attributes make education an important element influencing how moral issues are viewed and how they are likely to be resolved.

In general, Canada and the United States are similar in having a highly educated population, but there are critical differences, some going back generations and others more recent. Following the Second World War and aided by the GI Bill, the numbers of young people enrolled in post-secondary schools in the United States rose dramatically. In Canada, however, this did not begin until the late 1950s and early 1960s, when new colleges and universities were founded and old ones expanded (McQuillan and Van Brunschot 2011: 84–6). In 1951, the participation rate of eighteen- to twenty-four-year-olds in Canadian post-secondary schools was 6 percent. By 1975, it was 20 percent, approaching US levels (Statistics Canada 2014). In the period covered by our analysis, Canada began with a comparative educational disadvantage, but this has altered dramatically in recent years. By 2012, the United States ranked fourteenth among thirty-seven OECD countries in the percentage of twenty-five- to thirty-four-year-olds with post-secondary education. With 42 percent in this category in the United States, the latter was above the OECD average of 38 percent but below that of Canada with 57 percent (OECD 2012). Educational differences between the two countries then remain a possible factor in how moral conflicts have unfolded and require attention to changes over time. Given that, in general, more years of schooling are associated with more permissive outlooks and actions, changes in relative educational attainment in both countries lead us to expect that the United States will be more permissive at earlier periods and Canada more permissive in recent years.

Religion

Based on experiences of suppression in their home country, early English settlers in colonial America saw denominational differences as a source of conflict. When the United States was formed, those past experiences contributed to a founding constitution that separated church from state. In contrast, colonial Canada followed the mother country's practice, giving special recognition to the Church of England, later extended to the United Church. In addition, to build support from its newly conquered French settlers, the Roman Catholic Church was granted privileges in Quebec, some of which would spill over to other provinces. The result gave Catholic and mainline Protestant churches considerable and long-lasting influence over marriage, divorce, and education.

Today, both countries remain Christian by a large majority – 66 percent in Canada and 78 percent in the United States – and, in both, religious affiliation has become highly fluid (Pew 2008; Pew 2013). Both have also become similar in the proportions reporting no religious affiliation, rising from about 5 percent in 1970 to around 20 percent in 2012 (Pew 2013). The most permissive outlooks on moral issues are associated with the religiously unaffiliated (e.g., Langstaff 2011: 60), with Jews (e.g., Wald 2011), and, to some extent, with mainline Protestant churches (e.g., Hutchinson 2011; Olson et al. 2011).

Religion is both a source of difference between the two countries (e.g., Lipset 1990: 74–89) and a known factor in influencing how voters perceive issues and how their organized communities attempt to influence policy. Yet, unlike younger age, with its clear association with more permissive attitudes generally, an attribute shared only with the religiously unaffiliated, religious denominations tend to vary depending on the moral issue in question. For example, although Catholicism strongly affirms a right-to-life position when opposing abortion and capital punishment, that logic does not apply to its opposition to lax regulation of gun ownership (Semet and Ansolabehere 2011). Catholics themselves are often internally divided and inconsistent in beliefs and values (Fischer and Hout 2006). For example, while Catholic doctrine opposes homosexuality, lay Catholics are less opposed to same-sex marriage than conservative Protestants (Bendyna et al. 2001). Nowhere is the difference between the church and its members more apparent than in Quebec, where the Catholic Church had dominated the society from its origins. But beginning with the Quiet Revolution of the late 1950s and 1960s, Quebec was introduced to rapid social change and the sharp diminishment of the church's role in the province. Yet, despite the decline in religious practices, the church's cultural role has remained strong. This is evident in how other religions, specifically Islam, are now perceived as a serious threat and in the recent efforts of the pro-vincial government to introduce restrictions on the display of religious symbols. In response to current events, 78 percent of Quebecers polled affirmed it is "important to preserve historic Catholic symbols" and 56 percent agreed that "the Catholic religion should have special status in Quebec" (Gagnon 2013).

In general, evangelical Protestants are more consistently on the restrictive or punitive side of moral issues (Langstaff 2011; Shames et al. 2011; Lynerd 2014: 30). US research on state-level morality policies on issues like abortion (O'Connor and Berkman 1995), gay rights (Haider-Markel and Meier 1996), prohibition (Frendreis and Tatalovich 2010), and lotteries (Pierce and Miller 1999) further support such findings for evangelical Protestants. Donovan and Tolbert (2013) demonstrate that, in states where there have been referendums on same-sex marriage, the latter have been mobilized to act on their strong hostility. Yet evangeli-cal Protestants display some internal variations, for example, by gen-eration and race (Wilcox and Iida 2011: 115).

There are some differences in orientation by country, with United States overall both more politically conservative and activist (Harri-son 2014; Bean 2014). The religious makeup of the United States is proportionately more evangelical than that of Canada; the latter is more Catholic. We can anticipate, then, that national differences in the trajectory and contentiousness of moral issues will be related to the proportions and distributions of both Roman Catholic and evan-gelical Protestant groups within and between the two countries.

The Context of Moral Conflicts   93

However, given that restrictive views of moral issues are associated with Protestant evangelism more than with Catholicism, we expect that evangelical Protestants will exert a stronger influence on morality policy in the United States than Catholics will in Canada.

Race/Ethnicity

The ethnic and racial makeup of each country has had a profound foundational influence on its history and politics. For the United States, the experience of slavery left a lasting mark, continuing to affect the destiny of African Americans and their relations with the dominant white majority, and sustaining a culture that incorporates lingering racism. For Canada, the foundation was laid by the presence of French settlers remaining after the British conquest and their concentration in one sector of the country. The rights of francophones and the place of Quebec in the Canadian confederation remain dominant and frequently contentious influences on Canadian nationhood. These characteristics alone, even when they are not directly relevant to any of the moral issues selected for study here, are critical because of the ways they have molded both societies and given each its special character. In addition, at least in the United States, there is a strong racist component in how policies regarding capital punishment and marijuana have been administered. In a report to the Inter-American Commission on Human Rights, the American Civil Liberties Union (2014) reported on the significance of race in death-penalty sentences. Similarly, race accounts for a disproportionate share of African Americans arrested for marijuana violations (King and Mauer 2006).

Concentrations of other ethnic or racial groups, even when their interests are not specifically linked to the issues selected for study, are also likely to be relevant because of how they shape the political and social contours of each nation and how they bear on moralized issues in general. In taking this latter position, however, we are not adopting the view, expressed pejoratively by some Canadians, that the United States is a melting pot, while Canada remains a societally supported mosaic of different racial, linguistic, and ethnic groups. As others have demonstrated, that contrasting view of how the two countries have evolved does not take into account both similar trends in assimilation to the dominant culture and in barriers to that assimilation, or to the persistence of immigrant cultures (e.g., Reitz and Breton 1994). At the same time, early history was sufficiently formative to each country's development that we anticipate, in general, that some part of the differences in how Canada and the United States deal with moral issues is attributable to their different racial/ethnic histories.

Although the two countries remain major immigrant receivers, it is Canada that now has a larger proportion of its population that is foreign born – 20.6 percent compared to 12.9 percent in the United States (Statistics Canada 2013). Moreover, immigrant origins have changed. In the United States, in 1960, 75 percent of the foreign born came from Europe. By 2010, European-born immigrants were 12 percent, Asians were 28 percent, and those from Latin America, 53 percent (US Census Bureau 2012). In Canada, Asia is now the largest source of immigrants. The effects of these demographic shifts are expected to increase as the aging native white population is replaced by immigrants and their offspring. As of 2010, minorities (i.e., those not classified as non-Hispanic whites) were 36 percent of the US population, a share that is expected to rise to 45 percent by 2030. Within a similar time frame in Canada, visible minorities (an employment classification that excludes aboriginal people) increased from 16 percent to a predicted 31 percent (Torrey 2014: 15). The changing racial and ethnic makeup of both countries will likely have consequences for how moral issues are treated.

On the basis of past research, it can be expected that generation, education, religion, and race/ethnicity will all affect how moral issues develop and are resolved. Given differences in the demographic makeup of Canada and the United States, we can anticipate that all but generation will have an impact on differentiating moral policies in the two countries. These demographic variables and the expectations they lead to will not be directly tested in the chapters that follow, since the data required for that purpose are not critical to the central arguments of this volume. Instead, they will be treated collectively, as a kind of residual, to subsume the expectation that

H_{CI}: the United States will display more conflict over moral issues than will Canada.

Civil Society and Values

Another important way to assess modern states is through the nature and extent of their civil societies. Civil society is defined as the "non-governmental and not-for-profit organizations that have a presence in public life, expressing the interests and values of their members or others, based on ethical, cultural, political, scientific, religious or philanthropic considerations" (World Bank 2013). The importance of this kind of civil society was recognized early in the history of the United States by de Tocqueville (2000) as an essential element in sustaining democratic government. His argument underlies the continued importance attached to the right of citizens to freely unite into associations where they can protect their interests independent of governmental control.

The free associations that mark civil society have been conceptualized in varied ways. They may be termed voluntary associations (like PTAs or fraternal organizations), social movements (like the civil rights or women's), interest groups (like professional or religiously affiliated associations), or pressure or lobbying groups (like chambers of commerce or trade unions). We draw attention to these different concepts because they carry with them normative evaluations. For example, Skocpol (2003), beginning with an affirmation of how critical free associations have been in US civic life, notes both the decline in citizen participation and the rise of professionally administered lobbying groups concerned with delivering services to their clients. In their popular text, Cigler and Loomis (2011) examine both the positive and negative consequences of interest groups for the conduct of government. On the positive side, they are seen as ensuring that public concerns are made known to government. On the negative side, the lobbying of elected and appointed government personnel by advocacy groups is viewed as a source of corruption in the United States and a means for diminishing the quality of democratic governance (e.g., Gais 1996; Hansen 1991; Mills 1956). Pross (1986), a prominent student of pressure groups in Canada, presents his analysis without suggesting any negative implications and concludes that pressure groups are an important tool in ensuring democratic input into policymaking.

Similarly, social movements, including those that rely on non-institutionalized methods for expressing positions and influencing politics, may be evaluated in multiple ways. They may contribute to contention (Tilly and Tarrow 2006), reflect the weakness of oppositional groups attempting to bring about change (Mansbridge 1986), create a backlash (Piven and Cloward 1977), or successfully achieve their goals (Amenta 2006). These assessments are tied to internal variations in social movements and to the environments in which they operate.

We count ourselves among those who affirm the importance of civil society, manifested in the right of citizens to freely form associations independent of governing institutions. We will often use the concept of

NGO as a neutral term for describing and evaluating those associations, especially when we wish to avoid normative judgments. At the same time, we remain alert to both their positive and negative consequences.

Both the United States and Canada share the freedom to form associations and have a large number and variety of them. Yet there is a long-standing debate over which of the two countries has a greater propensity to participate in NGOs. As formulated by Lipset (1985: 141–2), the argument favored the United States, attributed to the latter's more individualistic and anti-statist culture rooted in that country's revolutionary origins. But challengers took issue with Lipset's emphasis on cultural sources of divergence and found little difference in contemporary rates of participation in NGOs (Curtis et al. 1989). In the end, Lipset (1990: 147–8) conceded that, at least on methodological grounds, it was difficult to defend the case that the two countries differed. We therefore do not anticipate that the comparative history of moral issues will be affected by national rates of participation in NGOs.

If numbers themselves are not relevant, what is important is the kind of NGOs present. At one level, both countries are similar in having comparable interest groups and social movements that either defend or oppose policies affecting each of the moral issues we consider. But beyond that superficial similarity, groups differ among themselves within and between countries. The social movement literature[2] will be our source for anticipating when the activities of diverse kinds of groups will give rise to national differences.

Groups, whether organized interests tied to established institutions or social movements challenging them, are all dependent on the resources they can mobilize in order to have an impact. Resources include active members, effective leadership, viable organizational structures, and ties with other groups that enhance their influence. Much attention is given to money as a critical resource, particularly since many US interest groups devoted to influencing policy are richly funded (Goidel, Gross, and Shields 1999). The electoral arena in Canada had been protected from what are, since the US Supreme Court ruling on *Citizens United v. Federal Election Commission* (2010), virtually unlimited infusions of outside money in the United States, especially from the deep pockets of super-PACs. In Canada, money was allotted

---

2 For a useful review of the literature focused on political consequences see Amenta et al. (2010).

through public funding and access to political advertising on radio and TV was tightly regulated. Although the Canadian situation changed after the 2011 election, when party funding was removed, campaign finance in the United States still remains much less regulated than in Canada (Boatright 2011; 2012). But taking into account all resources and not just financial ones, we predict that, compared to Canada,

H_{C2}: NGOs in the United States will have greater impact on the life history of moral issues.

Also relevant are the strategies that groups may employ. For example, Cress and Snow (2000) argue that effective strategies are those that identify a problem that needs solving and proposing a plausible solution. Strategies can vary depending on whether they are aimed at mobilizing supporters or at influencing policymakers, and what is effective in one context may be counter-productive in another (e.g., Mansbridge 1986). Persuasive strategies aimed at policymakers may use campaign contributions, lobbying activities, or the mobilization of voters. Social movements that deliberately choose protest actions may do so to threaten established authority or to persuade policymakers, both of which are more effective when a rapid response is expected (Amenta et al. 2010: 197).

Following Lipset's lead on value differences between Canada and the United States, the expectation would be that both institutionalized strategies, like campaigning, voter mobilization, and lobbying, and non-institutionalized ones, like protest demonstrations, are more prevalent and more effective in the United States. Support for this view can be found in early work by Presthus (1974) on interest group lobbying, where he concluded that US groups were more effective than Canadian ones. But later research has found evidence of cultural shifts, making Canadians and Americans more alike in values, particularly as the former have abandoned their deferential attitudes (Nevitte 1996). Smith (2005), focused on same-sex marriage, argues that Canadian groups were strategically more successful in achieving their goals. However, since she was not concerned with the influence of values on outcomes, we cannot make any direct connections. Although we anticipate that the strategies used by groups will affect the life history of moral issues, we cannot predict how these may be the source of significant differences between the two countries.

Amenta et al.'s (2010: 298) review of the conditions under which social movements are likely to have a political impact adds two further conditions. One is the political context within which such groups operate, which provides their crucial opportunity structure. The second relates to the likelihood of political mediation, in which state actors demonstrate a helpful openness to the goals for which groups are working, based on the benefits those actors anticipate. We concur in expecting that both political opportunities and mediation will have an impact on whether civic groups of all kinds are effective in influencing the course taken by moral issues. But because we see opportunities and mediation as characteristics of the political system, we reserve our discussion of them to the following section.

Political Institutions

As we just concluded, the effectiveness of those attempting to influence the course of moral issues is dependent on the political context in which they operate, where opportunities for action are linked to existing political institutions and to the mediation provided by institutional participants. Here we anticipate significant differences in impact on the course of moral issues because it is in the political arena where the two countries are most different. From the executive branch, to the operation of legislative bodies, political parties, the judiciary, and federalism, the two countries follow different arrangements and practices.[3]

In Canada, a prime minister representing a parliamentary majority is virtually all-powerful. Even a minority government does not entirely constrain a prime minister skillful enough to avoid alienating the opposition, who may then receive from it sufficient support to ensure passage of his party's legislative agenda. In the United States, even when the president is supported by a majority of his own party in both the House and Senate, there is no guarantee he will be able to achieve his program. Although the president may act as an important symbolic leader so that stands he takes on moral issues will be accorded new or augmented legitimacy, the prime minister can more directly affect the resolution of moral issues. Cabinet government in Canada augments the authority of the executive at the same time as cabinet positions vary in their influence. In particular, ministers of finance and justice are historically the most powerful. As a result, compared to the United States,

---

3 For an overview of the historical roots of these differences, see Kaufman (2009).

H_{C3}: executive authority in Canada is more likely to affect the resolution of moral issues.

The US legislature is more fractious than the Canadian one, lacking predictable and consistent partisan positions while providing a forum for individual members to promote pet projects and positions. Indeed, there is considerable expectation that the latter will sponsor legislation that favors particular constituents and interests. On the whole, the US legislature is a powerful one, certainly as compared to the Canadian (Tichenor 2012; White 2012). In Canada, there is virtually no scope for individual action, given that the parliamentary agenda is set by the prime minister and his cabinet and private member bills are rarely successful. Party discipline is almost complete and party leaders have no problem predicting the likelihood of bills passing (Haussman and Turnbull 2014). We are confident then in predicting that,

H_{C4}: compared to Parliament, Congress will provide more opportunities for moral issues to be given a powerful voice.

Politics in the United States is, for the most part, confined to two parties, Republican and Democratic, operating nationally and in each state. Local elections may be run on a non-partisan basis but even then, the partisan identity of candidates is often well known. Although smaller protest parties have been present at all federal levels of government and have, at times, had a major impact (e.g., Schwartz 2006), we concentrate on the two major parties. Both have loose organizational forms and are generally inclusive of a range of ideological positions. This has resulted in considerable organizational fluidity over time as each party has been challenged internally by those who want more ideological consistency, or externally by those who want to capture the party to represent their interests (Epstein 1986; Schwartz and Lawson 2005).

Although Canada also has two major parties, the Liberals and Conservatives, that have been the main competitors for national office throughout its history, it is more accurately described as a multi-party system. Other parties, representing special interests, like farmers or Quebec nationalists; or ideological perspectives, like the CCF, NDP, or Reform, have all played governing roles in the provinces and major oppositional ones in Parliament. Those parties may be more tightly organized than the two older ones, but all play their legislative roles in a similarly disciplined manner (Cross 2004). Given the relative ease with which new political parties with distinct agendas may form and compete in Canada and how this affects the performance of all parties, we are led to hypothesize that

H$_{C5}$: the two major parties in the United States will be more open to addressing moral issues than will their counterparts in Canada.

In US politics, parties come to own issues through processes that push them to emphasize topics compatible with past positions and appealing to the constituencies they wish to attract (Petrocik 1996; Egan 2013). The potential for issue ownership provides an incentive for NGOs to use one of the parties as a vehicle for furthering its goals. For parties, issue ownership can be a way to play a mediating role with NGOs that it wishes to include among its supporters. But because the two main US parties are typically not highly disciplined, this leaves room for individuals, whether legislators or candidates for office, to play an independent mediating role with respect to issues, using them to advance their own careers. In Canada, protest parties, tied to special interests, are more likely to be directly linked to issue ownership. But because they are often at a disadvantage in competing for office with the two major parties, the latter remain motivated to make their own claims to issue ownership. Yet, in comparing the two countries with regard to moral issues, we expect that

H$_{C6}$: issue ownership will be more prominent in US parties.

The federal system in both countries divides areas of responsibility between the central and provincial/state governments and provides multiple entry points for those interests trying to influence government. In both settings, venue shopping by NGOs will be affected by the opportunities inherent in federalism and by the availability of congenial partisan politicians (Constantelos 2010: 477).

The smaller number of provinces in Canada, the absence of a powerful senate to represent provincial interests within Parliament, and the unique position of Quebec as the homeland of the French-speaking minority have all contributed to the relatively greater power of provinces versus the national government compared to the power differences between states and the central government in the United States. Although Field (1992) appears to qualify this generalization, based on the strength of states' rights in the United States, she also acknowledges the greater flexibility of the Canadian system, with its lesser concern with legalisms and greater willingness to negotiate across levels. But differences in the division of responsibilities by level of government, most notably through the presence of a single criminal code in Canada compared to state variations in the United States (Thomas 2014), affect the likelihood of where moral issues will emerge. They lead us to expect that, compared to Canadian provinces,

H_{c7}: US states will be the more likely venue for the appearance of moral issues.

Referring back to chapter 2, we note that the final resolution of prohibition took place at the national level in both countries and subsequent governmental efforts to regulate alcohol devolved to local levels. Yet, in Canada, alcohol retained its special quality to engage fundamental issues of federalism, ensuring that it would, in some sense, remain on the federal agenda in a way foreign to how federalism operates in the United States. When moral issues are the subject of election debate, the greater distortions in the US electoral map and the reinforcing potential of simultaneous elections could tend to compensate for those issues' state-centered venue and lead to more opportunities for issues to be addressed at the national level. However, in Canada, federal responsibility for criminal law virtually guarantees that, whenever moral issues of right and wrong enter the legal arena, they will be national issues. As a result,

H_{c8}: opportunities for the nationalization of moral conflicts will be greater in Canada.

In Canada, the judicial system is presumed to be removed from partisan politics, at least to the extent that judicial appointments are not subject to legislative scrutiny and approval (Kerans 2014: 201–4). Although judges in the United States, particularly at the national level, are considered activist, playing a distinct role in legislative interpretations and enforcement, this was not the traditional evaluation of Canadian high-court justices. But the advent of the Constitution Act changed that and the Canadian courts, particularly through their interpretations of guarantees in the Canadian Charter of Rights and Freedoms, have become significant actors in moral conflicts. In this way they have come to participate in what has been argued as a general trend: "In many jurisdictions with a constitutional bill of rights or a constitutional division of powers, morality policy and judicial power have become mutually reinforcing" (Snow 2014). As a result, we anticipate

H_{C9}: a greater role for US courts in adjudicating moral conflicts along with declining differences between the two countries after 1984.

This review of differences between Canadian and US political institutions leads us to rest much of our subsequent analysis on the premise that institutions matter, despite some claims to the contrary (e.g., Montpetit et al. 2007: 268). Each of the political institutions described is expected to play a critical role in the history of moral conflicts, with those in the United States having greater effect on that history.

Impact of the National Environment

This chapter has reviewed differences between Canada and the United States that can be presumed to have an impact on the life course of moral issues. Demographic differences are those population characteristics that influence how issues are perceived and the groups likely to be mobilized to act on them. Selected differences in civil society and accompanying values affect the likelihood of mobilizing and the strategies selected to exert influence. In comparison to demography and civil society, we anticipate political institutions in both countries to be the most critical factor affecting how moral issues emerge and develop. Those institutions are also the greatest source of relevant differences between the countries. Because of the numerous ways in which they shape opportunities for action, we expect that US institutions will have a greater impact on the history of moral issues than will be the case in Canada.

None of the characteristics reviewed are totally fixed but change with changing conditions, legislation, and court decisions. Among demographic changes, we pointed to the shift in the distribution of the more highly educated from the United States to Canada. We also observed how the ethnic/racial composition of the population in both countries has altered over time. Value patterns have changed as well, with Canadians ones becoming more similar to those in the United States. Within the political arena, the courts in Canada have become more activist and therefore more like those in the United States. These changes alert us to the importance of history not only in tracing the life course of issues but also in affecting those features of the social and political environment that impinge on the issues.

Known differences between the United States and Canada in demography, culture, and politics that are expected to influence moral issues have been presented in this chapter in relatively uncomplicated ways, without reference to the two factors that add to complexity and provide the rationale for this volume. Only in combination with the phases through which moral issues evolve and the unique attributes of the issues themselves can the national context lead us to a comprehensive explanation of the history of moral conflicts. Now, having described all the factors involved to enable such an explanation, we can proceed in the following chapters to describe and analyze how that explanation evolves.

REFERENCES

Amenta, Edwin. 2006. *When Movements Matter: The Townsend Plan and the Rise of Social Security*. Princeton, NJ: Princeton University Press.

Amenta, Edwin, Neal Caren, Elizabeth Chiarello, and Yang Su. 2010. "The Political Consequences of Social Movements." *Annual Review of Sociology* 36 (1): 287–307. https://doi.org/10.1146/annurev-soc-070308-120029.

American Civil Liberties Union. 2014. *Racial Disparities in Sentencing*. Written submission to the Inter-American Commission on Human Rights. 153rd Session, 27 October.

Bean, Lydia. 2014. *The Politics of Evangelical Identity*. Princeton, NJ: Princeton University Press. https://doi.org/10.1515/9781400852611.

Bendyna, Mary E., John C. Green, Mark J. Rozell, and Clyde Wilcox. 2001. "Uneasy Alliance: Conservative Catholics and the Christian Right." *Sociology of Religion* 62 (1): 51–64. https://doi.org/10.2307/3712230.

Boatright, Robert G. 2011. *Interest Groups and Campaign Finance Reform in the United States and Canada*. Ann Arbor: University of Michigan Press. https://doi.org/10.3998/mpub.2485161.

Boatright, Robert G. 2012. "The End of the Reform Era? Campaign Finance Retrenchment in the United States and Canada." *The Forum* 10 (2). https://doi.org/10.1515/1540-8884.1440.

Cigler, Allan J., and Burdett Loomis, eds. 2011. *Interest Group Politics*. 8th ed. Thousand Oaks, CA: CQ Press.

Constantelos, John. 2010. "Playing the Field: Federalism and the Politics of Venue Shopping in the United States and Canada." *Publius* 40 (3): 460–83. https://doi.org/10.1093/publius/pjq010.

Cress, D.M., and David A. Snow. 2000. "The Outcomes of Homeless Mobilization: The Influence of Organization, Disruption, Political Mediation, and Framing." *American Journal of Sociology* 105 (4): 1063–104. https://doi.org/10.1086/210399.

Cross, William. 2004. *Political Parties*. Vancouver: UBC Press.

Curtis, James E., Ronald D. Lambert, Steven D. Brown, and Barry J. Kay. 1989. "Affiliation with Voluntary Associations: Canadian and American Comparisons." *Canadian Journal of Sociology* 14 (2): 143–61. https://doi.org/10.2307/3341288.

de Tocqueville, Alexis. 2000. *Democracy in America*. Ed. and trans. Harvey C. Mansfield and Delbra Winthrop. Chicago: University of Chicago Press. https://doi.org/10.7208/chicago/9780226924564.001.0001.

Donovan, Todd, and Caroline Tolbert. 2013. "Do Popular Votes on Rights Create Animosity toward Minorities?" *Political Research Quarterly* 66 (4): 910–22. https://doi.org/10.1177/1065912913478839.

Egan, Patrick J. 2013. *Partisan Priorities: How Issue Ownership Drives and Distorts American Politics*. New York: Cambridge University Press. https://doi.org/10.1017/CBO9781107337138.

Epstein, Leon. 1986. *Political Parties in the American Mold*. Madison: University of Wisconsin Press.

Field, Martha A. 1992. "The Differing Federalisms of Canada and the United States." *Law and Contemporary Problems* 55 (1): 107–20. https://doi.org/10.2307/1191759.

Fischer, Claude S., and Michael Hout. 2006. *Century of Difference: How America Changed in the Last One Hundred Years*. New York: Russell Sage Foundation.

Frendreis, John, and Raymond Tatalovich. 2010. "'A Hundred Miles of Dry': Religion and the Persistence of Prohibition in the U.S. States." *State Politics & Policy Quarterly* 10 (3): 302–19. https://doi.org/10.1177/153244001001000305.

Gagnon, Michelle. 2013. "Quebec's Values Charter Forcing Rethink of Catholicism, Religious Identity." *CBC News*, 13 October.

Gais, T. 1996. *Improper Influence: Campaign Finance Law, Political Interest Groups, and the Problem of Inequality*. Ann Arbor: University of Michigan Press. https://doi.org/10.3998/mpub.14656.

Goidel, Robert K., Donald A. Gross, and Todd G. Shields. 1999. *Money Matters: Consequences of Campaign Finance Reform in U.S. House Elections*. Lanham, MD: Rowman & Littlefield.

Haider-Markel, Donald P., and Kenneth J. Meier. 1996. "The Politics of Gay and Lesbian Rights: Expanding the Scope of Conflict." *Journal of Politics* 58 (2): 332–49. https://doi.org/10.2307/2960229.

Hansen, J.M. 1991 (1919). *Gaining Access: Congress and the Farm Lobby*. Chicago: University of Chicago Press.

Harrison, Trevor W. 2014. "Populist and Conservative Evangelical Movements: A Comparison of Canada and the United States." In *Group Politics and Social Movements in Canada*, ed. Miriam Smith, 201–24. Toronto: University of Toronto Press.

Haussman, Melissa, and Lori Turnbull. 2014. "Legislatures and Parties: Heightened Divisions since the 1990s." In *Canada and the United States: Differences That Count*, ed. David M. Thomas and David Biette, 163–85. 4th ed. Toronto: University of Toronto Press.

Hurka, Steffan, Christian Adam, and Cristoph Knill. 2016. "Is Morality Policy Different? Testing Sectoral and Institutional Explanations of Change." *Policy Studies Journal*, forthcoming (early view, https://doi.org/10.1111/psj.12153).

Hutchinson, Roger. 2011. "Focusing, Framing, and Discerning: The United Church of Canada and the Same-Sex Marriage Debate." In *Faith, Politics, and Sexual Diversity in Canada and the United States*, ed. David Rayside and Clyde Wilcox, 177–88. Vancouver: UBC Press.

Kaufman, Jason. 2009. *The Origins of Canadian and American Political Differences*. Cambridge, MA: Harvard University Press.

Kerans, Hon. Roger P. 2014. "Two Nations Under Law." In *Canada and the United States: Differences That Count*, ed. David M. Thomas and David Biette, 186–206. 4th ed. Toronto: University of Toronto Press.

King, Ryan S., and Marc Mauer. 2006. "The War on Marijuana: The Transformation of the War on Drugs in the 1990s." *Harm Reduction Journal* 3: 6–17.

Langstaff, Amy. 2011. "A Twenty-Year Survey of Canadian Attitudes towards Homosexuality and Gay Rights." In *Faith, Politics, and Sexual Diversity in Canada and the United States*, ed. David Rayside and Clyde Wilcox, 49–66. Vancouver: UBC Press.

Lipset, Seymour Martin. 1985. "Canada and the United States: The Cultural Dimension." In *Canada and the United States: Enduring Friendship, Persistent Stress*, ed. Charles F. Doran and John H. Sigler, 109–60. Englewood Cliffs, NJ: Prentice-Hall.

Lipset, Seymour Martin. 1990. *Continental Divide: The Values and Institutions of the United States and Canada*. New York: Routledge.

Lynerd, Benjamin T. 2014. *Republican Theology: The Civil Religion of American Evangelicals*. New York: Oxford University Press. https://doi.org/10.1093/acprof:oso/9780199363551.001.0001.

Mansbridge, J.J. 1986. *Why We Lost the ERA*. Chicago: University of Chicago Press.

Martinez, Michael D. 2014. "Turning Out or Tuning Out? Electoral Participation in Canada and the United States." In *Canada and the United*

States: Differences That Count, ed. David M. Thomas and David Biette, 142–62. 4th ed. Toronto: University of Toronto Press.

McQuillan, Kevin, and Erin Gibbs Van Brunschot. 2011. "The Educational Attainment of Canadians." In *The Changing Canadian Population*, ed. Barry Edmonston and Eric Fong, 83–98. Montreal and Kingston: McGill-Queen's University Press.

Mills, C. Wright. 1956. *The Power Elite*. New York: Oxford University Press.

Montpetit, Eric, Frederic Varone, and Christine Rothmayr. 2007. "Regulating ARTs and GMOs in Europe and North America: A Qualitative Comparative Analysis." In *The Politics of Biotechnology in North America and Europe*, ed. Eric Montpetit, Frederic Varone, and Christine Rothmayr, 263–86. Lanham, MD: Lexington Books.

Nevitte, Neil. 1996. *The Decline of Deference: Canadian Value Change in Cross-National Perspective*. Peterborough, ON: Broadview Press.

O'Connor, Robert E., and Michael B. Berkman. 1995. "Religious Determinants of State Abortion Policy." *Social Science Quarterly* 76 (2): 447–59.

OECD. 2012. "United States – Country Note." *Education at a Glance: OECD Indicators*. www.oecd.org/edu/eag2012.

Olson, Laura R., Paul A. Djupe, and Wendy Cadge. 2011. "American Mainline Protestantism and Deliberation about Homosexuality." In *Faith, Politics, and Sexual Diversity in Canada and the United States*, ed. David Rayside and Clyde Wilcox, 189–204. Vancouver: UBC Press.

Petrocik, John R. 1996. "Issue Ownership in Presidential Elections, with a 1980 Case Study." *American Journal of Political Science* 40 (3): 825–50.

Pew Research. 2008. *U.S. Religious Landscape Survey*. (1 June). Washington, DC: Pew Research Center.

Pew Research. 2013. *Canada's Changing Religious Landscape*. (27 June). Washington, DC: Pew Research Center.

Pierce, Patrick A., and Donald E. Miller. 1999. "Variation in the Diffusion of State Lottery Adoptions: How Revenue Dedication Changes Morality Politics." *Policy Studies Journal: The Journal of the Policy Studies Organization* 27 (4): 696–706. https://doi.org/10.1111/j.1541-0072.1999.tb01997.x.

Piven, Frances F., and Richard A. Cloward. 1977. *Poor People's Movements: Why They Succeed, How They Fail*. New York: Random House.

Presthus, Robert. 1974. "Interest Group Lobbying in Canada and the United States." *Annals of the American Academy of Political and Social Science* 413 (1): 44–57. https://doi.org/10.1177/000271627441300105.

Pross, A. Paul. 1986. *Group Politics and Public Policy*. Toronto: Oxford University Press.

Reitz, Jeffery G., and Raymond Breton. 1994. *The Illusion of Difference: Realities of Ethnicity in Canada and the United States*. Toronto: C.D. Howe Institute.

Schlozman, Kay L., Sidney Verba, and Henry E. Brady. 2012. *The Unheavenly Chorus: Unequal Political Voice and the Broken Promise of American Democracy.* Princeton, NJ: Princeton University Press. https://doi.org/10.1515/9781400841912.

Schwartz, Mildred A. 2006. *Party Movements in the United States and Canada: Strategies of Persistence.* Boulder, CO: Rowman & Littlefield.

Schwartz, Mildred A., and Kay Lawson. 2005. "Political Parties, Social Bases, Organization, and Environment." In *The Handbook of Political Sociology: States, Civil Societies and Globalization,* ed. Thomas Janoski, Robert Alford, Alexander Hicks, and Mildred A. Schwartz, 266–86. New York: Cambridge University Press.

Semet, Amy, and Steven Ansolabehere. 2011. "Profiling and Predicting Opinions on Gun Control: A Comparative Perspective on the Factors Underlying Opinion on Different Gun Control Measures." Paper presented at the Conference of Empirical Legal Studies. Evanston, IL: Northwestern University Law School. https://doi.org/10.2139/ssrn.1884661.

Shames, Shauna L., Didi Kuo, and Katherine Levine. 2011. "Culture War? A Closer Look at the Role of Religion, Denomination, and Religiosity in US Public Opinion on Multiple Sexualities." In *Faith, Politics, and Sexual Diversity in Canada and the United States,* ed. David Rayside and Clyde Wilcox, 29–48. Vancouver: UBC Press.

Shrestha, Laura B., and Elayne J. Heisler. 2011. *The Changing Demographic Profile of the United States.* Washington, DC: Congressional Research Service (31 March).

Skocpol, Theda. 2003. *Diminished Democracy: From Membership to Management in American Civic Life.* Norman: Oklahoma University Press.

Smith, Miriam. 2005. "The Politics of Same-Sex Marriage in Canada and the United States." *PS: Political Science and Politics* 38 (2): 225–8.

Snow, Dave. 2014. "Does Federalism Matter for Morality Policy? The Case of Assisted Reproductive Technologies and Embryo Research in Canada." Paper presented at the Canadian Political Science Association Annual Meeting, St Catharines, ON.

Statistics Canada. 2006. "Median Age, 1941 to 2011." Catalogue no. 96F0030XIE200102. http://www41.statcan.gc.ca/2006/3867/htm/ceb3867_000_3-eng.htm.

Statistics Canada. 2013. "Canada's Population Estimates: Age and Sex, 2013." *Annual Demographic Estimates: Canada, Provinces and Territories.* 91–215-X.

Statistics Canada. 2014. *Historical Statistics of Canada: Section W: Education.* Modified 2014-07-02. Archived content. For inquries, infostats@statscan.gc.ca.

Thomas, David M. 2014. "Past Futures: Federalism under Stress." In *Canada and the United States: Differences That Count,* ed. David M. Thomas and David Biette, 93–115. 4th ed. Toronto: University of Toronto Press.

Tichenor, Daniel J. 2012. "Democracy's Wartime Deficits: The Prerogative Presidency and Liberal Democracy in the United States." In *Imperfect Democracies: The Democratic Deficit in Canada and the United States*, ed. Patti Tamara Lenard and Richard Simeon, 204–25. Vancouver: UBC Press.

Tilly, Charles, and Sidney Tarrow. 2006. *Contentious Politics*. Boulder, CO: Paradigm Press.

Torrey, Barbara Boyle. 2014. "Population Tectonics: Life and Death in North America." In *Canada and the United States: Differences That Count*, ed. David M. Thomas and David Biette, 3–22. 4th ed. Toronto: University of Toronto Press.

US Census Bureau. 2012. "The Foreign-Born Population in the United States: 2012." www.census.gov/content/dam/Census/library/publications/2012/acs/acs-19.pdf.

Wald, Kenneth D. 2011. "Paths from Emancipation: American Jews and Same-Sex Marriage." In *Faith, Politics, and Sexual Diversity in Canada and the United States*, ed. David Rayside and Clyde Wilcox, 239–54. Vancouver: UBC Press.

White, Graham. 2012. "The 'Centre' of the Democratic Deficit: Power and Influence in Canadian Political Executives." In *Imperfect Democracies: The Democratic Deficit in Canada and the United States*, ed. Patti Tamara Lenard and Richard Simeon, 226–47. Vancouver: UBC Press.

Wilcox, Clyde, and Rentaro Iida. 2011. "Evangelicals, the Christian Right, and Gay and Lesbian Rights in the United States: Simple and Complex Stories." In *Faith, Politics, and Sexual Diversity in Canada and the United States*, ed. David Rayside and Clyde Wilcox, 101–20. Vancouver: UBC Press.

World Bank. 2013. "Defining Civil Society." http://go.worldbank.org/4CE7WO46KO.

Chapter Five

The Emergence of Moral Conflicts

Forms of Conflict

Morally infused policies, expressed as regulation of or restrictions on behavior, make up a substantial part of the legal codes of Canada and the United States, as they do of all legal systems. Sustained by the values dominant in a society, such laws may exist for long periods without evoking noticeable opposition. It is only when concerted opposition appears, demanding change in the status quo, that we can speak of the emergence of moral conflicts. That is, issues are transformed from being one-sided to two-sided (Meier 1994: 246–7).

The form that opposition takes varies by issue. We noted in the case of prohibition that, even when alcohol use was most extensive and uninhibited, there was still some regulation, mainly through tax levies, but also through local laws on public drunkenness. Conflict emerged first in the advocacy of greater restrictions, culminating in national prohibition, and later in the opposing direction, when prohibition was replaced with lighter regulation at the subnational level. In somewhat analogous ways to those later changes, opposition to long-established policies on abortion, marijuana use, and same-sex relations has aimed to decriminalize or ultimately legalize those activities.

Capital punishment, like abortion, same-sex relations, and marijuana use at the time when all were most severely regulated and punished, has a lengthy history of acceptance. But, unlike those issues, it has gone through several cycles of rejection and acceptance. Over the course of US history, individual states have abolished the death penalty, only to reinstate it (Greenberg 2000). Our research, while mindful of this history, dates the contemporary emergence of opposition to capital punishment to the late 1960s and early 1970s, signaled by the uptick in media coverage in both countries (see figures 3.3 and 3.4).

At one stage, pornography involving adults was associated with protest similar to that in the cases of abortion, marijuana, and same-sex relations, that is, it was intended to loosen or do away with restrictions. But once the issue was reframed as child pornography, then opposition moved to a restrictive stance. It is in this sense that pornography is like prohibition in having two directly opposing foci of conflict at different times. As we did in the case of prohibition, we look for signs of emergence in the initial conflict that was generated by efforts to remove restrictions on pornography and find them in the 1960s.

The regulation of firearms has a very different history and meaning in Canada and the United States, as was summarized in chapter 3. Even though Canada has a lengthy record of restrictions on gun ownership and a much lower incidence of gun violence than the United States, both countries display similar ambivalence about gun control, with demands for more or less control fluctuating over time. For our purposes, we treat the emergence of conflict in the 1960s in the United States and the 1970s in Canada.

The six issues that form the basis of our analysis present themselves differently, depending on the form opposition takes. But, in all instances, we equate critical demands for change in the historical definition of a moral issue as a turning point, marking the emergence of conflict. Yet history does not always unfold in such distinct ways that make the turning point either highly visible or easily distinguishable from other phases. We can identify emergence after the fact, although it may not stand out sharply when it occurs because it is often more of a process than a distinct event.

This chapter is organized to test the five hypotheses about emergence that were generated from the case of prohibition with support from the literature on social movements, contentious politics, and policymaking. Emergence is expected to follow from

- large-scale social changes,
- possible triggering events,
- collective action challenging the status quo,
- collective actors' social status, and
- tactics supported by rich resources.

Environmental Change

The first hypothesis predicted that "moral conflicts are likely to emerge from large-scale social and political changes." Indeed, vast social, economic, and political changes, set in motion by the Second World War, continued to exert their influence on Canada and the United States, as they did worldwide, and produced virtually revolutionary outcomes beginning in the 1960s. Among the noteworthy changes, particularly in the United States, was a greatly enlarged generational cohort, able to enroll in the expanded number and size of post-secondary educational institutions, where their concentration made subsequent mobilization relatively easy. Women, now increasingly better educated, often found themselves out of the labor force after wartime participation and isolated in suburban communities. African Americans, who had begun to make progress toward increased equality, at least outside the South, were now mobilized to press for greater civil rights. Meanwhile, an unpopular war was being waged in Vietnam that formed the basis for much of the alienation of young people. The consequence of these developments was a milieu in which long-established values and practices were no longer taken for granted and where nothing was safe from questioning. This questioning applied particularly to authority. Everything, from the roles of women, race relations, drug use, and expressions of sexuality, was now a subject of contention. Although this description of a world in flux applies best to the United States in this period, it was also echoed in Canada, even if to a lesser extent and sometimes later than in the former. It is therefore easy to conclude that, helped by a destabilized environment, challenges to existing laws and practices in regard to abortion, marijuana, pornography,[1] and same-sex relations emerged at around the same time in both countries.

Two issues – capital punishment and gun control – were less strongly affected by the tumult of the 1960s, displaying instead the continuing impact of a much earlier turbulent environment. In both countries, that environment left a strong and continuing preference for the death penalty applied to capital offenses. At the same time, opposition to capital punishment in the United States has a lengthy cyclical history. Haines (1996) identifies four periods when abolition was active. The first was in

---

1 Friedman (2000: 4–5) argues that opposition to strict regulation of obscenity had already appeared by the 1930s and gained momentum after the Second World War.

the mid to late nineteenth century and reflected the reformist zeal of the post–Civil War period. The second, from the late nineteenth to the early twentieth centuries, is associated with the Progressive movement. He dates the third to the mid-twentieth century, when post–Second World War reform was prominent. The last period begins around the 1970s and shows the effects of the civil rights era. In Canada, as well, there had been periodic attempts to abolish capital punishment through the first half of the twentieth century (Chandler 1976), gaining momentum after the Second World War (Ryan 1969). These latter developments in both countries allow us to use the end of the 1960s and beginning of the 1970s as a time frame for examining the more recent emergence of a two-sided debate on capital punishment.

In the United States, the heritage of its War of Independence, western expansion, and Civil War, coupled with constitutional guarantees, all sustained a history of widespread gun ownership that continues to be defended up to the present. But, like opposition to capital punishment, advocacy of gun control has been cyclical, responsive to fatal shooting episodes. In Canada, early imposition of federal authority over western development and the existence of a single criminal code helped keep firearms from acquiring a mystique like that in the United States. In the absence of clear markers for emergence, we follow the pattern formed by other moral conflicts and begin our examination in the 1960s. For the United States we designate the emergent period to be between 1963 and 1968, covering the assassinations of President John F. Kennedy in November of the earlier year and later, those of Senator Robert Kennedy and Dr Martin Luther King. That was also a time of high media coverage (figure 3.5; Smith 1980: 300).

Triggering Events

When the conflict potential of an issue is revealed through one or more dramatic and disruptive events, the latter can serve as triggers to emergence by bringing the issue to public attention, mobilizing people to take collective action, and prodding political actors to recognize new political concerns. But the absence of distinct triggers for prohibition and the current reluctance of social movement theorists to see them as essential to the emergence of contention left us to hypothesize that, while triggers may be important, they are not critical factors in emergence.

Two of the six issues were aided in their emergence by triggers in both Canada and the United States, and two others experienced a trigger in the United States. Issues with similar triggering mechanisms were capital punishment and gun control. The United States was also affected by triggers that challenged prevailing restrictions on abortion and same-sex relations. These results support our restrained approach to the significance of triggers, particularly in Canada.

Abortion

In 1962, Sherri Finkbine provided the dramatic case that opened abortion to public debate. While pregnant, she had taken thalidomide and only later learned that the drug could cause severely malformed fetuses. She petitioned a local hospital for an abortion and the *Arizona Republic*'s front-page, black-bordered headline account quickly found its way to front pages across the nation and worldwide. When a local prosecutor threatened legal action, the hospital she had engaged refused to proceed with the abortion. Finkbine had to travel to Sweden, where, despite criticism by the Vatican, she aborted the fetus (Finkbine 1967). Shortly after, a Gallup Poll asked: "As you may have heard or read, an Arizona woman recently had a legal abortion in Sweden after having taken the drug thalidomide, which has been linked to birth defects. Do you think this woman did the right thing or the wrong thing in having this abortion operation?" Fifty-two percent agreed with her decision (Tatalovich and Daynes 1981: 116).

In Canada, the deforming effects on fetuses from a rubella epidemic were a factor in the Canadian Medical Association's efforts to expand the use of abortions (Brodie at al. 1992: 28). News of the effects of thalidomide use had also spread to Canada (Halfmann 2011: 43). Yet there is no evidence that either were triggering events analogous to what happened in the United States.

Capital Punishment

Capital punishment in Canada was established in the colonial era and moves to seek its abolition reached Parliament as unsuccessful private members' bills at various times (Chandler 1976). In 1959, a single criminal case appeared to serve as a trigger for abolition. It involved fourteen-year-old Steven Truscott, sentenced to be hanged for the rape and murder of twelve-year-old school friend Lynne Harper. Truscott was condemned, despite a recommendation for mercy by the trial jury, because death was the only penalty prescribed for the crime of murder. The Government gave Truscott a temporary reprieve to allow him to appeal, and in January 1960 his death sentence was commuted to life imprisonment. Eventually he was paroled and judicial review of his conviction concluded that there had been a miscarriage of justice, although he was never formally declared innocent. Truscott's death sentence provoked much public debate about capital punishment, leading to the highest level of support for abolition. The majority position in public opinion polls from 1943 to 1975 was opposed to abolishing the death penalty, but there was some loosening in 1960, when 41 percent favored abolition (Fattah, 1976).

In the United States, the case of Caryl Chessman, executed by the State of California in 1959, served to stimulate concern about abolishing the death penalty, evident from a spike in media coverage during 1959–60 (see figure 3.3). Chessman had been convicted of robbery, kidnapping, and rape at a time when California had a "Little Lindbergh Law," where any crime involving kidnapping with bodily harm was considered a capital offense. Chessman spent nearly twelve years on death row (a US record at that time), during which time he publicized his case through letters, essays, and four books, of which one became a movie. Chessman's public outreach launched a worldwide movement to spare his life, and Governor Edmund Brown heard appeals from such authors and intellectuals as Aldous Huxley, Ray Bradbury, Norman Mailer, Dwight MacDonald, and Robert Frost as well as former first lady Eleanor Roosevelt and Evangelical leader Billy Graham.

Gun Control

Agitation for gun control in both countries has been highly sensitive to shooting massacres or the assassination of political leaders. In the early 1930s, a combination of such events became triggers in the United States. Shootings among warring gangs involved in illegal alcohol trafficking became a source of alarm among the public and political leaders. Then, in 1933, newly inaugurated President Franklin Delano Roosevelt was riding in an open-air car in Miami when an assassin shot at him. The assassin missed his target but killed the mayor of Chicago, a fellow passenger. But support for gun control in the United States has cycled through many such recurring triggers, to be followed by decline and then resurgence in public and political attention. Not only does that make it difficult to select a particular trigger as the date for the emergence of moral conflict, but, as we have already indicated, the cycles of attention also obscured the impact of the social and political environment on timing. To say that moral conflict emerged in the 1960s is necessarily imprecise, given the short-lived effect of shooting triggers.

Gun control did not emerge as an issue in Canada until the early 1970s, triggered by two school shooting incidents. On 27 October 1972, at a high school in Ottawa, eighteen-year-old Robert Poulin opened fire on his classmates with a shotgun, killing one and wounding five before killing himself. On 28 May 1975, sixteen-year-old Michael Slobodian brought two rifles to his high school in Brampton, Ontario, and began firing in a boys' washroom, where he killed one student. He then entered a classroom, where he killed an English teacher and wounded thirteen more students before committing suicide. These shocking events produced a spike in media coverage (see figure 3.6) and a call for compulsory registration of all firearms from 83 percent of those surveyed by the Gallup Poll (*Globe and Mail* 1975).

Same-Sex Relations

The treatment of same-sex relations in the United States is the final case in which triggering events had an effect on the emergence of moral conflict. In June 1969 the New York City police raided the Stonewall Inn, a Greenwich Village gay bar. Although such raids on establishments serving the gay community were not uncommon, this time the impact was dramatic. Martin Duberman (1993: xv), an activist in the gay rights movement, considers the Stonewell experience "*the* emblematic event in modern lesbian and gay history," and political scientists Button, Rienzo, and Wald (1997: 25) agree that it was "a crucial catalyst to the mass political mobilization of lesbians and gay men." Nothing comparable to Stonewall occurred in Canada and whatever spillover there was did not generate the same magnitude of response.

Challenging Groups

The third hypothesis tied emergence to the appearance of collective action that challenges prevailing practices and their underlying values, with the intention of limiting behavior viewed as undesirable. That action may come from already existing interest groups, aroused to defend their positions. As actors in a contentious environment, interest groups, with an acknowledged claim to defending specific groups and interests, can bring an aura of legitimacy to whatever issues they advocate. Interest groups representing those of high status, like the legal and medical professions and religious authorities, carry especially strong weight in redefining moral boundaries. Social movements have their own advantage by projecting high levels of enthusiasm while being single-minded in pursuit of their goals. Acting singly or together, interest groups and social movements can mark the full entry of a moral issue into a field of conflict regardless of whether or not they are the primary initiators of its emergence. Overall, compared to Canada, the United States is more consistent in its display of collective opposition to all the restrictive or punitive versions of our array of moral issues, with interest groups taking the lead in most issues. Yet, even in the United States, the impact of collective action has varied by issue.

Abortion

The legal profession played a role in redefining abortion in the United States, signaled by the American Law Institute's (1959) recommendation permitting abortions when the mother or child would otherwise be harmed or as a result of rape. The medical profession, however, was comparatively slow in speaking out in favor of new legal definitions (Bates and Zawadski 1964: 115; Halfmann 2011). However, by the end of the 1960s, numerous healthcare, women's, and religious organizations added their voice to reform or repeal state anti-abortion laws: the American Medical Women's Association (1969), American Public Health Association (1969), American Protestant Hospital Association (1970), American Baptist Churches (1968), Presbyterian Church in the United States (1970), American College of Obstetricians and Gynecologists (1970), and the United Church of Christ (1971), among others (Tatalovich and Daynes, 1981: 66–7).

Social movements in the United States also added to the voices advocating change by demanding that all abortion laws be repealed. Among them, the burgeoning women's movement saw abortion rights as part of the repertoire of its rights agenda (Rossi 1969: 338–46). More narrowly focused, the National Association for Repeal of Abortion Laws (NARAL) was founded in 1969 by activists under Lawrence Lader (1973), a longtime advocate of legalized abortions (Lader 1966). Its precursor was the Association to Repeal Abortion Laws (ARAL), active in California as a movement to help women obtain illegal abortions (Solinger 1998: 75).

In Canada, both the legal and medical professions took a lead in promoting abortion reform. In 1953 Dr Daniel Cappon advocated a study of attitudes toward abortion to the Canadian Psychiatric Association, meeting in conjunction with the Canadian Medical Association (CMA), to prepare physicians to help women who did not want to carry a child to term (*Globe and Mail* 1953). Organized medicine quickly took an active role in proposing legal changes (Halfmann 2011). In 1961 the Canadian Bar Association entertained a proposal that the law be eased to allow women who were raped to obtain legal abortions (*Globe and Mail* 1961b). Inspired by this professional advocacy, the leading English-language newspaper, the *Globe and Mail* (1962a), came to advocate abortion reform, editorializing that "doctors across the country have called for an amendment to the Code permitting them to use abortion when it is necessary for broad physical and mental reasons. It is time Canada took this civilized step." In 1963 and 1964 the Canadian Bar Association tabled resolutions endorsing legal abortions for therapeutic reasons, as did the Ontario Medical Association the following year. Moving beyond such resolutions were the actions of many hospitals that, on their own initiative, were making expansive definitions of what constituted therapeutic abortion (Stewart 1967).

Social movement activity appeared in Canada but not until the end of 1967, when change in abortion laws was already moving to the policy agenda. We leave an account of that activity to the following chapter on establishment, and here conclude that, in Canada, interest groups alone took the lead in the emergence of abortion reform.

Capital Punishment

If we date the current emergence of opposition to capital punishment in the United States to sometime around 1960, when media coverage peaked over the execution of Caryl Chessman (see figure 3.4), we are left with only modest evidence of concurrent supporting groups (Dicks 1991). Most prominent was the NAACP Legal Defense Fund (2015), which took up the cause of abolition in the 1960s. In addition, some early leaders of the American Civil Liberties Union, an organization in the forefront in the fight for civil liberties generally, were strongly opposed to capital punishment. However, efforts to include that opposition as part of the organization's expansion of civil rights issues in the 1960s were a source of conflict within the ACLU (Walker 1999: 262).

In Canada, according to Ryan (1969: 81), "after the Second World War, opposition to the death penalty gained support, at first among a few religious leaders, lawyers, and correctional workers and others, and later among larger groups." Although support had been expressed by the *Globe and Mail* (1961a), on the whole, Canada presents an even weaker case than the United States for the importance of interest groups and social movements as opponents seeking to undo the death penalty. Nevertheless, we can conclude that they did play some role.

Gun Control

Those citizens of the United States who favored restrictions on gun ownership remained outside any mobilized groups until the 1970s. Although the assassination of President Kennedy had the potential for the emergence of a popular movement for gun control, there was no sustained response at that time (Goss 2006: 35). Only beginning in 1974 were five national gun control groups founded, supplemented by an increase in the number of such groups at the state level (Goss 2006: 40–2). Other groups appeared even later (Spitzer 2015: 115, 116, 118). The absence of large-scale mobilization into social movements that could lead to pressure for supportive legislation is attributed to the low salience of gun control in affecting how its advocates vote in state and national elections (Schuman and Presser 2013) and to the strategic weaknesses present in current movements (Goss 2006).

Laws in Canada had long restricted access to firearms. The 1892 Criminal Code required individuals to have a basic permit to carry a pistol; in 1919–20, an amendment to the Criminal Code required individuals to obtain a permit to possess any firearm; and, in 1934, the first registration requirement for handguns was established. Nevertheless, Canada has not been immune to acts of violence, and those in 1972 and 1975 mark the emergence of gun control as a moral conflict. But, just as in the United States, attention quickly declines, to await the next mass shooting. No mass movements appeared, and support for control was confined to organized interests. One of those was the Ontario Association of Chiefs of Police, which resolved that all firearms be registered, all sales be recorded, and all purchasers be required to have a government certificate to buy a gun. Another was the *Globe and Mail* (1975), editorializing that "there is a growing problem of violence in Canada, a violence problem linked to guns. It is, in part, a problem exacerbated by the too-easy access to firearms that our present laws permit."

Marijuana

Although a two-sided public debate about the morality of marijuana use in the United States first appeared in the 1960s, professional organizations were voicing concerns even earlier. In the mid-1950s, a joint study of narcotics by the American Bar Association and the American Medical Association criticized the punishment approach and favored drug clinics, maintenance dosages of drugs, and rehabilitation. Although that study was attacked by the Federal Bureau of Narcotics and effectively suppressed (Musto 1973: 232), it signaled the direction those professions were taking. By the early 1960s, mental health professionals, concerned with how the issue symbolized a serious generational divide, worked to redefine drug abuse as a health problem (Meier 1994: 43). State legislatures began to take up the challenge by moving the conflict onto their political agenda. In 1968, Alaska, California, and Vermont reduced their penalties for possession of marijuana (Rosenthal 1977: 62) and, by the end of 1970, thirty-two states had done so (Meier 1994: 43).

The use of marijuana itself was promoted by a mass movement made up of young people. Many were college students and some were artists. New York's Greenwich Village, San Francisco's Haight-Ashbury, and Berkeley, California, were critical nodes for the diffusion of what became a cultural revolution that involved much more than marijuana (Howard 1969; Gitlin 1987). The principal challenge to how marijuana had been defined as an illegal substance came from this youth movement.

Canada did not experience the same magnitude of disruption that the cultural revolution of the 1960s brought to the United States. To the extent that there was any collective action aimed at promoting the use of marijuana, it was confined to the youth movement like the one appearing in the United States and elsewhere in the world (Schwartz 1981: 79; Owram 1996). Although there was great concern about the criminalization of young people experimenting with marijuana, there was even greater concern about its presumed addictive properties and its use as a gateway to other drugs (Spurgeon 1964). It was such fears that kept both law enforcement officials and the medical profession from opposing any pathway to legalization (*Globe and Mail* 1963). Changing approaches from professional organizations would not come until later, after the emergent phase. We see Canada, then, as initially lacking organized challengers.

Pornography

In both Canada and the United States, the leading precedent on pornography had been the "Hicklin Rule" of 1868. As interpreted by Lord Cockburn: "The test of obscenity is this, whether the tendency of the matter charged as obscene is to deprave and corrupt those whose minds are open to such immoral influences, and into whose hands the publication may fall."

A one-sided definition of the immorality of pornography dominated, supported in the United States by the courts and community and religious groups. Some of the latter traced their origins to the late nineteenth century, like the WCTU, Boston Society of Morals and Religious Instruction of the Poor, American Association for the Prevention of Licentiousness and Promotion of Morality, and, most prominently, the New York Society for the Suppression of Vice (Kobylka 1991: 24). The religious underpinnings of the modern anti-pornography movement were established in the 1930s with the founding of two agencies of the Catholic Church – the National Legion of Decency and the National Office for Decent Literature – to monitor motion pictures and books.

The transformation of pornography into a two-sided issue came in the 1950s through the efforts of legal scholars, civil rights groups, book publishers, and artists. Prominent legal scholars included William Lockhart and Robert McClure (1954; 1955), who argued that obscene materials were "relatively harmless" and they criticized the US Supreme Court for evading the core issue, that censorship was a violation of the First Amendment. Interest groups opposing the prevailing position on pornography, as compiled by Daynes (1988: 63), include the American Library Association, American Jewish Congress, Association of American Publishers, Authors League of America, Committee on Constitutional Liberties, Council for Periodical Distributors Association, Metropolitan Committee for Religious Liberty, and the National Lawyers Guild. At the forefront were the ACLU and its state affiliates.

The Canadian environment was, like the one in the United States, empty of significant social movements at the time opposition to old standards for evaluating obscenity emerged. In addition, there appears to have been little in way of advocacy from existing interest groups. The *Globe and Mail* (1959) was among the few public voices at this time, and it was a relatively muted one:

We believe that any general campaign against pornography should be postponed until the Federal authority, either by ruling of the Supreme

Court or by a revision of the Criminal Code, provides a clear and workable definition – if one is possible – of obscenity. Even when this is done, such a campaign needs careful watching. Moreover, there must be considerable care as to who is permitted to exercise supervision. History shows that censorship has often produced far greater evils than those it was designed to correct.

Same-Sex Relations

Same-sex relations, though always present, were often treated as though they did not exist and in an atmosphere that discouraged discussion. Prior to the Stonewall Inn raid, activists concerned with changing laws were judged to be few and with limited political influence. Afterwards, however, mobilization took off.

Almost immediately following Stonewall, countless new lesbian and gay liberation organizations came into being. Mobilized by the women's movement, lesbians became a greater force in the new gay movement. More radical in tone and tactics than previous homosexual organizations, these new political groups not only challenged antigay policies but focused on sexual oppression more generally (Button et al. 1997: 25).

In their battle to change a punitive legal environment, these social movements were allied with groups like the American Civil Liberties Union and the American Law Institute, whose Model Legal Code urged decriminalization of same-sex relations (Kane 2003: 316, 318).

In Canada, there were few voices in defense of homosexuals during the 1950s or 1960s. Consequently, a debate at a Toronto law conference in 1962 between Oxford University legal scholar H.L.A. Hart and Rev. Elliott MacGuigan of the Willowdale Jesuit Seminary drew wide attention (*Globe and Mail* 1962b). MacGuigan argued that the criminal law should reflect social mores, but Hart disagreed, saying the criminal code should not enforce moral principles. Furthermore, he viewed homosexuality as a victimless crime. The debate prompted the *Globe and Mail* to publish a four-part series by Alan Mewett (1962), law professor at Queen's University, which essentially agreed with the Hart position. This series began a slight trend of increased media coverage on homosexuality and quiet advocacy by the *Globe and Mail* (1967), approving of the decriminalization that had already been adopted in Great Britain, and urging "more public discussion of a problem that probably involves more Canadians than most of us care to acknowledge. And perhaps it is also time for Canadian politicians to consider if they are retaining a law that enshrines the prejudices of another era."

Social movements advocating liberation of gays and lesbians from legal restrictions grew in Canada, most noticeably during the 1970s, that is, after the 1969 decriminalization (Smith 2008: 35–6). Yet there were signs of earlier groups. For example, in 1964 a new organization formed to aid homosexuals, the Homophile Reform Society, requested a meeting with Prime Minister Lester B. Pearson to discuss removing section 149 of the Criminal Code, which made homosexual acts illegal (*Globe and Mail* 1964).

Overview

Our prediction that collective action will be critical to the emergence of moral conflicts is supported, but with issue and country variations. The weakest role played by interest groups and social movements in enabling the two-sided perspective that underlies conflict was with respect to gun control and, to a lesser extent, to capital punishment and pornography. Leading the struggle to redefine moral issues were legal and medical groups, civil rights organizations, and, in the United States with regard to abortion and marijuana, individual states. Interest group leadership in Canada was, overall, weaker and centered in the medical and legal professions with regard to abortion and only in the latter for same-sex relations. Social movement leadership in Canada was also weaker, entering the conflict after it was already underway.

Social Status

Our analysis of prohibition in chapter 2 noted how the relation between a social movement and its social base could be beneficial when that base captured the symbolic nature of the moral conflict in which it was engaged. That is, the participation of Protestant clergy and laypersons, who were themselves dedicated to abstention from alcohol, along with reformed drinkers, dramatized the moral position taken by these social actors personally in ways that enhanced the message they preached. We then broadened the connection by also including interest groups. That allowed us to recognize that high-status challenging groups, regardless of type, can lend legitimacy to their cause. For example, physicians can pass on some of their acknowledged dedication to promoting health and well-being to any issue that they define as within their professional purview. Lawyers can do the same in their symbolic role as upholders of legal norms. These additional observations led us to hypothesize that the identity of collective factors would aid the emergence of specific positions on moral conflicts. As we wrote in chapter 2, this occurs when the positions taken by those actors serve in "highlighting their own social status and contrasting it with other population groups associated with morally undesirable behavior."

Lawyers have been important in both countries as advocates for changing punitive laws on abortion and same-sex relations. The same is true for physicians with regard to abortion. Through their professional identity, lawyers in the United States have enhanced the legitimacy of the fight for changing the law dealing with pornography and, along with physicians, with marijuana. The more active presence of the legal and medical professions in moral conflicts in the United States also gives their members the role of moral exemplars who represent the right or correct views in that country.

The ability to draw on a dedicated social base in social movements is strongest in tying women to abortion, youth to marijuana, and gays and lesbians to conflict over same-sex relations in both countries. But the advantages these bring are not unequivocal. In societies where, politically, men are more highly valued over women, adults over youth, and straight people over homosexuals, identification between lower-status groups and issues can hamper the latter's acknowledgment as critical while enhancing conflict and blocking resolution. In the fight for prohibition, in contrast, advocates could point to their distinctive moral virtue as teetotalers.

The absence of a clearly defined social base linked to relatively high social status has been an obstacle to leaders when opposing capital punishment, gun control, and pornography. This has affected both the emergence of those issues and, as we will examine in the following chapter, their placement on the policy agenda. There we will elaborate on why capital punishment and especially pornography became established through an inside-access model of agenda setting rather than through the outside-initiative model based on mass mobilization. In the United States, in addition, weak advocacy by those opposed to permissive gun laws is directly related to the absence of an obvious social base available for mobilization. As Goss (2006) argues, this absence exemplifies the classic collective action problem in trying to mobilize disparate individuals to solve a problem that does not directly affect them. In contrast, opponents of gun control can readily mobilize an existing gun culture in rural southern and western areas of the country (Spitzer 2015: 7–14), a base much stronger in the United States than in Canada (McLean 2015).

In summary, support for H_{P4} is less clear cut than we would prefer, given the mixture of high-status groups like the legal and medical professions with lower-status ones like women, youth, and gays and lesbians in support of new approaches to abortion, marijuana, pornography, and same-sex relations. But given the presence of the higher-status ones in both countries for all issues, we still conclude that status mattered.

Organizational Resources

The final hypothesis on emergence predicted that groups, whether interest groups like professional organizations or social movement organizations, would be more effective in introducing their position on moral issues where they had an array of organizational resources. For example, when established professional organizations enter a moral conflict, they do so with the advantage of multiple existing resources. These include a nation-wide presence with local branches or chapters, money, prestige, and influence. Organizations concerned with civil rights also bring with them crucial experience as litigators. In the United States, such interest groups were important in the emergence of all issues except for gun control and had relatively weak representation in the struggle over capital punishment. Similar access to organizational resources occurred in Canada, especially with regard to abortion and same-sex relations, but with considerably less effect on other issues.

In our analysis of the life history of prohibition, we observed the powerful impact of social movements tied to Protestant evangelical churches and their incorporation of new roles for women. Additional confirmation of how social movements in general serve as agents of change, including the commitment of movement members even in the face of setbacks, encouraged us to anticipate that new social movements would play similar roles in other moral conflicts. Strong evidence for such connections was found for abortion, marijuana, and same-sex relations. In Canada, however, those social movements came somewhat later, after the issues that inspired them first emerged, and their impact appears to have been weaker. To some extent, this can be explained by differences between the two countries in their civic culture and political institutions, a topic examined in the conclusion to this chapter. Yet they also point to some of the disadvantages inherent in social movements in general, regardless of national setting. As Goss (2006) demonstrates in her analysis of the modest impact of the gun control movement, movements need money and the influence that comes from well-placed sponsors, neither of which are easy to acquire. No contemporary social movement had the organizational resources of those promoting prohibition, and consequently did not play as decisive a role in conflict emergence. But given that our overall assessment makes only binary distinctions, we treat all issues as benefiting from organizational resources.

Meeting Expectations about Emergence

We began by hypothesizing five conditions that would lead to the emergence of conflict over moral issues. For the most part, our findings support expectations along with some variation tied to the specific content of an issue, how the issues emerged in the two countries, and how well they conform to the experiences of prohibition.

H_{P1} postulated that moral conflicts are likely to emerge from large-scale social and political changes, an expectation fulfilled by all our issues in both countries. The importance of triggering events, H_{P2}, was less uniform. In Canada, triggers were factors in the emergence only of capital punishment and gun control. While those issues also were responses to triggers in the United States, in that country triggers additionally played a role in the emergence of conflict over abortion and same-sex relations.

The remaining three hypotheses all deal with the impact of collective action. H_{P3} predicted the importance of such action for conflict emergence and was supported for all issues in the United States. In Canada, it did not have the same significance for marijuana and pornography. In addition, collective action, while present, was a relatively weak factor in the emergence of same-sex relations as a two-sided issue. H_{P4} pointed to the impact that the higher status of organized challengers could have in leading to emergence. For our issues, such status factors played some role, although less strongly than in the case of prohibition. Similarly, while H_{P5} drew attention to the benefits accruing to collective actions that could draw on rich resources, their presence was less prominent than was true in the emergence of prohibition.

Unlike the example of prohibition, where social movements were the critical actors, issues in our sample demonstrated the impact of interest groups, principally in the form of professional organizations.

The latter were able to arouse attention to their causes because they were resource-rich in prestige, funding, geographic spread, and prior experience in dealing with the media and political institutions. In Canada, they were reinforced by one national English-language daily that not only reported on issues but took a role in shaping them. The social movement that led the fight for prohibition benefited from a moral standing and organizational base among Evangelical churches that lent it stature in the broader community, and religious organizations continue to play a role in the emergence of contemporary moral issues. When the latter emerged, comparable resources were still out of reach for movements of youth, women, or homosexuals, although they were available to other supportive interest groups.

Compared to Canada, the emergence of issues in the United States relied more on triggers, was affected by more pervasive and stronger collective action, and, although about the same in benefiting from the status of change advocates, relied somewhat more on the rich resources of collective actors. These differences follow from expectations developed from the description of the two societies presented in chapter 4. There we hypothesized (H_{C1}) that the demographic makeup of the United States would make it more prone to conflict over moral issues. Here we interpret that to mean that one factor aiding the generation of such conflict is an added sensitivity to instances of overt turmoil. Those kinds of triggers are not totally unknown in Canada, but they are less frequent. Differences in the civic culture between the two countries was demonstrated in the United States by the somewhat greater efficacy of collective action in affecting all issues (H_{C2}). Strategically, however, impact from the status of collective actors was only somewhat stronger in the United States, although they were better able to draw on richer resources in that country.

In understanding the emergence of moral conflicts, the experiences of prohibition prove to be an efficient model for predicting how contemporary issues become politicized into moral conflicts. Out of thirty possible hypothesized relations in each country, twenty-eight were supported in the United States and twenty-four in Canada. Of those relations we treat as supporting expectations, we recognize a relatively weak link with the status of challenging groups and pornography in both countries. In Canada, we also judged the positive association between challengers in the early struggle over same-sex relations to be relatively weak. The overall ability to predict and explain emergence is an important first step in our overall theory of phase development.

REFERENCES

American Law Institute. 1959. *Model Penal Code: Tentative Draft No. 9*. Philadelphia:
American Law Institute.
Bates, Jerome E., and Edward S. Zawadski. 1964. *Criminal Abortion*. Springfield,
IL: Charles C. Thomas.
Brodie, Janine, Shelley A.M. Gavigan, and Jane Jensen. 1992. *The Politics of
Abortion*. Toronto: Oxford University Press.
Button, James W., Barbara A. Rienzo, and Kenneth D. Wald. 1997. *Private Lives,
Public Conflicts: Battles over Gay Rights in American Communities*. Washington,
DC: CQ Press.
Chandler, David B. 1976. *Capital Punishment in Canada*. Toronto: McClelland
and Stewart.
Daynes, Byron W. 1988. "Pornography: Freedom of Expression or Societal
Degradation?" In *Social Regulatory Policy: Moral Controversies in American
Politics*, ed. Raymond Tatalovich and Byron W. Daynes, 41–73. Boulder, CO:
Westview Press.
Dicks, Shirley, ed. 1991. *Congregation of the Condemned: Voices against the Death
Penalty*. Buffalo, NY: Prometheus Books.
Duberman, Martin. 1993. *Stonewall*. New York: Dutton.
Fattah, Ezzat Abdel. 1976. *The Canadian Public and the Death Penalty: A Study
of a Social Attitude*. Unpublished paper, Criminology Department, Simon
Fraser University.
Finkbine, Sherri. 1967. "The Lesser of Two Evils." In *The Case for Legalized
Abortion Now*, ed. Alan F. Guttmacher, 15–25. Berkeley, CA: Diablo Press.
Friedman, Andrea. 2000. *Prurient Interests: Gender, Democracy, and Obscenity in
New York City, 1909–1945*. New York: Columbia University Press.
Gitlin, Todd. 1987. *The Sixties: Years of Hope, Days of Rage*. New York: Random
House.
Globe and Mail. 1953. "Psychiatrist Urges Study of Attitude toward Abortion."
16 June.
Globe and Mail. 1959. "Beware of Censorship." 30 April.
Globe and Mail. 1961a. "Experiment in Public Opinion." 26 May.
Globe and Mail. 1961b. "Lawyers Back Modified Laws for Abortions."
1 September.
Globe and Mail. 1962a. "Time to Be Civilized." 22 June.
Globe and Mail. 1962b. "Professors Differ on Punishment." 29 September.
Globe and Mail. 1963. "Local Agencies Veto Legalizing of Marijuana."
9 November.
Globe and Mail. 1964. "Seek to Form Society to Aid Sex Deviants." 25 July.

Globe and Mail. 1967. "Homosexuality and the Law." 8 July.

Globe and Mail. 1975. "Two Voices Worth Heeding." 27 June.

Goss, Kristin A. 2006. *Disarmed: The Missing Movement for Gun Control in America.* Princeton: Princeton University Press.

Greenberg, David. 2000. "The Unkillable Death Penalty." *Slate,* 2 June. http://www.slate.com/articles/news_and_politics/history_lesson/2000/06/the_unkillable_death_penalty.html.

Haines, Herbert H. 1996. *Against Capital Punishment: Anti-Death Penalty Movement in America, 1972–1994.* New York: Oxford University Press.

Halfmann, Drew. 2011. *Doctors and Demonstrators: How Political Institutions Shape Abortion Law in the United States, Britain, and Canada.* Chicago: University of Chicago Press. https://doi.org/10.7208/chicago/9780226313443.001.0001.

Howard, John Robert. 1969. "The Flowering of the Hippie Movement." *Annals of the American Academy of Political and Social Science* 382 (1): 43–55. https://doi.org/10.1177/000271626938200106.

Kane, Melinda D. 2003. "Social Movement Policy Success: Decriminalizing State Sodomy Laws, 1969–1998." *Mobilization: An International Quarterly* 8 (3): 313–34.

Kobylka, Joseph F. 1991. *The Politics of Obscenity: Group Litigation in a Time of Legal Change.* New York: Greenwood Press.

Lader, Lawrence. 1966. *Abortion.* Indianapolis, IN: Bobbs-Merrill.

Lader, Lawrence. 1973. *Abortion II: Making the Revolution.* Boston: Beacon.

Lockhart, William, and Robert McClure. 1954. "Literature, the Law of Obscenity, and the Constitution." *Minnesota Law Review* 38 (March): 320–4.

Lockhart, William, and Robert McClure. 1955. "Obscenity in the Courts." *Law and Contemporary Problems* 20 (4): 587–607.

McLean, Dylan S. 2015. "Guns in the Anglo-American Democracies: Explaining an American Exception." *Commonwealth and Comparative Politics* 53 (3): 233–52. https://doi.org/10.1080/14662043.2015.1051287.

Meier, Kenneth J. 1994. *The Politics of Sin: Drugs, Alcohol, and Public Policy.* Armonk, NY: M.E. Sharpe.

Mewett, Alan. 1962. "Morality and the Criminal Law." *Globe and Mail,* 15 October. https://doi.org/10.2307/825323.

Musto, David F. 1973. *The American Disease: Origins of Narcotic Control.* New Haven, CT: Yale University Press.

NAACP Legal Defense Fund. 2015. naacpldf.org/history.

Owram, Doug. 1996. *Born at the Right Time: A History of the Baby Boom Generation.* Toronto: University of Toronto Press.

Rosenthal, Michael P. 1977. "Legislative Response to Marihuana: When the Shoe Pinches Enough." *Journal of Drug Issues* 7 (1): 61–77. https://doi.org/10.1177/002204267700700106.

Rossi, Alice S. 1969. "Abortion and Social Change." *Dissent* 16: 338–46.

Ryan, Stuart. 1969. "Notes: Capital Punishment in Canada." *British Journal of Criminology* 9 (1): 80–5. https://doi.org/10.1093/oxfordjournals.bjc.a049201.

Schuman, Howard, and Stanley Presser. 2013. "The Gun Control Paradox." *Contexts* 12 (2).

Schwartz, Mildred A. 1981. "Politics and Moral Causes in Canada and the United States." *Comparative Social Research* 4: 65–80.

Smith, Miriam. 2008. *Political Institutions and Lesbian and Gay Rights in the United States and Canada*. New York: Routledge.

Smith, Tom W. 1980. "The 75% Solution: An Analysis of the Structure of Attitudes on Gun Control, 1959–1977." *Journal of Criminal Law & Criminology* 71 (3): 300–16. https://doi.org/10.2307/1142702.

Solinger, Rickie. 1998. *Abortion Wars: A Half Century of Struggle, 1950–2000*. Berkeley: University of California Press.

Spitzer, Robert J. 2015. *The Politics of Gun Control*. Boulder, CO: Paradigm Publishers.

Spurgeon, David. 1964. "Drug Addiction of Teen-Agers." *Globe and Mail*, 8 June.

Stewart, Walter. 1967. "How the Hospitals Broke the Great Abortion Silence." *SW Magazine*, 6 May.

Tatalovich, Raymond, and Byron W. Daynes. 1981. *The Politics of Abortion*. New York: Praeger Publishers.

Walker, Samuel. 1999. *In Defense of American Liberties: A History of the ACLU*. 2nd ed. Carbondale, IL: SIU Press.

Chapter Six

Establishment

A moral issue is considered established when it becomes the topic of wide-spread public concern and is incorporated into the government's policy agenda. A number of different kinds of actors may play a role in this establishment, including the media; the public, principally in its organized capacity; and specific political actors. The latter can be political parties, legislatures and their committees, the executive, the judiciary, or individual politicians. One goal of this chapter is to identify the most important actors affecting establishment and their links to particular issues and national settings.

We used our examination of prohibition in chapter 2 as a means to generate five general hypotheses about the processes through which issues become established. They include

- effects of continuing pressures from groups that had already con- tributed to issue emergence,
- stimulus from prior legitimation,
- mobilization and impact of partisan connections,
- initiatives by authoritative actors, and
- use of atypical means.

Here we test those hypotheses to see how well our six contemporary issues conform to what was found in an unusual case that occurred under very different circumstances. The results of these current analy- ses further expand understanding of the evolution of moral conflicts in two adjacent countries.

Continuing Pressures

Just as social movements and interest groups played a critical role in bringing their concerns to the attention of both the public and political actors, their continuing demand for change is hypothesized to be a factor in ensuring that those concerns are given a place on the political agenda. The presence of such organized group pressures can be found for all issues in both countries, but they have been less visible and effective with respect to gun control. In addition, Canada differs from the United States in demonstrating even less organized pressure for gun control as well as for opposition to capital punishment, lessened restrictions on pornography, or LGBT rights.

Abortion

In Canada, as the medical and legal professions continued their advocacy for abortion reform in the late 1960s, new pressure came from organized women's groups. Testifying before the Standing Committee on Health and Welfare in 1967, the Women's Liberation Group favored abortion on request and the Canadian Abortion Law Reform Association endorsed provisions for therapeutic abortions. Even more focused was the Association for the Modernization of Canadian Abortion Laws (AMCAL), founded in 1968 to support therapeutic abortion in cases of physical or mental health of the mother; rape, when there was a high probability of retardation or malformation of the unborn child; or because of serious hereditary disease (*Globe and Mail* 1968a). The Canadian Association for Repeal of the Abortion Law (CARAL), a coalition of pro-choice activists, appeared in 1973, united by their opposition to continuing restrictions that remained despite the 1969 law that had opened the door to legal abortions (see chapter 3).

In the United States, as well, both the legal and medical professions kept up their pressure, as did existing social movements. Legal scholars, in particular, played an important role, producing a systematic litigation strategy to shape the Supreme Court deliberations (Faux 2000). Preparation of historical research on early abortion practices by Cyril C. Means (1968; 1971) were designed to influence the Supreme Court, and Justice Harry Blackman was said to have read both articles.

Capital Punishment

Canada continued a modest pattern of organized support for abolition of the death penalty. The Canadian Society for the Abolition of the Death Penalty was established in 1964 (*Globe and Mail* 1964a). It was not until well into the 1960s that major religious organizations took an official stand against capital punishment (Jayewardene

1972: 376). The *Globe and Mail* (1964b) affirmed its long opposition to capital punishment while urging parliamentary support for its position. It continued to press Prime Minister Pearson to table an abolitionist bill and demonstrate his leadership on the issue (*Globe and Mail* 1967).

In the United States, continuing support for the abolition of the death penalty was slow to build, but it was invigorated in reaction to the Supreme Court ruling in *Gregg v. Georgia* in 1976 that held capital punishment to be constitutional. That year marked the formation of the National Coalition to Abolish the Death Penalty, a partnership among a number of existing organizations. It also stimulated support for abolition among major religious organizations.

Gun Control

Despite a lengthy history of public support for federal government control over the registration and sale of firearms (Erskine 1972; Spitzer 2011), organized group pressure to control the sale and possession of firearms in the United States still remains weak, especially in comparison to the power of the National Rifle Association. Pro-control groups that now exist include the Brady Campaign, named in honor of Jim Brady, who was shot in an assassination attempt against President Reagan in 1981. It represented the effort of an existing organization, the National Council to Control Handguns, formed in 1974, to gain favorable publicity through association with both Brady and President Reagan. Another is Americans for Responsible Solutions, founded in 2012 after the previous year's shooting of Gabrielle Giffords, then a Democratic congresswoman. Here, too, there were expectations that the name of a prominent political figure would increase the group's impact. In 2006, New York City mayor Michael Bloomberg and Boston mayor Thomas Menino, along with thirteen other mayors, co-founded Mayors Against Illegal Guns and, in 2013, merged with Moms Demand Action. The following year, the two groups began Everytown for Gun Safety. Today, as groups favoring gun control continue to organize, they look for new strategies that de-emphasize the symbolism denoted by control for ones that focus on the need to reduce gun violence (Ball 2013).

Among Canadian contrasts with the United States, presented in the previous chapter, were low levels of organized protest, and these differences continue. When acts of violence caused by firearms occur, they tend to produce statements from authorities, like police chiefs or newspaper editors, rather than lead to mobilization of the public. Only in 1991 did the Coalition for Gun Control form to press the government for gun control legislation.

Marijuana

In Canada, the healthcare professions continued their pressure for change. The Ontario Medical Association passed a resolution urging legalization of marijuana possession, as did the Canadian Medical Association, which also called for an end to prison sentences for possession of marijuana (as well as some other drugs) (*Globe and Mail* 1971). Voicing such opinions was encouraged by new opportunities opened by the government's creation of the Commission of Inquiry into the Nonmedical Uses of Drugs (also known as the Le Dain Commission) in 1969. The Canadian Mental Health Association's brief to the commission agreed that "generally jail sentences should be avoided for young people found guilty of drug offenses." But a less permissive position still prevailed in the Canadian Psychiatric Association's opposition to legalization, on grounds that drug or alcohol abuse should not be accepted as normal or desirable for society (Hartley 1971).

The legal profession and related professional associations were another important source of pressure. By 1978 the Canadian Bar Association pressed for legalization, as did the Canadian Criminology and Corrections Association. It was a view even expressed by Mr Justice Antonio Lamer in his capacity as chairman of the Law Reform Commission of Canada.

Those who took a strong position in support of decriminalization included the *Globe and Mail* (1968b), which urged the government to "take the drug out of the Narcotics Control Act list and place it in a new restricted drug category under the Food and Drug Act." In a similar vein, the United Church of Canada stated that "a fine or imprisonment is not an appropriate solution for the casual marijuana user," who should be given "compulsory treatment" under the Mental Health Act (Hartley 1971).

In the United States, organized pressure for change gained publicity with the founding of the National Organization for the Reform of Marijuana Laws (NORML) in 1970. Its founder, Keith Stroup, was aided in beginning the organization by a $5000 grant from the Playboy

Foundation. It continues its activities through a grassroots network of 135 chapters and over 550 lawyers.

Pornography

Canada continued a pattern of little organized pressure to change the law on obscenity. One of the few public voices raised in favor was that of the *Globe and Mail* (1959), although its message was one of caution:

> Tradition has it that Voltaire once wrote to an author in trouble with the authorities: "I disapprove of what you say, but I will defend to the death your right to say it." This newspaper has somewhat similar feelings in the case of the "girlie magazines" now under attack in this city. We hold no brief for these publications nor for those who deal in them. But we do believe in a free press and freedom of speech generally; and the current "anti-pornography" campaign holds a threat to both.

Another important spokesperson against censorship was the chief librarian of the Toronto Public Libraries, Henry Campbell. In 1961, he refused to turn over to the Customs Department the library's copies of Henry Miller's *Tropic of Cancer*, although his decision was overturned by the library board (French 1965).

In the United States, the struggle for change in defining pornography took place in the courts. The groups mobilized to aid that struggle were listed in the previous chapter. But given that the number of cases that reached the highest court was relatively limited – averaging 3.8 cases per year in the 1960s and 3.0 in the 1970s – the scope for group influence was also limited.

Same-Sex Relations

Organized pressure in favor of protecting and advancing the rights of LGBTs increased and became more broadly accepted after initial social movement activities to publicize the cause helped the issue's emergence. In the United States, a primary objective of the well-organized gay rights movement was repeal of state anti-sodomy legislation (Rayside 1998; 2008). The success of this litigation campaign can be attributed to the mobilization of gay and lesbian groups at the national, state, and local levels across the country. It was aided, as well, by existing legal defense organizations.

In Canada, there was no national gay rights organization until EGALE was formed in 1986. Yet local groups were important, especially in Montreal and Vancouver, and activists had staged a demonstration on Parliament Hill in 1971. Those groups brought a number of test cases before provincial human rights commissions, of which that of John Damien was pivotal. Damien, a jockey and racing steward fired by the Ontario Racing Commission because he was homosexual, appealed to the Ontario Human Rights Commission. Although he lost and then filed a wrongful dismissal suit that was settled years later, Smith (1999: 52) argues that "the Damien case was the *cause célèbre* of the gay political community in the mid to late seventies and, from the beginning, gay liberation activists saw the potential of the case to mobilize its own constituency."

Prior Legitimation

A new issue or approach to one can be helped on the road to its establishment on the national agenda through laws and procedures that convey its existing legitimacy. For example, in both countries, this could be the result of committee hearings or special commissions that give voice to the two-sided nature of moral conflicts. Legitimation can even be enhanced through failed legislation, such as that introduced through private member bills in the Canadian House of Commons. Private member bills played this role with respect to abortion, capital punishment, pornography, and same-sex relations.

In the United States, issue legitimation could come about through legislative or judicial actions at the state level. Such an outcome is virtually impossible in Canada, given that all the issues we consider come under the authority of its single criminal code. Yet, even there, some flexibility is possible from judgments rendered by provincial courts or from the powers reserved to the provinces, like that over marriage. In general, however, evidence of prior legitimation as a result of state-level actions is strongest in the United States.

Abortion

In the United States, state legislative reforms between 1966 and 1972 made a legitimating contribution to new approaches to abortion. During that period, fourteen states reformed their abortion laws to more or less accord with the recommendations of the American Law Institute (itself a legitimator) and four states (Alaska, Hawaii, New York, and Washington) repealed their original laws to make abortion an elective medical procedure.

Litigation undertaken by legal defense groups was an even stronger source of legitimation. Legal challenges nullified the California anti-abortion law in 1969 (*People v. Belous*, 1969) and the restrictive law governing the District of Columbia (*US v. Vuitch*, 1969) was broadened to include health considerations.

In Canada, private member bills were one source of legitimation for a policy of decriminalized abortion. Two of these (Bills C-122 and C-136) were introduced by NDP Members of Parliament in 1966 and 1967 and were referred to the Standing Committee on Health and Welfare. During this same period, a third (Bill C-136) was sponsored by a Liberal MP. Another source was the Standing Committee on Health and Welfare itself. Late in 1967, it issued an interim report acknowledging that the existing law was unclear and that the Criminal Code needed amendment to allow for therapeutic abortions (Tatalovich 1997: 32–3).

Capital Punishment

In Canada, the abolition of capital punishment gained legitimacy through activities that involved the government in stages. Beginning in 1914, MP Robert Bickerdike introduced a private member's bill supporting abolition. Unsuccessful, he tried again in 1915, 1916, and 1917 (Chandler 1976: 17). Abolition was not debated again in the House of Commons until 1924, when a bill favoring abolition was defeated on a free vote. In 1950 and 1953, private members' bills were introduced which, though unsuccessful, led to creation of a joint committee of the Senate and House in 1955. Even though the committee recommended retention of the death penalty, acknowledgment of abolition's legitimacy as an alternative public policy was now clearly established (Ryan 1969).

In the United States, in 1950, forty-five of the forty-eight states imposed capital punishment. Today that has declined to thirty-one states, of which most have rarely or never executed a condemned person. Since 1977, the five states with the largest number of executions account for more executions than the other forty-five states combined (Baumgartner et al. 2008: 37). This legitimation of the shift away from capital punishment signaled by the actions of individual states is also reflected in the softening of American attitudes toward capital punishment (Baumgartner et al. 2008).

Gun Control

Although gun control in the United States involves state, local, and national governments, historically the states have been most important. At the same time, state gun laws have varied greatly with respect to restrictiveness, as comparison of state gun laws demonstrates (Lester and Murrell 1982; Vernick and Hepburn 2003). Today gun control involves "venue shopping" by anti-gun and pro-gun advocates, with the former focused on the need for national legislation to regulate all guns in all states and the latter seeking to carve out rights for gun owners in specific states (Reich and Barth 2017). By 2014, forty-one states responded to lobbying by the National Rifle Association (NRA) by enacting legislation requiring local police to grant carry permits to anybody who applies unless the person is a convicted felon (Spitzer 2015: 68).

Given the long history of restrictions on some types of gun ownership in Canada (Royal Canadian Mounted Police 2012), and the monopoly exercised by the federal government in regulating ownership, there has been little room for sustained opposition to control. In a sense, then, the two-sided nature of control is particularly weak in Canada. Yet there has been some legitimating potential for opponents to gun control located among sportsmen and aboriginal people. The latter can make the greatest claim for concessions as evident from provisions of the Firearms Act of 1995, which expressly sought to not limit aboriginal rights to long arms (Renke 2006).

Marijuana

The legitimacy of new approaches to marijuana was first signaled in the United States. There, President Kennedy sponsored a White House Conference on Drug Abuse in 1962. He also appointed an Advisory Commission on Narcotic and Drug Abuse in 1963 whose report favored reduced minimum mandatory sentences, more funding for research and treatment programs, and separating marijuana from classification with other addictive narcotics. In addition, in 1968, Alaska, California, and Vermont reduced their penalties for possession of marijuana (Rosenthal 1977: 62) and, by the end of 1970, thirty-two states had done so (Meier 1994: 43).

Both nations established commissions to investigate the problem of drugs: the Commission of Inquiry into the Nonmedical

Uses of Drugs in 1969 in Canada and the National Commission on Marihuana and Drug Abuse in 1970 in the United States. Both legitimated the two-sided debate over drug policy. Although the two reports (Canadian Government Commission of Inquiry 1972; National Commission on Marihuana and Drug Abuse 1973) recommended legal changes that would lessen penalties for possession and use of marijuana, neither government was then prepared to follow that advice.

Pornography

In the United States, legitimacy for changed conceptions of pornography stemmed from decisions in the lower courts that dissented from adherence to the long-established Hicklin Rule (see chapter 3). The most celebrated case that rejected the Hicklin Rule came in *United States v. One Book Called "Ulysses"* (1963), the latter the celebrated work by James Joyce. A United States District Court held that *Ulysses* was not obscene, a judgment affirmed by the Circuit Court of Appeals, and a ruling some scholars viewed as the beginning of the end of the Hicklin Rule in the United States (Green 1963: 673).

Further legitimation for a more accepting view of pornography was signaled by President Lyndon Johnson's appointment in 1968 of a Commission on Obscenity and Pornography. The commission's report (Commission on Obscenity and Pornography 1970) concluded that viewing of pornographic materials was essentially harmless to adults and undeserving of punishment.

In Canada, although obscenity is defined by the Criminal Code, provinces exert some influence through local censorship boards, zoning laws, and their empowerment to enforce the law. Historically, results have differed across provinces, given cultural variations among them (Casavant and Robertson 2007).

Nationally, legitimation for greater acceptance of pornography came, ironically, from the Senate Committee on Salacious and Indecent Literature, where hearings were held in 1952 and 1953 in response to objections about the wide availability of pulp and pocket magazines picturing female nudity (Charles 1966: 251). In his representation before this committee, future justice minister E. Davie Fulton argued for more explicit standards for defining obscenity than were currently used in applying the Hicklin Rule. Such a change would, in fact, allow for narrower standards.

The two-sided debate over policies toward obscenity has evolved to distinguish those materials that were deliberately degrading, especially when they involved representations of children. Legitimation for this new definition came from nine private member bills that were referred to the Standing Committee on Justice and Legal Affairs. The committee, in turn, in its March 1978 report, incorporated these new concerns with degradation and the exploitation of children. However, the committee's recommendations, although present in newly proposed legislation, did not make it past tabling.

Same-Sex Relations

In the United States, encouraged by appeals from the gay rights movement to repeal laws that discriminated against gays and lesbians (Rayside 1998; 2008), the path to sexual freedom would proceed at the state level. Illinois was the first to repeal its anti-sodomy laws in 1961. From then through the 1970s, twenty-two additional states and territories did so. Others, like Arkansas, Idaho, and Alaska, vacillated among repeal, reinstatement, and court decisions. By the end of 2002, thirty-six states and the District of Columbia had repealed their anti-sodomy statutes (Kane 2003: 315), twenty-six through legislative repeal and ten by intervention of state high courts.

There were no comparable events in Canada, nor were they constitutionally possible. Reinforcement of the criminal nature of homosexual acts by the Supreme Court in 1967 may have, instead, helped legitimate an opposing perspective. The case involved Everett George Klippert, who was convicted in the Northwest Territories on four charges of gross indecency. His sentence to an indefinite period of imprisonment, upheld by the Supreme Court by a 3–2 vote, preceded a turning point away from such punitive treatment of same-sex relations.

Although there is both federal and provincial protection of human rights in Canada, Quebec was the first province to include sexual orientation in its Human Rights Code in 1977, a move other provinces were slow to follow. Still, it was provincial human rights commissions that were the venue for test cases by "the gay and lesbian communities as levers for political action. They served as a rallying cry and as an assertion of the entitlement to equality" (Smith 1999: 3). From our perspective, cases brought before the commissions were also a legitimating prelude to national establishment of LGBT rights.

Partisan Connections

A link between moral issues and partisanship can play a critical role in whether they become established under three possible conditions. In one, the major established parties make every effort to avoid becoming entangled in the issue, something both of the two main political parties in Canada and the United States tried to do initially with respect to prohibition. That is, there is bipartisan agreement to prevent establishment. In another, the two major parties adopt opposing positions and each becomes associated with ownership of one side of the issue. The third possibility is when both parties agree on how the issue should be handled. As we hypothesized in chapter 2, establishment is eased when at least one party takes a position.

In general, policy differences between the two US parties outweigh agreements. Yet, on capital punishment and marijuana, differences are relatively muted.

In Canada, the Liberals and Conservatives had many fewer manifesto planks on moral conflicts than did the US major parties (see appendix 2). It is NDP platforms that have the most frequent references to abortion (pro-choice position) and gay rights (full commitment to sexual equality). The Liberals have taken positions in the direction of easing restrictions, but they have done so through legislation, that is, through inside access, in the case of abortion, capital punishment, adult pornography, or same-sex rights (discussed in the following section). This has short-circuited much of the partisan rancor that can accompany establishment. As a result, neither of the two major parties wants to reopen debate on these issues. Party polarization has emerged on gun control, specifically with Liberals defending and Conservatives wanting to abolish the long-gun registry. Child pornography is apparently a bipartisan concern in Canada as it is in the United States. Bipartisanship had existed on marijuana to the extent that both governing parties tried to avoid dealing with decriminalization. This recently changed when the Liberal Party and its leader, Justin Trudeau, endorsed legalization.

Abortion

Halfmann (2011: 131–65) argues that the most fundamental reason why abortion was so polarizing and combative in the United States compared to Canada (or Great Britain) was because of the greater porosity of the major political parties in the former, making them more open to outside influences. The two major US parties remain internally diverse as a result of reliance on party primaries and caucuses, candidate-centered elections, and loose campaign finance laws, all of which make it easy for organized interests to penetrate the inner circles of party decision making. Since 1980 the Democrats have become as reliably pro-choice in their party platforms as the Republicans have become committed to a pro-life policy agenda (see appendix 2).

When Justice Minister Pierre Trudeau introduced legislation to liberalize access to abortion in 1968, NDP MPs were strong supporters, while Conservatives were allowed to suspend party discipline and vote at will. Liberal backbenchers were described as "unusually quiet and somewhat uneasy during the abortion debate" (Morton 1992: 24). Although Trudeau "never approved a free vote, party leaders claimed that no Liberals were being forced to vote against their conscience." The only concession made by Trudeau occurred near the end of the third reading, when "he allowed a free vote on a motion to completely eliminate clause 18, the abortion provision" (Morton 1992: 26). That motion failed and the entire legislative package of changes in the Criminal Code was enacted.

The contours of partisan division on abortion were now apparent, and they would become even sharper as a result of court challenges and Supreme Court rulings that, by the 1980s, nullified the existing federal law on abortion. Following the Conservatives' strong electoral victory in 1988, Prime Minister Brian Mulroney formed a caucus committee of pro-life and pro-choice MPs to find a compromise on abortion. The resulting Bill C-43 would recriminalize abortion, but still offered broad grounds for allowing the procedure. When the bill was tabled in the Commons in November 1989, Mulroney implored those on both sides to the controversy to compromise, but allowed a free vote only to his party's backbenchers. "Cabinet Ministers and those aspiring to Cabinet were sent a clear message to hold their noses and pass the bill" (Brodie et al. 1992: 99). Despite being a free vote, party affiliation was the determining factor in the final vote, when 83 percent of Conservatives voted in favor while 88 percent of Liberals and 98 percent of New Democrats voted in opposition (Overby et al. 1998).

Capital Punishment

In Canada, abolition of the death penalty occurred under a Liberal government during the 1976–7 parliamentary session. It was supported by the leadership of both the Conservative and NDP parties. To the extent that such apparent consensus made establishment relatively easy, it was tied to earlier procedural measures. Following Prime Minister Pearson's 1963 election, his cabinet used executive authority to commute every death sentence to life imprisonment. Initially presiding over a minority government, his successor, Pierre Trudeau, continued this cautious policy by renewing the moratorium on capital punishment for another five years. At that time, now with a majority Liberal government, a bill was introduced to remove the death penalty from the Criminal Code (Thompson 2008: 174–5).

Republicans have included a plank in their party platforms endorsing capital punishment more often than Democrats. However, Democrats have never explicitly disavowed use of the death penalty. This diffidence is explained by Baker (2014) as a result of assumptions about public sentiments. "For Democrats, opposition to the death penalty has been considered politically untenable at the national level ever since Michael S. Dukakis cost himself support with a clinical answer during a 1988 presidential debate about whether he would support it if his wife were raped and killed."

Gun Control

In Canada, where handguns have a long history of required registration, gun control has not been a strongly partisan issue. But efforts to expand oversight to long guns, begun under a Conservative government in 1990, were a source of division within Conservative ranks. Justice Minister Kim Campbell introduced Bill C-80, only to have it fail second reading because of opposition from her own caucus and then die on the order paper. Only later would a revised bill pass with cross-party support. But the initial controversy over long-gun registration does reveal some continuing sources of partisan division, with the Liberals and NDP more consistently pro-control.

The seven US federal laws passed limiting gun ownership, beginning with the National Firearms Act of 1934, all occurred under Democratic administrations. Yet the powerful symbolism invoked by the Second Amendment has made it difficult for either of the two major US parties to present a clear policy that would limit gun ownership. At best, in recent years, Democratic platforms speak of the need for "reasonable regulation" while still defending the right to own and use firearms. The Republican Party, however, presents itself as an even more determined defender of the Second Amendment by avoiding calls for restrictions.

Marijuana

In Canada, the NDP has been the one party consistently in favor of decriminalizing possession of marijuana, beginning with the introduction of its bill in Parliament in 1971 after the Le Dain Commission had reported (Larsen 2012). The Liberal Party's stand has been more mixed but, with the 2015 election of a Liberal government, the new prime minister has promised that marijuana reform will be an early policy objective.

Openness to decriminalizing marijuana has an association with the Democratic Party, although party leaders have often been reluctant to press the issue. For example, during the 1972 presidential election, Democratic candidate George McGovern was labeled the "amnesty, abortion and acid" candidate. While he did favor reduced penalties for marijuana and ending prison terms for minor drug violations, McGovern pointedly denied ever advocating legalized marijuana (Kovach 1972). Republican attachment to a more punitive stance can be linked with President Nixon's 1971 War on Drugs, a slogan and policy carried on by President Reagan. But given that the National Commission on Marijuana and Drug Use, appointed by President Nixon, favored decriminalizing possession, it is difficult to associate this issue with sharply divided partisanship. This has come to be the case as some Republicans have embraced the medicinal claims for marijuana use.

Party platforms give an even stronger picture of how official partisanship has been limited (see appendix 2), illustrating the difficulty of overcoming the one-sidedness of the issue. From 1968 through 2012 both major parties had an anti-drug plank that usually emphasized enforcement, particularly against drug traffickers. At the same time, Republicans were much more likely to mention marijuana and to specifically oppose the decriminalization or legalization of any drug, marijuana included, with the strongest language used in 1992: "We oppose legalizing or decriminalizing drugs. That is a morally abhorrent idea, the last vestige of an ill-conceived philosophy that counseled the legitimacy of permissiveness." The Democrats briefly mentioned marijuana in 1984 and opposed legalization of any narcotic in 1988, saying "the legalization of illicit drugs would represent a tragic surrender in a war we intend to win."

Pornography

In 1970, the commission appointed by President Johnson issued a report on pornography that downplayed its potential to be a pernicious influence and advocated for less restrictions. In 1986, the Attorney-General's Commission on Pornography, appointed under the Reagan administration, essentially repudiated the recommendations of the earlier report. In doing so, it extended a long series of Republican platforms that have condemned pornography. Evidence for partisan divisions is not strong, however, and mirrored public opinion. From his review of polls, Downs (1989: 24) concluded that "citizens balance the competing values of sexual morality and freedom, reflecting a reasonable awareness of the clash of values in this area of public policy." Since 1996, the Democrats have limited their planks to shielding children from pornographic materials, putting both parties in the same policy position.

Partisan differences on pornography in Canada are now more muted, with neither of the two older parties interested in reopening debates about adult pornography and both united on the need to control child pornography.

Same-Sex Relations

From 1984 through 2004, Democratic platforms always included a statement against discrimination based on sexual orientation; Republican ones never did so. In 1992, all the Democratic presidential contenders favored ending the ban on gays serving openly in the armed services (Vaid 1995: 160). Republicans did not raise the issue (McFeely 2002: 239). Every GOP platform from 1992 through 2012 included opposition to same-sex marriage or had a defense of traditional heterosexual marriage. Democrats in 2008 and 2012 explicitly endorsed same-sex marriage.

In Canada, the NDP has been the single party most consistently in favor of same-sex rights. Under Pierre Trudeau, the Liberals were more supportive of such rights than the Conservatives. Given changes in law and in court rulings, neither party has shown any interest in reopening debate on the subject.

Authoritative Leadership

One way that issues are established is through the inside access available to authoritative leaders in any of the three branches of government.

This can occur under three possible conditions. In one, political leaders take the initiative in proposing relevant legislation, possibly even bypassing many of the steps otherwise associated with the process of emergence. In another, the initiators are politicians who assume or aspire to leadership roles through their entrepreneurial skills as spokespersons on behalf of an issue. A third possibility follows from the leadership that emanates from judicial rulings that newly define the parameters of an issue.

Dealing only with initial establishment of the two-sided version of a moral issue, in Canada, the political leadership pathway was prominent in establishing five of the six issues considered – abortion, capital punishment, marijuana, pornography, and same-sex relations. In the United States, decisions by the courts have been the leading political mechanism, affecting abortion and pornography.

Abortion

Actions of the US courts were the principal route to establishing a two-sided view of abortion. The restrictive law governing the District of Columbia (*US v. Vuitch*, 1969) was broadened to include health considerations in a case eventually heard by the US Supreme Court in 1971. The landmark litigation was *Roe v. Wade* (1973), which constitutionalized abortions during the first trimester of a pregnancy and shifted abortion permanently onto the policy agenda of government at all levels.

In Canada, the initiative to transform how abortion was treated came from Justice Minister Pierre Trudeau when he introduced legislation to amend the Canadian Criminal Code (Criminal Law Amendment Act, 1968–9). The new legislation legalized therapeutic abortions done in hospitals.

Capital Punishment

Judgments about capital punishment in the United States have been formulated by the courts, beginning with interpretations from state-level ones. With individual states the normal venue for such punishment, the nationalization of this issue has remained limited. In other words, the effects of authoritative leadership have lacked potency in establishing a two-sided conception of capital punishment.

National leadership has been prominent in Canada from two sources. Initially, establishment was aided by the action of individual Members of Parliament who introduced private member bills without benefit of placement on the governing party's agenda. Later, party leaders in the governing party, both Liberal and Conservative, took the initiative to help establish the issue as a concern of the national government.

Gun Control

Canada, despite its lengthy history of legislation to control gun ownership, has had its own encounters with mass shootings. Following the 1975 school shootings in Ontario, ministers in the Liberal government of Pierre Trudeau announced that action would be taken. Both Justice Minister Ronald Basford and Solicitor General Warren Allmand promised that new gun control legislation would be introduced to the House of Commons within a few weeks (*Globe and Mail* 1975), although little followed from their pronouncements. Kim Campbell's leadership of the Conservatives on long-gun registration turned out to be a divisive factor within her own party. We interpret these events as indicators that authoritative leadership had relatively minor impact.

In the United States, authoritative leadership favoring gun control has been especially weak. During President Roosevelt's tenure, the Justice Department advocated national handgun registration, but to no effect. When regulatory laws have been passed in Congress, these have normally followed significant instances of gun violence, like those during prohibition or following mass shootings. But the more usual pattern is for mass shootings to provoke strong outcries for regulation followed by inaction (Fleming 2012). Although President Kennedy's assassination appeared to lead to greater receptivity to gun control, that sentiment soon dissipated. For example, even though President Lyndon B. Johnson stood behind the gun control effort of the 1960s, his lobbying efforts to enact the Gun Control Act of 1968 have been described as "minimal" (Spitzer 2011: 175) compared to his enormous impact on landmark social welfare legislation. President Obama's speech on the need for better gun control, following the San Bernardino, California, attack on 2 December 2015, was one of many he gave after mass shootings, but with little effect.

Marijuana

To address marijuana, the Liberal government's health minister, John Munro, appointed the Canadian government Commission of Inquiry in 1969 (also known as the Le Dain Commission). He instructed the commissioners to produce an interim report within six months. The report was delayed, ostensibly deliberately, to allow the minister to convince his colleagues specifically concerned with issues of law and enforcement, Solicitor General George McIlraith and Justice Minister John Turner, of the desirability of positions taken in the report. He was not only unsuccessful in this but had to modify his public account of what changes the government would be likely to make (Waring 1970).

Not until 1976, two years after the Le Dain Commission offered its recommendations that would allow personal use (although that use still had the potential for police seizure), did the Liberal government announce a change in policy. Justice Minister Otto Lang then stated that the government was committed to shifting marijuana from the Narcotics Control Act to the Food and Drug Act and that simple possession would not warrant a jail sentence. Although the change did not represent a wholehearted about-face from previous policy, it did signal the beginning of an altered approach, though one that would still take years to evolve under different administrations. Stronger political leadership that will move to legalize marijuana in Canada has a new potential with the 2015 election of Prime Minister Justin Trudeau, who made legalization one of his campaign promises. Overall, although changes have been slow, we consider marijuana to have been affected by authoritative leadership.

Although greater openness to decriminalizing marijuana in the United States has an association with the Democratic Party, there has been little party leadership on the issue. There is an even stronger reluctance to address it on the part of Republican leaders.

Pornography

Pornography in the United States was redefined in a 1957 legal case that reached the Supreme Court. That case offered a new, legally validated definition of obscenity that would supersede previous ones (Strub 2013). There had been earlier controversies over how to define obscenity, but none had such far-reaching effects. This landmark case, *Roth v. United States* (1957), involved a New York bookseller, Samuel Roth, who had been convicted of mailing obscene sexual advertisements, a sex magazine called *Good Times*, and a book entitled *American Aphrodite*. Now the highest court gave its official repudiation of the long-prevailing Hicklin Rule (Friedman 2000: 16).

In Canada, Justice Minister E. Davie Fulton took the lead in redefining obscenity, incorporated into the Criminal Code in 1959. The law stipulated that "any publication a dominant characteristic of which is the undue exploitation of sex, or of sex and any one of more of the following subjects, namely crime, horror, cruelty and violence, shall be deemed obscene." Ironically, the intent was to broaden the definition of pornography to make it easier for the courts to prosecute violations, as Fulton had made clear earlier, when testifying as an Opposition member to a Senate Committee on Salacious and Indecent Literature (Charles 1966: 251). The results, however, led to a narrowing of how pornography was treated. This became evident from two pivotal cases. In the first, the Canadian Supreme Court in 1962 overturned the Quebec Appeals Court decision that D.H. Lawrence's *Lady Chatterley's Lover* was obscene. In the second, on a 5–4 vote, the high court in *Regina v. Brodie* (1962) applied the new Fulton standard of obscenity to throw out a conviction.

Same-Sex Relations

Justice Minister Pierre Trudeau's legislation to amend the Canadian Criminal Code included the decriminalization of same-sex relations. The latter change was justified by Trudeau on grounds that "the state has no business in the bedrooms of the nation" (McLaren and McLaren 1998). In this case, we have a particularly clear example of how authoritative leadership represents an inside-access form of establishment.

In the United States, increased congressional attention came in the 1980s with an upsurge of congressional hearings (twenty-one in contrast to eight in the 1970s). These were stimulated by the AIDS outbreak and by opposition to gay rights, most forcefully expressed by Senator Jesse Helms (R-NC). Helms was instrumental in ensuring that no federal funding from the Centers for Disease Control went to private groups or state and local governments "to provide AIDS education, information, or prevention materials and activities that promote or encourage, directly or indirectly, homosexual activities" (Ellis and Kasniunas 2011: 95). Helms also played a role in almost derailing early attempts to include sexual orientation in federal hate crime legislation when he opposed a coalition of racial, ethnic, gender, religious, and homosexual organizations that advocated incorporating hate crimes into the federal criminal code (Jacobs and Potter 2000). The two-sided establishment of policies related to same-sex relations was constrained by pressures from such negative assessments, exemplified by President

Clinton's compromise over homosexuals in the military through a rule of "Don't ask, don't tell, don't pursue" (Horvitz 1993) and his reluctant signature of the Defense of Marriage Act in 1996, defining marriage as the union of a man and a woman (Baker 2013).

Atypical Measures

Of all the contemporary issues we consider, none has followed the path of prohibition in the United States by first becoming law through a constitutional amendment and then undoing the law by another constitutional amendment. Yet the experience of prohibition did alert us to the possibility that moral conflicts would likely be associated with atypical procedures even when these did not lead directly to establishment (H_{P10}). They could include executive orders and referendums that, while institutionalized, can still be considered unusual because of their infrequent occurrence. Yet only in Canada do we find instances of atypical measures. Three issues were addressed through free votes – abortion, capital punishment, and same-sex relations – and they, along with pornography, benefited as well from the impetus of private member bills. These can be considered atypical because they deviate from a basic principle of responsible government, that the cabinet has the support of the majority in Parliament, upheld through the practice of party discipline (Franks 1997). For example, in assessing free votes in the case of same-sex marriage, leading to the passage of the Civil Marriage Act in 2005, Overby et al. (2011) report that those votes were even more unusual because of evidence of strong constituency influence rather than that of the more common partisanship.

In addition, Canada manifested other inclinations to flout tradition when faced with moral conflicts. For example, the last attempt to pass legislation regulating abortion by the Conservative government suffered an unusual defeat in 1990. Although Prime Minister Mulroney allowed a free vote for all but his cabinet, Bill C-43 was unappealing to both pro-life and pro-choice MPs and barely passed in the House of Commons. Defeat came, instead, in the Senate, where the prime minister also permitted a free vote. There the vote was tied 43–43. The tie was unprecedented in the history of the Senate and was the first defeat of a government bill in that chamber in thirty years.

Capital punishment provoked a demand for a non-traditional approach by the government of Quebec. There Justice Minister Claude Wagner, backed by Premier Jean Lesage, urged that a national referendum be held on capital punishment. In opposing such a move as contrary to the practice of parliamentary government, the *Globe and Mail* (1965) expressed fear that an "illogical cry for the ultimate revenge" would motivate Canadians, especially following the federal government's decision to commute the death sentence of Leopold Dion, convicted of slaying a thirteen-year-old boy and accused of murdering three other boys while on parole for earlier sex crimes. This was also a period when francophones were less abolitionist than anglophones (Chandler 1976: 105–8).

Assessing Establishment

Three of the five processes we hypothesized as leading to establishment were generally supported across all six issues and in both countries. These were:

H_{P6}, which predicted that active groups, by continuing pressure, could bring about establishment;

H_{P7}, that the entry of moral issues would be eased when prior laws and procedures have acknowledged their legitimacy as subjects of policy;

H_{P8}, that the establishment of moral issues proceeds when at least one major party takes a position.

The prediction that atypical means would be a route to establishment (H_{P10}) was found to be true only in Canada, affecting abortion, capital punishment, pornography, and same-sex relations. In addition, prior legitimation of these issues came about through private member bills in Canada. In contrast, such legitimation was most likely to come from actions at the US state level. The latter supports the expectation of H_{C7} that US states will be the more likely venue for moral issues. Chapter 4, comparing Canada and the United States, did not directly anticipate these findings, including the significance of private member bills. Earlier, we had confidently predicted in H_{C4} that, compared to Parliament, Congress would provide more opportunities for moral issues to be given a powerful voice. Our findings do not so much refute the hypothesis but demonstrate the special quality of moral issues to overcome the normal operation of responsible government. Normally, Congress does provide more opportunities, and the restrictions that are part of parliamentary policymaking can only be breached under the unusual power of moral conflicts.

Gun control stood apart with the weakest support for the hypothesized relations, especially in regard to authoritative leadership in both countries. Where such leadership was present for other issues, in the United States, it came from court actions; in Canada, from executive leadership. In predicting the importance of executive authority in Canada in H_{C3}, we emphasized how it would be more likely to affect resolution of moral conflicts. Our findings in this chapter make it evident that it is equally prominent in the establishment of moral issues. Meanwhile, the greater role for the courts in the United States remained important to the establishment phase without much of the predicted diminishment in the difference between the two countries in this regard (H_{C9}).

We summarize support for hypothesized relations by classifying them as either supportive or not, downplaying the significance of degrees of support. But such nuances are worth some consideration. For example, Canada displayed somewhat less organized pressure with respect to capital punishment, gun control, pornography, and same-sex relations. That gives modest support to the expectation in chapter 4 (H_{C2}) that NGOs would have greater impact in the United States.

Similarly disregarded in our classification, the United States, in contrast to Canada, manifests greater conflict associated with establishing the two-sided nature of moral issues, particularly regarding abortion, gun control, and same-sex marriage as well as marijuana. This difference was anticipated in H_{C1} and attributed to the changing ethnic and racial makeup of both countries, reflecting, in turn, prior histories in dealing with the challenges of major demographic changes. In addition, Canada also presents a more muted environment for partisan divisions on moral issues, tied to greater circumspection by party leaders in pursuing the issues themselves. That is, as anticipated in H_{C5}, US parties are more open to taking on moral issues, and, as in H_{C6}, individual parties are more inclined to assume ownership of particular issue positions.

All the issues considered became part of the policy agenda in both countries, fulfilling our main criterion for establishment. However, the five pathways to establishment that we had anticipated, based on the experiences of prohibition, were supported more strongly in Canada than in the United States. In Canada, we found support for twenty-seven out of thirty possibilities (90 percent). In the United States, only twenty were supported (67 percent).

A second criterion of establishment, introduced at the outset of this chapter, is that of widespread public concern. It can be discerned through the extent of coverage by major newspapers. A comparison, first introduced in chapter 3, reveals considerable variation by issue and country (with the caveat about the comparability of media coverage on abortion, gays, and marijuana noted in appendix 1). Only abortion (figures 3.1 and 3.2) supports high levels of coverage in the two countries, with the first major upsurge about a decade earlier in the United States. In Canada, capital punishment, gun control, and pornography all remain relatively low in media attention compared to the United States. In the case of pornography, the peak in attention in the 1970s (figure 3.9) does not even approach that amount of coverage until the mid-1980s in Canada (figure 3.10). Both marijuana (compare figures 3.7 and 3.8) and same-sex relations (figures 3.11 and 3.12) present pictures of relatively low interest in the United States compared to Canada.

When juxtaposed with all the other signs of establishment found, the extent of public interest manifested by newspaper coverage supports the higher level of public controversy in the United States, affecting the extent to which most issues have become established as two-sided controversies. Our next task is to examine the progress of these issues as they continue to engage the political world.

REFERENCES

Baker, Peter. 2013. "Now in Defense of Gay Marriage, Bill Clinton." *New York Times*, 25 March.
Baker, Peter. 2014. "Obama Orders Policy Review of Executions." *New York Times*, 2 May.
Ball, Molly. 2013. "How the Gun-Control Movement Got Smart." *The Atlantic*, 7 February.
Baumgartner, Frank R., Suzanna L. De Boef, and Amber E. Boydstun. 2008. *The Decline of the Death Penalty and the Discovery of Innocence*. New York: Cambridge University Press. https://doi.org/10.1017/CBO9780511790638.
Brodie, Janine, Shelley A.M. Gavigan, and Jane Jenson. 1992. *The Politics of Abortion*. Toronto: Oxford University Press.
Canadian Government Commission of Inquiry. 1972. *The Report of the Canadian Government Commission of Inquiry into the Non-Medical Use of Drugs*. Ottawa: Information Canada.
Casavant, Lyne, and James R. Robertson. 2007. *The Evolution of Pornography Law in Canada. (CIR 84–3E)*. Ottawa: Library of Parliament, Law and Government Division.

Chandler, David B. 1976. *Capital Punishment in Canada*. Toronto: McClelland and Stewart.

Charles, W.H. 1966. "Obscene Literature and the Legal Process in Canada." *Canadian Bar Review* 154: 242–92.

Commission on Obscenity and Pornography. 1970. *Report of the Commission on Obscenity and Pornography*. Washington: Government Printing Office.

Downs, Donald Alexander. 1989. *The New Politics of Pornography*. Chicago: University of Chicago Press.

Ellis, Margaret E., and Nina Therese Kasniunas. 2011. "Gay Rights: Nature or Nurture?" In *Moral Controversies in American Politics*, ed. Raymond Tatalovich and Byron W. Daynes, 80–109. 4th ed. Armonk, NY: M.E. Sharpe Publishers.

Erskine, Hazel. 1972. "The Polls: Gun Control." *Public Opinion Quarterly* 36 (3): 455–69. https://doi.org/10.1086/268023.

Faux, Marian. 2000. *Roe v. Wade: The Untold Story of the Landmark Supreme Court Decision That Made Abortion Legal*. Lanham, MD: Cooper Square Press.

Fleming, Anthony K. 2012. *Gun Policy in the United States and Canada*. New York: Continuum International Publishing.

Franks, C.E.S. 1997. "Free Votes in the House of Commons: A Problematic Reform." *Policy Options* 18 (November): 33–6.

French, William. 1965. "Who Killed Censorship?" *Globe and Mail*, 9 October.

Friedman, Andrea. 2000. *Prurient Interests: Gender, Democracy, and Obscenity in New York City, 1909–1945*. New York: Columbia University Press.

Globe and Mail. 1959. "Beware of Censorship." 30 April.

Globe and Mail. 1964a. "Society Wages War on Death Penalty." 28 July.

Globe and Mail. 1964b. "At Last an Open Vote on Capital Punishment." 4 December.

Globe and Mail. 1965. "No Substitute for Debate." 27 December.

Globe and Mail. 1967. "The Repugnant Rope." 24 April.

Globe and Mail. 1968a. "AMCAL Campaigns for End to Abortion's Barbarisms." 22 March.

Globe and Mail. 1968b. "Sense for the Drug Laws." 19 October.

Globe and Mail. 1971. "Doctors Offer a Sound Lead." 12 June.

Globe and Mail. 1975. "School Shootings Show Need for Gun Control, Basford Says." 29 October.

Green, Bernard. 1963. "Federalism and the Administration of Criminal Justice: The Treatment of Obscenity in the United States, Canada, and Australia." *Kentucky Law Review* 51 (Summer): 667–702.

Halfmann, Drew. 2011. *Doctors and Demonstrators: How Political Institutions Shape Abortion Law in the United States, Britain, and Canada*.

Chicago: University of Chicago Press. https://doi.org/10.7208/chicago/9780226313443.001.0001.

Hartley, Norman. 1971. "Canadian Psychiatrists Oppose Marijuana's Legalization." *Globe and Mail*, 20 February.

Horvitz, Paul F. 1993. "'Don't Ask, Don't Tell, Don't Pursue' Is White House's Compromise Solution: New U.S. Military Policy Tolerates Homosexuals." *New York Times*, 20 July.

Jacobs, James B., and Kimberly Potter. 2000. *Hate Crimes: Criminal Law and Identity Politics*. New York: Oxford University Press.

Jayewardene, C.H.S. 1972. "The Canadian Movement against the Death Penalty." *Canadian Journal of Criminology and Corrections* 14: 366–90.

Kane, Melinda D. 2003. "Social Movement Policy Success: Decriminalizing State Sodomy Laws, 1969–1998." *Mobilization: An International Quarterly* 8 (3): 313–34.

Kovach, Bill. 1972. "McGovern Scores Nixon Job Stand in a Bid to Labor." *New York Times*, 5 September.

Larsen, Dana. 2012. "Canada's NDP: Forty Years of Fighting to End the War on Marijuana." www.cannabisculture.com/content/2012/07/12/canadas-ndp-forty-years-fighting-end-war-marijuana.

Lester, David, and M.E. Murrell. 1982. "The Preventive Effect of Strict Gun Control Laws on Suicide and Homicide." *Suicide & Life-Threatening Behavior* 12 (3): 131–40. https://doi.org/10.1111/j.1943-278X.1982.tb00935.x.

McFeely, Tom. 2002. "Getting It Straight: A Review of the 'Gays in the Military' Debate." In *Creating Change: Sexuality, Public Policy, and Civil Rights*, ed. John D'Emilio, William B. Turner, and Urvashi Vaid, 236–44. New York: St Martin's Press.

McLaren, Angus, and Arlene Tigar McLaren. 1998. *The Bedroom and the State: The Changing Practices and Politics of Contraception and Abortion in Canada, 1880–1996*. 2nd ed. Toronto: Oxford University Press.

Means, Cyril C. 1968. "The Law of New York Concerning Abortion and the Status of the Foetus, 1664–1968: A Case of Cessation of Constitutionality." *New York Law Forum* 14 (Fall): 411–515.

Means, Cyril C. 1971. "The Phoenix of Abortional Freedom: Is a Penumbral of Ninth-Amendment Right about to Arise from the Nineteenth-Century Legislative Ashes of a Fourteenth-Century Common-Law Liberty." *New York Law Forum* 17: 335–410.

Meier, Kenneth J. 1994. *The Politics of Sin: Drugs, Alcohol, and Public Policy*. Armonk, NY: M.E. Sharpe.

Morton, F.L. 1992. *Morgentaler v. Borowski: Abortion, the Charter, and the Courts*. Toronto: McClelland and Stewart.

National Commission on Marihuana and Drug Abuse. 1973. *Drug Abuse in America: Problem in Perspective*. Second report. Washington: US Government Printing Office.

Overby, L. Marvin, Christopher Raymond, and Zeynep Taydas. 2011. "Free Votes, MPs, and Constituents: The Case of Same-Sex Marriage in Canada." *American Review of Canadian Studies* 41 (4): 465–78. https://doi.org/10.1080/02722011.2011.623234.

Overby, L. Marvin, Raymond Tatalovich, and Donley T. Studlar. 1998. "Party and Free Votes in Canada: Abortion in the House of Commons." *Party Politics* 4 (3): 381–92.

Rayside, David. 1998. *On the Fringe: Gays and Lesbians in Politics*. Ithaca: Cornell University Press.

Rayside, David. 2008. *Queer Inclusions, Continental Divisions: Public Recognition of Sexual Diversity in Canada and the United States*. Toronto: University of Toronto Press. https://doi.org/10.3138/9781442688896.

Reich, Gary, and Jay Barth. 2017. "Planting in Fertile Soil: The National Rifle Association and State Firearms Legislation." *Social Science Quarterly* 98 (2): 485–99.

Renke, Wayne. 2006. "Gun Control." In *The Canadian Encyclopedia*.

Rosenthal, Michael P. 1977. "Legislative Response to Marihuana: When the Shoe Pinches Enough." *Journal of Drug Issues* 7 (1): 61–77. https://doi.org/10.1177/002204267700700106.

Royal Canadian Mounted Police. 2012. "History of Firearms Control in Canada: Up to and Including the Firearms Act." http://www.rcmp-grc.gc.ca/cfp-pcaf/pol-leg/hist/con-eng.htm.

Ryan, Stuart. 1969. "Capital Punishment in Canada." *British Journal of Criminology* 9 (1): 80–5. https://doi.org/10.1093/oxfordjournals.bjc.a049201.

Smith, Miriam. 1999. *Lesbian and Gay Rights in Canada: Social Movements and Equality Seeking, 1971–1995*. Toronto: University of Toronto Press.

Spitzer, Robert J. 2011. "Gun Control: Constitutional Mandate or Myth?" In *Moral Controversies in American Politics*, ed. Raymond Tatalovich and Byron W. Daynes, 161–95. 4th ed. Armonk, NY: M.E. Sharpe Publishers.

Spitzer, Robert J. 2015. *The Politics of Gun Control*. Boulder, CO: Paradigm Publishers.

Strub, Whitney. 2013. *Obscenity Rules: Roth v. United States and the Long Struggle over Sexual Expression*. Lawrence: University Press of Kansas.

Tatalovich, Raymond. 1997. *The Politics of Abortion in the United States and Canada: A Comparative Study*. Armonk, NY: M.E. Sharpe Publishers.

Thompson, Andrew W. 2008. "Uneasy Abolitionists: Canada, the Death Penalty, and the Importance of International Norms, 1962–2005." *Journal of*

Canadian Studies / Revue d'Études Canadiennes 42 (3): 172–92. https://doi.org/
10.3138/jcs.42.3.172.
Vaid, Urvashi. 1995. *Virtual Equality: The Mainstreaming of Gay and Lesbian
Liberation.* New York: Anchor Books.
Vernick, Jon S., and Lisa M. Hepburn. 2003. "State and Federal Gun Laws:
Trends for 1970–99." In *Evaluating Gun Policy,* ed. Jens Ludwig and Philip J.
Cook, 345–411. Washington: Brookings Institution Press.
Waring, Gerald. 1970. "Political Snafus Surround Release of LeDain Report."
Canadian Medical Association Journal 103 (2): 117.

Chapter Seven

Continuity, Decline, Resurgence

Moving among Phases

Once established, moral conflicts may proceed along a more or less direct path toward resolution. Such continuity is an important process and a measure of the durability of contention, but it is not, in itself, a distinct phase requiring explanation. It is used here to draw attention to the fact that some issues have the capacity to keep moving on, either through continuing conflict or by reaching an end stage without much digression. Other issues will demonstrate more volatility, passing through phases of decline or resurgence. But all three concepts are related in the sense of capturing some aspect of an issue's potential life course. At this point in our analysis, continuity is more like a residual category for subsuming stasis; decline and resurgence describe dynamic processes of change.

Decline

Decline in an issue's relevance may affect its two-sided conflictual basis or only one side. The latter is more likely to occur when the older, more restrictive or punitive side of the dueling arguments begins to lose its potency. This happened in the case of prohibition. Yet such decline does not preclude the potential of the older side to push back against its opposition. Decline may be temporary, followed by resurgence, only to be followed by additional periods of decline. Or it may be the harbinger of resolution, as happened in Canada following authoritative action on abortion, capital punishment, pornography, and same-sex relations, and discussed with more detail in the following chapter. Indicators of decline can be found in media coverage, first presented in chapter 3, and in party platforms (see appendix 2).

Evidence of Decline

Canada and the United States had an initial decline in attention to abortion at about the same time in the 1970s. In Canada, this reflected a political resolution and partisan retreat from the issue. Media coverage climbed to a peak in the mid-1970s, then dropped through the early 1980s. A second period of attention then began, only to decline sharply after 1990 (see figure 3.2). In the United States, once abortion became included in party platforms, it stayed there. Media attention climbed until 1970, then fluctuated up and down until it had a major increase in 1992 and relatively persisting decline since (see figure 3.1).

A more consistent pattern of decline was evident for capital punishment in Canada, both in media coverage (see figure 3.4) and in party platforms. The Conservatives' mention of capital punishment was present only in their 1962 and 1963 platforms; the Liberals' only in 1979. Media coverage declined in the mid-1970s, when government action resolved the issue. But support for the death penalty persists among the public, especially Conservative voters, and Prime Minister Stephen Harper continued to link himself with those views, telling an interviewer in 2011 of his personal support (Lilley 2011). In the United States, capital punishment had modest ups and downs in coverage, with most occurring in the mid-1970s and 1980s and a somewhat uneven long-term decline since (see figure 3.3). It has appeared in party platforms from 1972 onward.

Gun control drew attention from the Liberals in the 1979 campaign, but it remained absent from the Conservative agenda. Media coverage declined in the mid-1970s, with a short increase during the mid-1990s, and a steep one in 2008 (see figure 3.6). In the United States, gun control coverage had two sizable peaks in 1968 and 1998; otherwise, coverage has been of relatively modest proportions (see figure 3.5). However, the issue itself shows no signs of departing from party platforms.

In Canada, official attention to marijuana from the Conservatives ended in 1963 and resumed in 1993. The Liberal platform contained a reference to marijuana in 1979, but then omitted mention until 1993. But media coverage went down earlier, in 1968, with fluctuations among relatively low levels of coverage until a sharp upsurge in about 2005 (see figure 3.8). The earlier rise and fall occupied a similar period to that in the United States. In the latter country, the highest interest in marijuana, combining articles about arrests and policy debates, took place between 1968 and 1978. Subsequent decline has had only slight interruptions (see figure 3.7). Drugs of all kinds, including marijuana, have remained a topic in party platforms since their beginning in 1968.

Canadian parties were distinct in their attention to pornography. The Conservative platform addressed pornography in 1963 and then was silent on the topic until 1984. When the Liberals turned their attention to pornography in 1979, they also included objections to the exploitation of children, a perspective that we consider part of a new framing. Yet media coverage was low, rising briefly in 1984 and then quickly dropping until reaching a sharp peak in 2008 (see figure 3.10). In the United States, pornography received its greatest coverage in 1976; its drop after that has had only minor rebounds, even with new concern about child pornography (see figure 3.9). Of the six issues, only pornography had a brief hiatus from partisan attention in the United States, indicated by its absence from the 1980 platforms. Reference to pornography has appeared much more often in Republican platforms. But, once the focus shifted to the involvement of children, this led to similar partisan outlooks, as it did in Canada (see appendix 2).

Media coverage on same-sex relations in Canada had concentrated on scandal and police raids and that did not decline until after 1982 (see figure 3.12). Meanwhile, the entire issue was avoided by all political parties until the 1993 campaign, when it was present in the Liberal platform, then in the Conservative one in 2004, and in both major parties' platforms in 2006. The NDP, however, has been most consistent in its inclusion from 1993 until 2015. Despite the conflict surrounding same-sex relations, media coverage in the United States was relatively light and therefore evidence of meaningful decline is difficult to discern (see figure 3.11). The topic was not included in party platforms until 1984, the latest appearance of all six issues. This new attention to same-sex relations then became a regular feature of party platforms (see appendix 2, table 2). Once the issue was reframed to emphasize the right to marriage during the 2004 election (Green 2011), it rose in contentiousness and in media attention. In the case of the latter, coverage ebbed and flowed in company with election cycles.

A summary of the patterns of ebb and flow in attention to the six moral causes analyzed here points to enduring differences between Canada and the United States. In Canada, evidence of declining concern is manifested by absence from the major parties' platforms and some form of resolution through policy change. This has occurred for all issues except for marijuana and it too promises to be resolved by the Liberal government elected in 2015. Media coverage does not perfectly align with policy outcomes, since the former is likely to be affected by dramatic events and therefore displays more uneven patterns of rise and decline.

In the United States, once a moral issue is included in party platforms, it remains there in some form, even if it may be subject to reframing. That country presents something of a puzzle, where, for all the issues we examine, continuing conflict is played out in the partisan arena. At the same time, with the possible exception of same-sex relations, evidence of declining concern is apparent through uneven media attention. Yet the lack of synchronization between partisan and media concerns is, in itself, a sign of volatility that directs us to delve further into the processes of change.

As we have done for other phases, we begin by looking back at the experiences of prohibition. They generated three hypotheses leading to expectations that decline occurred because of

- association with outmoded or untenable positions,
- high costs, or
- counter-movement effectiveness.

Because contemporary issues display more unevenness in their decline, we can anticipate that the explanatory power of these hypotheses may be limited. In particular, early authoritative resolution in Canada in the wake of establishment, even when that resolution continued to be challenged, was the main factor affecting the decline of abortion, capital punishment, pornography, and same-sex relations. Yet distinguishing those issues and countries where the hypotheses do apply from those where they do not suggests additional reasons for decline.

Old Positions

In analyzing the emergence of moral conflicts in chapter 5, we were alerted to how differing value positions stimulated the shaping of issues into two-sided controversies. As that contention continues, a changing environment may make one side of the argument less tenable. That happened in the case of prohibition, when the political and economic changes of the time helped make moderate alcohol consumption more socially accepted than total abstinence (Gusfield 1986: 135–6). The experience of prohibition led us to hypothesize the generality of a similar process, with changes preceding the decline of an issue's salience. We find support for the hypothesis (H_{P11}) for all six issues in Canada but not for three of them in the United States, where abortion, capital punishment, and same-sex relations remained unaffected.

As we observed in the first period of declining attention to abortion in Canada, it accompanied what appeared to be the end of the issue on the policy agenda. The second period of rise and decline was tied to challenges by Dr Morgentaler to existing regulations and then to their resolution (see chapter 3).

In the United States, greater coverage of abortion was stimulated by events like abortion clinic violence and court actions. Decline in attention came as a majority of the public remained relatively satisfied with the status quo and unaffected by court decisions that followed after *Roe v. Wade* (Luks and Salamone 2008: 99). Substantive findings from various polling organizations since 1950 indicate: (1) public support for abortions under "hard" therapeutic conditions is higher than under "soft" socio-economic conditions while less than a majority approves of abortions as a purely elective procedure, (2) many restrictions (like waiting periods or informed consent) that pro-choice advocates find onerous are perfectly reasonable for most Americans, and (3) although most people support *Roe v. Wade* as the law of the land, a sizable minority does not (Strickland, 2011: 14–18; Luks and Salamone 2008). These results suggest that, in the United States, the continuity in partisan attention and the absence of major change beyond the initial definition of legalization, while helping keep media coverage low, have not diminished abortion's salience.

Reasons for declining interest in capital punishment could reflect doubts about the morality of taking the life of even a murderer and about the deterrent capacity of the death penalty. However, in both countries, decline occurred in the face of persisting public approval of capital punishment. In opinion polls from 1943 through 1975, the year before abolition occurred in Canada, a majority, ranging from 51 to 73 percent, opposed abolishing the death penalty (Fattah 1976). Similarly, in the United States, from 1936 through 1960, majorities told Gallup interviewers they favored capital punishment and that level of support continued through 2009 (Steel and Steger 2011: 51). Despite these similarities in public views, however, decline in media attention in Canada was specific to the resolution of the issue, marking its ending on the political agenda. In the United States, capital punishment demonstrated resistance to change.

Drops in coverage of gun control in the United States have previously been attributed to the after-effects of specific events (see chapter 3). These continue to shape the ebb and flow of attention and the issue's continuing salience. In Canada, peaks and valleys in media attention on firearms are largely attributable to legislative activities, but the mobilization of conflicting values also played a role in the most recent shift in attention, associated with controversy over long-gun registration (see chapter 3). Repeal of the long-gun registry was a top legislative priority for Stephen Harper's Conservative government, elected in 2011. Opponents of the registry saw it as an infringement on the freedom to hunt and on the tourist trade, which relied on those who came to Canada for that purpose. It divided rural and urban Canada (Austen 2009) with moral and symbolic overtones which deeply polarized the policy debate (Simpson 2010). Divisions related to criminalizing ordinary citizens, effects on federal–provincial relations, and dispute over the government's right to collect and retain personal records. Once the gun registry was abolished in 2012, with little prospect of revival (*Guelph Mercury* 2012), the issue was resolved, and we can expect it to be followed by a drop-off in interest.

Although marijuana has gone through extremes of acceptance and rejection from the public and from policymakers, it generated only modest media coverage in the United States. Greatest attention was given over the decade beginning in the mid-1960s, mainly generated by the increased drug arrests that accompanied that era's cultural revolution. Subsequently, growing acceptance of marijuana use for medical purposes and, in particular, rejection of harsh penalties for possession, have lowered the issue's contentious tenor even as policies remain unresolved (see chapter 3). In effect, social changes have been more meaningful for decline than have primarily political ones.

In Canada, early patterns of attention to marijuana had been similar to those in the United States, and for similar reasons. But later, attention increased, then had a marked decline in 1985, only to rise to an unprecedented level in 2007, encouraged by the volume of drug-related arrests. Partisan governments have given the issue its saliency and contentiousness, with the Conservatives consistently opposed to loosened restrictions. The attention decline in the 1980s took place during a period of Conservative rule when government policy enjoyed public support, with fewer than one-third of those surveyed favoring legalization (MacKinnon 2001). The last upsurge in attention began its decline just prior to the 2015 election of a Liberal government, pledged to decriminalization. If this policy is enacted, it should mark the resolution of marijuana as a moral conflict.

Of all the issues we deal with, pornography appears as the least contentious, never arousing the same kind of media or political attention as have the others. Institutional support for restrictions on pornography that involved adults gave way to much narrower definitions of what constituted an offense. We can interpret the drop in media attention in the United States as a sign of how loosened views of obscenity itself had become an accepted part of the national culture.

A similar assessment of pornography can be made for Canada, where media coverage was even lower. Although Canadian coverage sharply increased in 2008, showing the effect of reframing as child pornography, there was no parallel increase in the United States to reflect the same reframing. Reframing had begun in the 1970s (to be discussed further under "Resurgence" and in chapter 8, on resolution), and the momentary surge in attention was quickly followed by its decline. Once political parties in both countries agreed to restrictions on child pornography, the result was resolution of conflict.

Widespread acknowledgment of the sheer existence of gay, lesbian, and transgender individuals within the population and their presence in all walks of life has constituted a revolutionary change in the public sphere. Moral disapproval of same-sex relations has sharply declined in both countries, with even greater acceptance in Canada (Andersen and Fetner 2008). In the United States, however, some reservations remain.

> Overwhelming majorities of Americans have … come to believe that gay people deserve equal employment rights, including employment in the military, medicine, and politics and (to a lesser extent) as teachers or clergy. Yet on aspects of gay rights that have to do with gay relationships and sexuality, Americans are less supportive, and their opinions have changed more slowly. (Egan et al. 2008: 236)

These changes, even with their limits, give us reason to expect that they will be associated with declining salience. Yet, in the United States, evidence of decline is, at best, modest, a reflection of how relatively recent has been the establishment of same-sex relations on the policy agenda and a reminder of the issue's continuing contentiousness.

In Canada, modest increases in attention to same-sex relations were stimulated by the Supreme Court's supportive application of the Charter of Rights and Freedoms in the 1990s. Yet there was barely an uptick in coverage when the court first ruled on the equality of marriage rights. A changed environment and the political resolution of most relevant elements have ended the place of same-sex relations on the policy agenda.

High Costs

The lesson from prohibition was that the high cost extracted by its enforcement eventually contributed to its demise. Costs were both financial and moral, fostering the corruption of police forces and local governments. Prohibition demonstrated that even moral causes, buttressed by religious beliefs, are difficult to sustain when costs become overwhelming. The generality of that finding is most applicable to the case of marijuana[1] in both countries. However, H_{P12} has only limited relevance to the decline of the other contemporary issues we analyze, affecting, to a degree, reactions to gun control in Canada and same-sex relations in the United States.

The financial costs of enforcement and, even more important, the social ones produced by the arrest and incarceration of large numbers of young men, especially in minority communities, has been one factor in diminishing the argument for retaining the criminalization of marijuana possession and use. It has played a similar role in both countries. In Canada, the Senate Special Committee on Illegal Drugs (2002: 36) noted the unwarranted costliness of a punitive approach. It indicted the marijuana regulatory regime on three grounds:

- Billions of dollars have been sunk into enforcement without any greater effect. There are more consumers, more regular users, and more regular adolescent users;
- Billions of dollars have been poured into enforcement in an effort to reduce supply, without any greater effect. Cannabis is more available than ever, it is cultivated on a large scale, even exported, swelling coffers and making organized crime more powerful; and

---

1 Marijuana, along with gun control, are two issues that Hurka et al. (2016) consider to be latent moral issues without the same weight as strictly manifest ones that are unaffected by cost. We, however, find that nothing is gained by that distinction, particularly when they both remain among the most contentious issues we consider.

- There have been tens of thousands of arrests and convictions for the possession of cannabis and thousands of people have been incarcerated. However, use trends remain totally unaffected and the gap the [Le Dain] Commission noted between the law and public compliance continues to widen. It is time to recognize what is patently obvious: our policies have been ineffective, because they are poor policies.

Many of the arguments favoring decriminalization in the United States parallel those made in Canada, but pay even more attention to the social costs of the racist origins of laws against marijuana. Those laws were enacted "in an atmosphere of hysteria during the 1930s and that was firmly rooted in prejudices against Mexican immigrants and African-Americans, who were associated with marijuana use at the time. This racially freighted history lives on in current federal policy, which is so driven by myth and propaganda that it is almost impervious to reason" (Staples 2014).

Yet, despite the application of severe punishments, "criminalization has not affected general usage: about 30 million Americans use marijuana every year. Meanwhile, police forces across the country are strapped for cash, and the more resources they devote to enforcing marijuana laws, the less they have to go after serious, violent crime" (Wegman 2014).

In Canada, a significant reason given for opposing the long-gun registry was its history of costliness. The registry had been instituted in 1995 under the Liberal government of Jean Chrétien and projected to cost $2 million. Resources were to be obtained mainly from general revenues, with the remainder coming from license fees. But the auditor general of Canada, Sheila Fraser, estimated the registration program would cost more than $1 billion by 2004–5, with perhaps 15 percent of the cost being covered from license fees (Simpson 2010).

Cost, however, can be a two-edged sword in the sense that it can be used to buttress old positions and devalue new ones. The costliness of new programs, whether real or anticipated, can be presented as barriers to change, and hence undermine efforts to institute new practices or regulations. For example, opposition to the exclusion of gays and lesbians from the US armed services argued against the harm done by eliminating access to a pool of talented recruits. Between 1993 and 2011, over 14,000 were discharged for reasons of sexual orientation and each discharge was estimated to cost $50,000 (Glantz 2011). This was the period when "Don't ask, don't tell," instituted to restrain discrimination, was operative. When the regulation was repealed, arguments then appeared about fairness and the absence of any harm from military service by gays and lesbians. Those new arguments, a measure of social more than financial costs, still demonstrate the role of costs in issue decline.

Cost considerations with regard to the availability of abortion facilities have had little impact on the contentiousness of the issue itself. Despite rulings making abortion legal, the procedure remains difficult to obtain outside of major cities and in particular parts of each country (Keller and Yarrow 2013; Young 2014). Reasons underlying limits to access include the lack of training provided by medical schools and hospitals, the reluctance of hospitals to offer facilities, and, in the United States, the unwillingness of local authorities to contribute resources.

Countermovement Effectiveness

When prohibition began to decline as a viable policy option, some of the impetus for change came from the mobilization of new, opposing perspectives. That finding raised expectations that similar processes would be relevant in other moral conflicts. It was summarized in H_{P13} to associate countermovement effectiveness "with the ability to mobilize support through appeals to core values." Although countermovement activity did affect abortion, gun control, pornography, and same-sex relations, we do not see such activity as a factor in decline. Those issues better illustrate the tension between movements and countermovements, captured in predicting resurgence in H_{P15}, where success was attributed to whichever side was better able to claim legitimacy for its arguments.

Country and Issue Differences

From the perspective of decline, the interaction between the national setting and particular issues produces both expected and unanticipated findings. Factors leading to the decline of prohibition turned out to be weak predictors of decline in contemporary issues, reflecting the continuing volatility of the latter. Of the three factors premised on the experiences of prohibition, only the reassertion of old positions was supported for all issues in Canada and three in the United States.

Costs played a role in decline in two cases in both countries, while countermovements lacked discernible impact on all issues, regardless of national setting.

In general, expectations of decline in attention, when measured by partisan attention, held in Canada for all issues, but only for pornography in the United States. In effect, political institutions in the United States acted, as anticipated in chapter 4, to keep moral controversies on the policy agenda. For example, H_{C4} predicted that Congress would give more opportunities for the expression of moral controversies. The modest drop-off in media attention in the United States (not, however, affecting coverage of same-sex relations) had little relation to the stability of partisan contention. This supported H_{C5}, that the major parties in the United States would be "more open to addressing moral issues than ... their counterpart in Canada."

One reason for issue decline is continuing social change that makes one side of the moral controversy less tenable. That occurred for all issues in Canada, but not for abortion, capital punishment, gun control, or same-sex relations in the United States. Clearly, major changes were occurring simultaneously in both countries, so that cannot account for results in the United States. In the latter country, resistance to changing conceptions of the three issues was facilitated by all the demographic, civic, and political factors that differentiate the United States from Canada (see chapter 4).

Another possible reason for issue decline is the mounting costs of enforcement, a major factor in the decline of prohibition as a viable policy. In both countries, cost has made for a powerful argument only in the case of marijuana on some of the same grounds that effectively moved prohibition off the policy agenda. Although abortion restrictions have also been approached from the perspective of cost, cost arguments have not been particularly effective in countering them. Cost was, however, more persuasive in Canada in loosening gun control restrictions and played a modest role in changing policy in the United States regarding LGBTs in the military.

We found no support for the prediction that countermovements would be relevant to the decline in issue salience. This does not appear to be related to the weakness of countermovements in affecting changing conceptions of moral issues but to their inability to diminish the salience of the controversies with which they are engaged, as we demonstrate in the following section.

Resurgence

Once an issue has declined in attention and salience it may still be pulled back into active contention. Canada demonstrates this possibility in the sharpest detail. There, the decline in issue salience traced in the previous section accompanied resolution through parliamentary or court action in the case of all contemporary issues except for marijuana, and its resolution is shortly expected. Yet neither legislative nor court actions have been fully successful in preventing resurgence.

The transition to an issue's resurgence can take place in two ways. One is through a reframing of the issue so that new aspects are emphasized and new interests mobilized. Such reframing affected four issues in both countries: gun control, marijuana, pornography, and same-sex relations. Resurgence can also be interpreted to have occurred through attempts to curtail or recriminalize abortion, even though authoritative decisions loosening restrictions had taken place in both countries, although under much greater heat in the United States. Similarly, the re-emergence of calls for capital punishment can be observed in Canada.

Understanding why these forms of issue resurgence have occurred brings us back again to the insights we derived from the case of prohibition. These generated two hypotheses to account for renewed or intensified concern with moral issues. Resurgence is expected when

- the original problem becomes worse or
- movements are able to assert or reassert the legitimacy of their position.

Problem More Acute

The apparent worsening of a problem can be a powerful impetus to the resurgence of concern about an issue. Typically this occurs through a process of reframing, exemplified in both countries with respect to gun control, marijuana, and pornography. but not to the other issues.

Gun Control. Renewed mobilization around gun control produced greater support for lessened control. In Canada, as we discussed in the earlier section on costs, the introduction of a long-gun registry in 1995 under a Liberal government became an issue of partisan contention. When the registry was abolished in 2012, the Conservative government benefited from the counterattack against the registry that mobilized recreational hunters, native peoples, the tourist trade, and regional interests. These successfully combined to undermine the continuity of the existing policy by arguing for the rights of hunters and native peoples. Repeal of the registry was connected as well to opposition to increased governmental regulation over the sale and possession of firearms.

Opposition to gun control in the United States coincided with a drop in media attention spanning most of the first decade of the twenty-first century (see figure 3.5). Nevertheless, contention continued through the reframing efforts of gun-control opponents. They produced a new version of contested values, where advocates of gun rights have confronted the previous challenge to the prevailing gun culture by new interpretations of the Second Amendment. Loosened restrictions on gun ownership became reframed as the right to self-protection through gun ownership, a response to perceptions of increased threat from criminals and terrorists and an outgrowth of the Supreme Court ruling in *McDonald v. Chicago* (2010) that gave Second Amendment rights to the self-protective potential of gun ownership. The justices have gone further in placing even stun guns under this same protective umbrella (Andersen and Ellement 2016). As a counter to the argument that restrictions on access to gun ownership make the country safer, the reframed position has strengthened opposition to gun control. Earlier interpretations of that amendment saw it providing only a collective right to the firearms necessary to service state militias. But now states and localities must prove that gun laws are consistent with more recent high-court rulings and do not unduly infringe upon the new-found constitutional right. The new gun rights ethos is reflected in public opinion as well. For two decades, beginning in 1993, surveys by Pew found majorities who said it was more important to "control gun ownership" than to "protect the right of Americans to own guns." But by 2014, those positions reversed (Pew Research Center 2014b). Related changes have been tracked in Gallup polls, where majorities now believe that gun ownership makes for greater personal safety (Gallup Polls 2015).

Marijuana. The reframing of marijuana has taken place out of a combination of factors present in both Canada and the United States. Marijuana is now considered much less harmful than other proscribed drugs and more likely to be benign than are legal addictive drugs like alcohol and nicotine (Boffey 2014). Enforcement of marijuana laws results in life-altering and disproportionate criminal records for the young and those in minority communities and, as we discussed earlier, presents social and economic costs difficult to defend. Reframing that takes account of these adverse effects makes it possible to see continued criminalization of those in possession of marijuana as an indication of how the problem has worsened. Along the moral divide, defense of criminalizing marijuana is now depicted as without moral standing.

Pornography. Pornography has also been reframed, but in ways that abandon earlier efforts to change its definition and loosen restrictions. Initially, reframing linked pornography with violence against women, bringing feminists and religious conservatives to take similar positions (Whittier 2014). More effective arguments were crystalized in concern that broad access to pornographic materials had allowed the freedom to depict and circulate the sexual exploitation of children. In the United States, the landmark Supreme Court ruling was *New York v. Ferber* (1982), which upheld state laws regulating child pornography on child-abuse grounds but without providing any operational definition of what constituted obscenity. At the same time as the high court seemed to give its constitutional blessings to state and federal efforts to suppress child pornography, concern remained whether state law, as in the case of *Massachusetts v. Oakes* (1989), was "overbroad" and thus has a "chilling effect" on First Amendment rights of free expression. After *Ferber*, the twenty-one obscenity cases that reached the Supreme Court through 2008 included six on banning child pornography and four on shielding children from exposure to pornography on the Internet. Conservative court coalitions prevailed on six of these cases and liberal court coalitions won on four. Conservative rulings emphasized protection of children; liberal ones were protective of free speech.[2]

The judicial record comports with the assessment by law professor Amy Adler that the three-pronged war on pornography involves protecting minors from online web access, battling child pornography, and redeploying decades-old obscenity law "to make up for limitations and [judicial] defeats in the realms of child pornography law and the doctrine of 'harmful to minors'" jurisprudence. Moreover, there was much political pressure surrounding the issue, as indicated by the large number of pornography-related bills introduced into Congress, "almost all of them focus[ed] on technology and children" (Adler 2006–7: 706–7). Her assessment is supported by evidence that, while only 15 percent

---

2 The Supreme Court Database codes the direction of each decision as liberal or conservative based on a complicated system that includes the constitutional provision, party to the litigation, and the issue involved. For cases pertaining to "criminal procedure, civil rights, First Amendment, due process, privacy, and attorneys," liberal is "pro-person accused or convicted of crime, or denied a jury trial" and the reverse is conservative.

of all congressional hearings during 1950–79 were wholly or partly devoted to children and pornography, that percentage sharply increased to 72 percent from 1980 to 2010. In the following two years, children were the subject of all five congressional hearings on pornography.

Public opinion polls provide another indicator that pornography involving children is widely seen as a new and dangerous phenomenon. Asked in 1977 by a Time/Yankelovich, Skelly & White Poll (1977) whether court cases involving child pornography should be prosecuted under "child abuse laws" or "as any other case of pornography," 72 percent favored the former. By February of 1986, 91 percent told an ABC News/Washington Post Poll (1986) that pornography was harmful to children who viewed or read it. In July of that same year respondents were asked to compare the extent of child pornography since they were children and 80 percent said it had increased (Harris Survey 1986). A decade later, 82 percent of those surveyed by a Pew News Interest Index Poll (1996) favored banning child pornography from the Internet. A question in March 2005 about whether child pornography should be allowed as a form of free speech was rejected by 97 percent of those asked in a special Judicial Confirmation Survey (2005).

In sum, in the United States, all sources point to a new consensus on pornography affecting children. It is currently viewed by policymakers and the public as sufficiently evil to be undeserving of the constitutional protections of free speech.

In Canada, as well, there was a reframing of pornography to emphasize the violation of moral norms when children were involved. However, the issue's new form appears to have been viewed as less threatening than was the case in the United States. One indicator is the failure to revise the Criminal Code with respect to child pornography in a 1981 bill (Bill C-53). Apparently, many MPs, Liberals as well as Conservatives, did not believe that child pornography was a serious problem. The legislative deadlock prompted Justice Minister Jean Chrétien to storm out of a committee hearing. "You don't want to deal with it," he screamed. "If you want to have child pornography in every bloody store in the country, you vote for it" (Globe and Mail 1982a). But the Globe and Mail (1982b) shared parliamentarians' misgivings: "There have been objections from various groups – artists, magazine distributors, book publishers, writers and librarians – who think that the child pornography provisions are far too broad and that they could seriously affect all manner of material that the authors of the amendments did not have in mind."

Yet support for greater legal restrictions on pornography involving children continued, prompting several private members' bills and the appointment of a special parliamentary Committee on Sexual Offenses against Children and Youth (the Badgley Committee). However, its 1985 report debunked the view that any "epidemic" of child pornography existed in Canada. It argued that most of the latter was imported from the United States and comprised only a small fraction of all pornography entering the country. Nonetheless, the Badgley Committee recommended that the use of children in the production, manufacture, sale or distribution as well as mere possession of visual images of "explicit sexual conduct" of persons under age eighteen be criminalized (Report of the Committee on Sexual Offenses against Children and Youths 1985). In 1993, the outgoing Conservative government passed Bill C-128, incorporating those recommendations. This did not end the controversy in Canada, where challenges continued on artistic and civil libertarian grounds. These were followed by new legislation, as we go on to discuss in the next section and in the following chapter, ultimately ensuring that the issue had been successfully reframed as child pornography.

Assertions of Legitimacy

Resurgence may also follow from efforts to assert or reassert the greater legitimacy of one side of the moral debate, as experienced during the prohibition controversy and summarized in H_{P16}. In the case of abortion and capital punishment, there have been moves to reclaim earlier positions challenged by opponents. The previous discussion of gun control as an increasingly serious problem can also be interpreted as a sign of the renewed legitimacy of lessened restrictions on gun control. Same-sex relations were reframed to focus on the right to marriage, thus extending the original quest for decriminalization of those relations so as to include full normalization.

Abortion. The victory that *Roe v. Wade* presented to pro-choice forces was an immediate incentive in rallying pro-life interests, aided during those times when the Republicans had control of at least one branch of government. During the 1970s, congressional abortion hearings surged as pro-life forces and their congressional allies added anti-abortion restrictions to every conceivable public policy: healthcare for the indigent, foreign aid, legal services for the poor, health benefits for federal employees or military personnel, and family planning grants.

There were also efforts to limit federal court jurisdiction with respect to abortion cases and opposition to the confirmation of pro-choice federal judges and Supreme Court justices (Halfmann, 2011: 187–91).

Abortion was partially or wholly the subject of 71 hearings during the 1970s and not many fewer during the 1980s (70) and 1990s (65) before falling to 30 hearings from 2000–10. In the following three years, however, 23 more hearings were held, often prompted by debate over the prospect of mandatory birth control coverage under Obamacare. The only major pro-choice enactment to emerge from Congress was the Freedom of Access to Clinic Entrances Act (FACE) of 1994. In addition, a multitude of state laws attempted to regulate the timing, method, and procedures for abortions, which led to further litigation that reached the Supreme Court (see, for example, Kreitzer 2015; Boonstra and Nash 2014; Camobreco and Barnello 2008).

Webster v. Reproductive Health Services (1989) was the pivotal ruling that encouraged pro-lifers to hope that the Rehnquist Court would eventually reverse *Roe v. Wade*. The case involved an abortion clinic's challenge to a Missouri statute whose preamble declared that life begins at conception and that also required physicians to conduct viability tests prior to doing an abortion; two-parent notification for minors, although with an option of a judicial bypass; a forty-eight-hour waiting period for minors; and a prohibition against public funding for abortion counseling. By upholding the viability testing requirement and the ban on using public facilities or public person-nel for abortions, the Supreme Court moved away from the most exacting "strict scrutiny" standard employed since *Roe* and toward the "unduly burdensome" standard that Justice O'Connor advocated. As important as was the immediate outcome, *Webster*'s broader effect was to re-federalize abortion policy by signaling to state governments that the new Court majority would not evaluate abortion according to the strictest precedents.

The anniversary of *Roe v. Wade* on 22 January has been remembered by opponents organized into an annual March for Life. The march began in 1973 and continues, even growing in size, since then. Among conservative Christians, the fight against abortion remains a power-ful source of mobilization (Lynerd 2014: 30). In addition, anti-abortion movements have begun to change their rhetoric in order to align them-selves with pro-feminist positions. They do so by relying on female spokespersons and framing their arguments that abortion is harmful to women through the use of medical and scientific terms (Saurette and

Gordon 2015). These movements ensure the contentiousness of abortion and its continuing presence on the political agenda.

In Canada, although opposition to abortion remains among a minority of the population, resurgence has been limited since the Conservative government's failure in 1988 to recodify a law that had been undermined by the Supreme Court ruling in *R. v. Morgentaler* (1988). Some efforts at resurgence remained, however, among Conservatives, particularly after their merger with the Canadian Alliance. During his 2002 campaign to lead the Canadian Alliance, where right-to-life sentiments were strongest, Stephen Harper disavowed using abortion as a partisan litmus test and criticized his rival, Stockwell Day, for resurrecting the issue (*Globe and Mail* 2000). But, in their 2008 platform, the Conservatives' promise to "amend the Criminal Code to make the pregnancy of a woman an aggravating factor in sentencing if a woman is assaulted or killed" was, despite the disclaimer that it would not lead to any new legislative effort to regulate abortion (see appendix 2), an opening to renewed politicization. This was evident from Prime Minister Harper's support of a private member's bill (Bill C-484 – Unborn Victims of Crime Act) that fulfilled the party's platform promise. That bill passed its first two readings, but, in the face of unified opposition from abortion-rights advocates, the government withdrew its support and the bill died when a federal election was called in 2008. But after re-election, the Harper government sought to restrict abortions abroad by banning the use of foreign aid for that purpose. However, a majority of Canadians surveyed opposed the policy (Harris/Decima 2010). The public now accepts the reality that abortion has been resolved as a policy issue, as an Angus Reid Public Opinion (2013) poll reported, with 59 percent saying that there "is no point in re-opening a debate about abortion in Canada right now" compared to the 30 percent who believed "the discussion should be re-opened." Yet resurgence of opposition to abortion in Canada still retains some strength, signaled, as in the United States, by an annual March for Life on Ottawa. And, as in the United States, anti-abortion activists have changed their voice in order to speak in terms that appear more sympathetic to the concerns of women (Saurette and Gordon 2015). We leave fuller discussion of contention over abortion to the following chapter, where we assess the extent to which the issue has been resolved.

Capital Punishment. Capital punishment was abolished in Canada through legislation, first on a trial bases in 1967 and then permanently in 1976. Even so, there have been subsequent signs of resurgence. In late

1984, the Canadian Association of Chiefs of Police called for restoration of the death penalty. Since the general election that year, seven private members' bills to restore capital punishment were given first reading in Parliament. Pressed by Conservative backbenchers, Prime Minister Mulroney allowed a free vote on restoring capital punishment in 1987, even while making clear his intention to vote against restoration (*Globe and Mail* 1987). Restoration was defeated by a 127–48 vote.

Yet capital punishment still retained some resurgent qualities. Since it was abolished, Canada had a policy of automatically requesting clemency for any Canadian citizen sentenced to death in another country. But in the case of Alberta-born Ronald Allen Smith, on death row in Montana since the early 1980s, the Harper government announced that each clemency request from prisoners in democratic countries like the United States would be handled on a case-by-case basis. This was challenged by Liberal MP Judy Sgro in 2008, who tabled a non-binding motion that the government should resume the policy of automatically seeking clemency for Canadians facing the death penalty abroad, and it was passed by a coalition of all the opposition parties. In response to Smith's own appeal, the Federal Court of Canada in 2009 ruled in *Smith v. Canada (Attorney General)* that the government was required to apply the previous policy in the Smith case.

A second issue of remaining contention was whether Canada should extradite murderers to countries that impose the death penalty. This question prompted two contrary decisions by the Canadian Supreme Court. In *Kindler v. Canada* (1991), the high court sided with the Mulroney government and ordered the defendants extradited to the United States with no guarantee that they would not be put to death. But the controversy that followed that decision became more intense when the issue of extradition was revisited in the case of *United States v. Burns* (2001), involving two men charged with triple homicides in Washington State. Justice Minister Allan Rock agreed to their extradition without seeking any assurance that the death penalty would not be imposed. His decision was challenged as violating the guarantee of "fundamental justice" under section 7 of the Charter of Rights and Freedoms, but this time the Canadian Supreme Court voted 9–0 in the defendants' favor. The big difference between *Kindler* and *Burns*, according to Thompson (2008), was the globalized spread of abolitionist norms that were now firmly entrenched in the Canadian legal culture. The year 2007 was the twenty-fifth anniversary of the Charter, an occasion that prompted Ontario Court of Appeals Justice Marc

Rosenberg to declare that *Burns* ended any prospect for bringing back the death penalty. "It is because of the Charter that the criminal justice system is out from under the shadow of capital punishment" (*Globe and Mail* 2007). According to these views, resurgence is now unlikely to alter policy.

Resurgence in the United States took place in a more volatile setting, with state and federal involvement, and greater and more irregular media coverage (see figure 3.3). The frequency with which public opinion polls ask about capital punishment is another indicator of how it has risen as a contentious issue. Out of a total of 871 questions on capital punishment asked during 1950–2010, the average was 6.9 questions per year during the 1970s, when the Supreme Court vacated death rows in several states (*Furman v. Georgia*, 1972). Averages increased to 17.2 during the 1980s, 23.9 in the 1990s, and 34.1 during the 11 years of 2000–2010. Some of this new attention went along with changing patterns of congressional hearings, which went from 13 in the 1980s, to 19 in the 1990s, and 23 in the first decade of the 2000s. That rise accompanied the reassertion of support for the death penalty in Supreme Court decisions. In 91 decisions from 1977 through 2010, conservative majorities won 54 cases and liberal majorities prevailed in only 37. This reversal in fortunes with respect to capital punishment parallels the setbacks suffered by pro-choice forces after *Roe v. Wade*. Epstein and Kobylka (1992: 308) attribute these outcomes to a "tyranny of absolutes" that came to dominate the judicial strategies of both groups.

> By continuing to press for legal interpretations that would provide absolute and conclusive victories, both abolitionists and pro-choicers set the stage for their own defeat. Given unfavorable political environments – both in terms of subsequent appointments to the Court and continued state legislation in clear opposition to the command of the Court – it may be that these forces could not have maintained their victories over time even if they had strategically altered their argumentational postures.

Same-Sex Relations. The reframing of same-sex relations into a demand for full civil equality by allowing same-sex marriages was the final expansion of this issue in both countries. That is, it represented resurgence through building on the momentum from prior struggles for new rights rather than, as in the cases of abortion, capital punishment, gun control, or pornography, reasserting values that upheld earlier and more restrictive positions. Reframing took place in both countries around the same time.

In Canada, as in the United States, the struggle for same-sex marriage was not one that many activists in the gay rights movement initially pursued, fearing that it might deflect support from other essential rights (Elliott 2004: 609–10). But times were changing and some activists were beginning to challenge the status quo. In response, the federal government, which had constitutional authority over marriage and divorce, gave its rebuttal. It passed a resolution in 1999 reaffirming the definition of marriage as "the union of one man and one woman to the exclusion of all others." In the following year, that definition was included in a revised Bill C-23, the Modernization of Benefits and Obligations Act (2000). However, in *Halpern v. Canada* (2002), the Ontario Superior Court held the same-sex marriage ban to be discriminatory and a violation of the Equality Clause (section 15) of the Charter of Rights and Freedoms, a decision upheld by the Court of Appeal for Ontario (Elliott 2004), leading to similar rulings in all but one other province and two territories. During this period, the Commons Standing Committee on Justice and Human Rights was holding hearings on same-sex marriage and recommended that the federal government not appeal the Ontario Court of Appeal's ruling against the provincial ban. Once assured by the Supreme Court of the constitutionality of same-sex marriages and the continued protection of religious institutions to refuse their performance, the Liberal government of Paul Martin introduced legislation in 2005 (Bill C-38) allowing a free vote to all but the cabinet. After passage, Canada became the fourth country in the world to legalize same-sex marriage.

The changing policy environment had its counterpart among the Canadian public. By 2004, after five provincial or territorial courts had nullified bans on same-sex marriage, a majority supported allowing such marriages (Lehman 2006). However, during the 2006 national election campaign, Conservative Party leader Stephen Harper promised to reopen the debate. But, as far as the public was concerned, 66 percent felt that the same-sex issue was settled and should not be reopened (Lehman 2006: 63). Yet, on election, the Conservatives tabled a motion to reopen debate which was defeated 123 to 175. "The result was decisive," said Prime Minister Harper afterwards. "I don't see reopening this question in the future" (*Ottawa Citizen* 2006). The reframed expansion of same-sex relations into same-sex marriage had overwhelmed the opposition in Canada, where the issue has now been resolved.

Same-sex marriage redefined the gay rights movement in the United States after 2000 even more than in Canada and stimulated even greater conflict. But, like Canada, all the legal momentum behind same-sex marriage came from the judiciary, with Congress and most states fighting a rearguard action to defend traditional heterosexual marriage. The stimulus bringing the redefined issue to the fore was a ruling by the Hawaii Supreme Court in *Baehr v. Lewin* (1993) that refusal to recognize same-sex marriages would be unconstitutional in the absence of a compelling state interest for doing so. The state responded in 1997 by enacting legislation that provided reciprocal benefits to same-sex or opposite-sex adults living in partnerships.

In a backlash against the *Baehr* ruling, Congress enacted the Defense of Marriage Act (DOMA) in 1996. It had two objectives: (1) Section 2 would prevent states from being forced by the Full Faith and Credit Clause of Article IV in the Constitution to recognize same-sex marriages validly celebrated in other states and (2) Section 3 would define marriage in federal law (for tax and social benefits) as the union between one man and one woman. Individual states also took action between 1998 and 2009, when thirty-one held referendums on whether to legalize same-sex marriage and all but one (Arizona) banned them (Ellis and Kasniunas 2011: 87–8). Only New Hampshire and the District of Columbia, both in 2009, approved same-sex marriage by legislative enactment. In 2012, Maine, Maryland, Minnesota, and Washington became the first states to legalize same-sex marriage through referendums.

Legislative actions to deny marriage rights persisted at the same time as pro-marriage advocates continued their campaign through the courts. In 1999, the Vermont Supreme Court ruled that same-sex couples are constitutionally entitled to all the same guarantees and benefits of opposite-sex couples, followed by the state recognizing civil unions. Most significant was the ruling by the Massachusetts Supreme Judicial Council in *Goodridge v. Department of Public Health* (2003) that same-sex couples cannot be denied marriage rights. Even though the legislature did not follow up with reform of the marriage law, the state had to issue valid marriage licenses to gay and lesbian couples beginning in the spring of 2004. By 2009, Hawaii, Vermont, Massachusetts, Connecticut, and Iowa had legalized same-sex marriage through legal mandates issued by their state high courts. In the pivotal judicial ruling that undermined the legal rationale for same-sex marriage bans, the Supreme Court in *United States v. Windsor* (2013) struck down section 3 of DOMA as violating the Fifth Amendment. In 2014 the high court refused to review appeals from lower courts that had upheld same-sex marriage, and, by that action, the number of states with legal same-sex marriage jumped from nineteen to thirty-seven. The Supreme Court would overturn the remaining state bans in a ruling issued in *Obergefell v. Hodges* (2015).

During the period of political activity aimed at legalizing same-sex marriage, both the media and the public were swept along. Media coverage had its first uptick beginning in 1996, but surged during the 2004 national elections and after, to the point that same-sex marriage virtually dominated all media coverage about gay rights in the United States (see figure 3.11). Since 2000, polling on same-sex marriage has also ballooned, from only 16 questions during the 1990s to 593 between 2000 and 2010. The first question asked by the Gallup Poll in 1996 found 68 percent opposed and only 27 percent favoring same-sex marriages. Over time, opinions reversed, with 53 percent supporting same-sex marriage in 2011, rising to 60 percent in 2015 (McCarthy 2015). A similar opinion shift was documented by Pew Research Center (2014a). Results from state referendums showed that counties with larger numbers of Protestant fundamentalists were more strongly opposed to same-sex marriage, whereas counties with more Democrats, greater urbanization, and a more educated population were less opposed (Lofton and Haider-Markel 2007: 332–3). Most state bans on same-sex marriage were orchestrated by evangelical Christians (Lynerd 2014: 30). Movement-countermovement tensions remain mobilized over all issues regarding same-sex relations (Conger and Djupe 2016: 279).

Country and Issue Differences

All six issues showed some signs of resurgence in both countries, indicating the continuing viability of both sides of their underlying moral conflicts. For gun control, marijuana, and pornography in both countries, resurgence was preceded by perceptions that problems related to them had become worse, in support of H_{P14}. The other three issues were reinvigorated by heightened contention over one or other side of the underlying moral conflict. Conflict was mobilized through the active competition between movements and countermovements, anticipated in H_{P15}. That conflict involved a reassertion of the greater legitimacy of the older arguments defending restrictions on abortion, advocacy for capital punishment, and opposition to gun control. In contrast, only same-sex relations benefited from arguments to expand rights.

Altogether, out of twelve possibilities, seven hypotheses found support in both countries.

A particularly striking feature of resurgence is its dependence on reframing that gives a new and enlarged meaning to an issue. Yet reframing can work for either side of a conflict. In the case of those defending the absence of restrictions on gun ownership, a new rationale appeared in the form of how guns could protect against violence. Marijuana could be reframed to both emphasize how criminalization unfairly penalized youth and minorities and how its usage had desirable medical properties. Pornography, although it became a two-sided moral issue through advocacy of freedom from constraints, was then reframed in favor of greater restrictions to reflect new concerns about pornography that involved children. Same-sex relations moved in the direction of greater freedom by including the right to marriage. We see the importance of such reframing as yet another aspect of how moral conflicts regularly evolve and change.

Along with the great similarities in how issues developed in both countries were some anticipated differences. One was the greater degree of contentiousness in the United States, confirming H_{C1}. As we argued in chapter 4, this stems, in part, from the stronger connection with partisanship, where the two major US parties are clearly divided over moral conflicts. Findings here then support H_{C5}, on the greater openness to moral issues, and H_{C6}, on the greater likelihood of issue ownership. In addition, the United States provides many more opportunities for conflicts to be expressed through the way it structures federalism, with individual states multiplying the venues available (H_{C7}).

At the same time, the Canadian parliamentary system allows even issues that appear to be resolved to be reopened as a consequence of executive authority. This happened with abortion, capital punishment, and same-sex marriage when the Conservative Party, which had opposed broadened rights, formed the government, in support of H_{C3}. However, as these cases demonstrate, once practices are institutionalized through laws, court decisions, and public support, they are unlikely to be successfully re-engaged by a new party in power.

Finally, although there are reasons to expect decreased differences between the two countries in the political impact of the courts, courts in the United States continue to exert greater impact. In other words, H_{C9} was not supported.

Movement between Phases

The rationale for introducing continuity into the title of this chapter now suggests a paradoxical quality to that continuity. By juxtaposing the apparently opposed phases of decline and resurgence, we could highlight the continual movement that characterizes the life histories of moral issues. Issues move from one phase to another, refining and reframing their content, re-engaging moral positions and introducing new perspectives, finding new allies, and mobilizing old ones. Although the same issues are part of the policy agenda of Canada and the United States, they continue to be shaped by each country's own demographic pressures, history, and, especially, political institutions. What appears to be the resolution of conflict may not, in fact, be conclusive. How such uncertainty plays out takes us to the following chapter, which looks directly at resolution.

REFERENCES

ABC News/*Washington Post* Poll. 1986. The Roper Center for Public Opinion Research. https://ropercenter-cornell-edu.flagship.luc.edu/CFIDE/cf/action/ipoll/index.cfm.

Adler, Amy. 2006–7. "All Porn All the Time." *N.Y.U. Review of Law & Social Change* 31: 695–710.

Andersen, Robert, and Tina Fetner. 2008. "Cohort Differences in Tolerance of Homosexuality: Attitudinal Change in Canada and the United States, 1981–2000." *Public Opinion Quarterly* 72 (2): 311–30.

Andersen, Travis, and John R. Ellement. 2016. "Supreme Court Orders SJC to Reconsider Stun Gun Ruling." *Boston Globe,* 21 March.

Angus Reid Public Opinion. 2013. "Canadians Have Mixed Feelings on Abortion, but Shun a New Debate." 28 January.

Austen, Ian. 2009. "Gun Control Issue Reveals a Changing Canada." *New York Times*, 7 December.

Boffey, Philip M. 2014. "What Science Says about Marijuana." *New York Times*, 30 July.

Boonstra, Heather D., and Elizabeth Nash. 2014. "A Surge of State Abortion Restrictions Puts Providers – and the Women They Serve – in the Crosshairs." *Guttmacher Policy Review* 17 (1): 9–15.

Camobreco, John F., and Michelle A. Barnello. 2008. "Democratic Responsiveness and Policy Shock: The Case of State Abortion Policy." *State*

Politics & Policy Quarterly 8 (1): 48–65. https://doi.org/10.1177/153244000800800104.

Conger, Kimberly H., and Paul A. Djupe. 2016. "Culture War Counter-mobilization: Gay Rights and Religious Right Groups in the States." *Interest Groups and Advocacy* 5 (3): 278–300. https://doi.org/10.1057/s41309-016-0004-7.

Egan, Patrick J., Nathaniel Persily, and Kevin Wallsten. 2008. "Gay Rights." In *Public Opinion and Constitutional Controversy*, ed. Nathaniel Persily, Jack Citrin, and Patrick J. Egan, 234–66. New York: Oxford University Press. https://doi.org/10.1093/acprof:oso/9780195329414.003.0011.

Elliott, R. Douglas. 2004. "The Canadian Earthquake: Same-Sex Marriage in Canada." *New England Law Journal* 38 (3): 591–620.

Ellis, Margaret E., and Nina Therese Kasniunas. 2011. "Gay Rights: Nature or Nurture?" In *Moral Controversies in American Politics*, 4th ed., ed. Raymond Tatalovich and Byron W. Daynes, 80–109. Armonk, NY: M.E. Sharpe Publishers.

Epstein, Lee, and Joseph F. Kobylka. 1992. *The Supreme Court and Legal Change: Abortion and the Death Penalty*. Chapel Hill: University of North Carolina Press.

Fattah, Ezzat Abdel. 1976. *The Canadian Public and the Death Penalty: A Study of a Social Attitude*. Burnaby, BC: Criminology Department, Simon Fraser University, unpublished report.

Gallup Polls. 2015. "Guns." http://www.gallup.com/poll/1645/Guns.aspx.

Glantz, Aaron. 2011. "Veterans Battle to Regain 'Don't Ask, Don't Tell' Losses." *New York Times*, 30 April.

Globe and Mail. 1982a. "Chretien Walks Out After MPs Stand Firm on Porn Amendment." 16 July.

Globe and Mail. 1982b. "Loose Law on Child Pornography." 6 July.

Globe and Mail. 1987. "Death Penalty Debate: Capital Punishment a Repugnant Act, PM Tells Commons." 23 June.

Globe and Mail. 2000. "Why Restage the Battles? There Is No Compelling Reason to Reopen the Abortion and Death-Penalty Debates." 15 June.

Globe and Mail. 2007. "Ruling Ensures Death Penalty Won't Return, Conference Told." 13 April.

Green, John C. 2011. "The Politics of Marriage and American Party Politics: Evidence from the 2004 US Election." In *Faith, Politics, and Sexual Diversity in Canada and the United States*, ed. David Rayside and Clyde Wilcox, 300–15.Vancouver: UBC Press.

Guelph Mercury. 2012. "Gun Registry Rightfully Gone for Good." 7 December.

Gusfield, Joseph R. 1986. *Symbolic Crusade: Status Politics and the American Temperance Movement*. 2nd ed. Urbana: University of Illinois Press.

Halfmann, Drew. 2011. *Doctors and Demonstrators: How Political Institutions Shape Abortion Law in the United States, Britain, and Canada.* Chicago: University of Chicago Press. https://doi.org/10.7208/chicago/9780226313443.001.0001.

Harris/Decima. 2010. "Majority Opposed to Government's Position on Maternal Health." www.harrisdecima.ca/news/releases/201005/671-majority-opposed-government-s-position-maternal-health.

Harris Survey. 1986. The Roper Center for Public Opinion Research. https://ropercenter-cornell-edu.flagship.luc.edu/CFIDE/cf/action/ipoll/index.cfm.

Hurka, Steffan, Christian Adam, and Cristoph Knill. 2016. "Is Morality Policy Different? Testing Sectoral and Institutional Explanations of Change." *Policy Studies Journal,* forthcoming (early view, https://doi.org/10.1111/psj.12153).

Judicial Confirmation Survey. 2005. The Roper Center for Public Opinion Research. https://ropercenter-cornell-edu.flagship.luc.edu/CFIDE/cf/action/ipoll/index.cfm.

Keller, Michelle, and Allison Yarrow. 2013. "Interactive: The Geography of Abortion Access." *The Daily Beast,* 22 January. http://www.thedailybeast.com/the-geography-of-abortion-access.

Kreitzer, Rebecca J. 2015. "Politics and Morality in State Abortion Policy." *State Politics & Policy Quarterly* 15 (1): 41–66.

Lehman, Mark Warren. 2006. *Affect Change: The Increased Influence of Attitudinal Factors on Canadians' Support for Legal Same-Sex Marriage.* M.A. thesis, Department of Political Science, University of Toronto.

Lilley, Brian. 2011. "Most Canadians Say Death Penalty OK." *Toronto Star,* 25 January.

Lofton, Katie, and Donald P. Haider-Markel. 2007. "The Politics of Same-Sex Marriage versus the Politics of Gay Civil Rights: A Comparison of Public Opinion and State Voting Patterns." In *The Politics of Same-Sex Marriage,* ed. Craig A. Rimmerman and Clyde Wilcox, 313–40. Chicago: University of Chicago Press.

Luks, Samantha, and Michael Salamone. 2008. "Abortion." In *Public Opinion and Constitutional Controversy,* ed. Nathaniel Persily, Jack Citrin, and Patrick J. Egan, 80–101. New York: Oxford University Press.

Lynerd, Benjamin T. 2014. *Republican Theology: The Civil Religion of American Evangelicals.* New York: Oxford University Press.

MacKinnon, Mark. 2001. "Support Rising for Legalizing Marijuana, Poll Finds." *Globe and Mail,* 22 May.

McCarthy, Justin. 2015. "Record-High 60% of Americans Support Same-Sex Marriage." Gallup Poll, 19 May. http://www.gallup.com/poll/183272/record-high-americans-support-sex-marriage.aspx.

Ottawa Citizen. 2006. "Same-sex debate: 'Time to move on.'" 8 December.

Pew News Interest Index Poll. 1996. The Roper Center for Public Opinion Research. https://ropercenter-cornell-edu.flagship.luc.edu/CFIDE/cf/action/ipoll/index.cfm.

Pew Research Center. 2014a. "Changing Attitudes on Gay Marriage." 24 September. http://www.pewforum.org/2014/09/24/graphics-slideshow-changing-attitudes-on-gay-marriage/.

Pew Research Center. 2014b. "Growing Public Support for Gun Rights." 10 December. http://www.people-press.org/2014/12/10/growing-public-support-for-gun-rights/.

Report of the Committee on Sexual Offenses against Children and Youths. 1985. Ottawa: Department of Justice Canada.

Saurette, Paul, and Kelly Gordon. 2015. *The Changing Voice of the Anti-Abortion Movement: The Rise of "Pro-Woman" Rhetoric in Canada and the United States.* Toronto: University of Toronto Press.

Senate Special Committee on Illegal Drugs. 2002. *Cannabis: Our Position for a Canadian Public Policy.* Ottawa: Senate of Canada.

Simpson, Jeffrey. 2010. "The Gun Registry Has Taken On a Moral Hue That Won't Fade." *Globe and Mail,* 8 May.

Staples, Brent. 2014. "The Federal Marijuana Ban Is Rooted in Myth and Xenophobia." *New York Times,* 29 July.

Steel, Brent S., and Mary Ann E. Steger. 2011. "Death Penalty: Just Punishment or Legalized Homicide?" In *Moral Controversies in American Politics,* 4th ed., ed. Raymond Tatalovich and Byron W. Daynes, 45–79. Armonk, NY: M.E. Sharpe Publishers.

Strickland, Ruth Ann. 2011. "Abortion: Pro-Choice versus Pro-Life." In *Moral Controversies in American Politics,* 4th ed., ed. Raymond Tatalovich and Byron W. Daynes, 3–44. Armonk, NY: M.E. Sharpe Publishers.

Thompson, Andrew S. 2008. "Uneasy Abolitionists: Canada, the Death Penalty, and the Importance of International Norms, 1962–2005." *Journal of Canadian Studies / Revue d'Études Canadiennes* 42 (3): 172–92. https://doi.org/10.3138/jcs.42.3.172.

Time/Yankelovich, Skelly & White Poll. 1977. The Roper Center for Public Opinion Research. https://ropercenter-cornell-edu.flagship.luc.edu/CFIDE/cf/action/ipoll/index.cfm.

Wegman, Jesse. 2014. "The Injustice of Marijuana Arrests." *New York Times,* 28 July.

Whittier, Nancy. 2014. "Rethinking Coalitions: Anti-Pornography Feminists, Conservatives, and Relationships between Collaborative Adversarial

Movements." *Social Problems* 61 (2): 175–93. https://doi.org/10.1525/sp.2014.12151.

Young, Leslie. 2014. "Abortion Access Varies Widely across Canada." *Global News*, 26 November. globalnews.ca/news/1694095/abortion-access-varies-widely-across-canada.

Chapter Eight

The Resolution of Moral Conflicts

The Finality of Resolution

Moral conflicts are resolved when they are no longer present on the active policy agenda, the result either of political actions or of failure to bring about change. The latter can occur when social changes make the issue irrelevant, advocates fall short of resources to force change, or opponents have the power to prevent change. Such de facto resolution did not occur for any of the moral conflicts we analyzed. Instead, when there was resolution, it followed from either court decisions or new legislation.

All the moral conflicts we considered were similarly two-sided in Canada and the United States, with each side promoting its position as the morally correct one. Typically, the older position was more restrictive: against abortion, marijuana use, pornography, and same-sex relations. It went along with support for capital punishment and loose control over gun ownership, particularly in the United States in the latter case. The newer, opposing side stood for removal of restrictions on the first set of issues and their imposition on the second. When pornography was reframed as child pornography, however, the newer position became a restrictive one.

The previous chapter, tracing issue decline and resurgence, demonstrated the volatility of our issues. The road to a final resolution could be diverted by an issue's reframing as well as by continuing challenges to one or other side of the issue. The most dramatic illustration of how one resolution could be overturned and an opposing one institutionalized came from the history of prohibition. That history, particularly as it unfolded in the United States, led us to anticipate the turbulent life history of all moral conflicts. The three hypotheses we derived to account for the resolution of prohibition can now be tested for how well they apply more generally. They predict that

- the final resolution will be in the direction of the newer, challenging form of the controversy;
- the final resolution will represent more inclusive and fundamental values; and
- political parties will come to agree on the need for resolution and hence its direction.

Direction of Outcome

The struggle to resolve conflict over prohibition moved in two diametrically opposed positions, from criminalization to repeal. And both resolutions were achieved through the difficult and unusual avenue of constitutional amendments in United States and through relatively less difficult legislative action in Canada. This meant that, at separate periods, there was an authoritative resolution when each side of the moral controversy enjoyed its own period of success. Those outcomes upset the argument of advocacy groups that there is only one morally correct position. Instead, the strength of a position depends more on current conditions and on the political opportunities that open with major social and economic changes than on any intrinsic qualities of right and wrong or good and bad. New conditions and opportunities become stimuli for mobilizing social movements and interest groups to work for their objectives. It was this combination of factors that led prohibition to be successfully reframed as a policy that recognized local and individual preferences and allowed them to be expressed without severe sanctions. We extend that result to anticipate that the challenging view will be the ultimate stage of a moral issue's outcome.

Our expectation that changes in morality policy will abruptly introduce new and distinct adaptations runs counter to more usual expectations about policy change. For example, in the evolutionary perspective presented by Carmines and Stimson (1989: 12), the norm is for issues to change gradually. Yet there can be "cataclysmic adaptations," when dramatic events, including distinctive partisan platforms, produce sharply defined change linked to particular issues (Carmines and Wagner 2006). In that perspective, the content of issues becomes relevant, as it does for Hurka et al. (2016), who demonstrate the link between morality politics and punctuated equilibrium, in which policies on moral issues represent sharp breaks with the more usual and gradual process of change.

Canadian Resolution

In Canada, virtually all issues were resolved in their newer manifestation, as predicted in H_{P16}. Only marijuana remains on the policy agenda, and it is expected to exit through legislation. Legislation was the initial means to resolve conflict over abortion, although the current absence of legislation as a result of court rulings leaves the issue in an ambiguous state. Legislation also resolved capital punishment; gun control; pornography, including the involvement of children; and same-sex relations, including same-sex marriage. Court challenges, when they occurred, served to further support those policy changes.

The road to resolution was undergirded by activists and interests representing countermovements that challenge the old normative order. Currently, only a very small Canadian pro-life movement remains opposed to fully legalized abortions, a testament to the strength of the pro-choice countermovement that first began contesting restrictions on abortions. An association of chiefs of police is virtually the only group that now lobbies in favor of capital punishment compared to the multi-interest countermovement that coalesced around its abolition. The Canadian Supreme Court upheld anti-pornography laws that were championed by a feminist countermovement that persuaded the court that substantive "harm" to women would result from violent and degrading pornography. Except for the few, isolated voices that defend child pornography on free speech grounds, no countermovement has emerged against government suppression of child pornography. Growing demands for LGBT rights by a broad-based countermovement eroded and ultimately ended the traditional stereotypes of homosexuals as deviants and child molesters (Adam 1987; Marcus 1992), so that today the hard-core opposition to gay rights comes primarily from Protestant fundamentalists and social conservatives, of which there are many fewer in Canada than in the United States (Bean 2014; see also chapter 4).

The two remaining issues are associated with greater ambiguity, whether in emergence or outcome. Gun control in Canada was, from its outset, associated with the dominance of a relatively restrictive position. It is not surprising, then, that today the Coalition for Gun Control is much larger and more diverse than the countermovement represented by sportsmen and gun owners. Repeal of the long-gun registry, severely undermined by its high cost, has been one of the rare achievements of the pro-gun countermovement in Canada. Marijuana has, in contrast, been dominated by a restrictive perspective that emphasizes legal enforcement. Although the challenge mounted by those coming from the direction of public health eventually achieved a degree of policy success with medicalized marijuana, contention continues. It does so as a robust countermovement favors decriminalization of marijuana possession.

US Contention

In the United States, steps to remove barriers to legal abortion took place through the courts, but changes introduced continue to be challenged through the courts and through legislation at the state level. We could interpret the current situation then as either resolved in the new direction or not. But given the continuity of contention, we assign it a "no." Capital punishment appeared to be resolved in favor of its abolition through court rulings, but that proved to be unstable when challenges reached a Supreme Court that took more conservative positions and individual states continued to follow their own policies. Gun control remains contentious, subject to local and state legislation on both sides of the conflict and to judicial decisions that vary with the political leanings of the courts. Marijuana has declined as a subject of intense moral debate at a time when advocates successfully argue against its unfair penalization of particular demographic groups and for its medicinal properties. Yet it remains unresolved nationally, where marijuana is included among the most proscribed Schedule 1 drugs subject to the severest penalties under the federal Controlled Substances Act of 1970, although a small group of states permit its use for medicinal or even recreational purposes. Pornography, particularly when involving children, has been successfully resolved nationally through both legislation and court rulings. Same-sex relations remain contentious even as according those relations full protection has continued, most recently, with recognition of same-sex marriage. But this has occurred primarily through court interpretations affecting individual states. Even in light of the 2015 Supreme Court ruling in *Obergefell v. Hodges* (2015) that "nationalized" same-sex marriage, conflict remains (Haider-Markel and Taylor 2016).

In Canada, we argued that countermovements played a critical role in propelling most issues in a new direction. In the United States, this was true only for marijuana, pornography, particularly in its latest manifestation opposing child pornography, and same-sex relations, although with varying degrees of resolution. In contrast, social norms undergirding the death penalty, pro-life advocacy, and gun rights have not been overtaken by countermovements with greater legitimacy. This is one compelling explanation for why those specific moral conflicts continue in the United States. For example, a case can be made that the main reason why the United States has not adopted strict nation-wide gun controls is due to determined opposition from the National Rifle Association, aided by a pervasive "gun culture" throughout rural America, and coupled with the fact that anti-gun interests have been unable to organize an effective countermovement (Goss 2006). Compared to Canada, gun control groups have had little impact on policy (Fleming 2012: 5).

Canada, in a sense, is similar to the United States in displaying continuing contention after the introduction of authoritative actions. But, in contrast to conditions in the latter country, Canadian judicial or legislative decisions have not been subsequently and successfully limited in any major ways. Moreover, they remain anchored in the national domain. In the United States, in contrast, individual states are the arenas in which acceptance of new morality policies are more likely. This result is in keeping with the differences between the two countries anticipated in chapter 4: that moral issues will be more contentious in the United States (H_{C1}) and that individual states, as the likely venue for contention (H_{C7}), will hinder a national resolution (H_{C8}). These national differences are also reflected in each country's support for H_{P16}, where, in the United States, no conflict except over pornography, and possibly some aspects of same-sex relations, has been unequivocally resolved to favor the challenge to the original side of the controversy. Canada, in contrast, has resolved all but marijuana in the newer direction.

Dominant Values

By definition, morality politics deals with values that define whose interests and which conceptions of what is right or good should be dominant in the society. Prohibition illustrated the transformation of this dominance when legitimacy shifted from policies representing the sectarian values of Protestant evangelism to ones more broadly inclusive of a diverse society. Although policies were diametrically opposed, they were still rooted in similar conceptions of a political system based on the rule of law, representative of its population, and guided by fundamental values about democratic governance. In the United States, those values were incorporated into its constitution and, in particular, into the amendments codified as the Bill of Rights. In Canada at that time, conceptions of democratic governance were initially taken over from practices followed by the British parliament along with the written directives in the British North America Act (BNAA) that served as its written constitution. What had changed regarding prohibition was how those values were interpreted, for all the reasons we documented in chapter 2. Values about legitimate governance are, to be sure, very general and, while constitutive documents are fundamental to the affirmation of dominant societal values, they neither encompass all the values relevant to moral conflicts nor are themselves entirely immutable. In societies as diverse as Canada and the United States, value differences are associated with particular interests and groups and are subject to competition. Which values dominate at a given time will be affected by changes in the social and political environment and in the composition of legislative and judicial bodies that interpret and enforce them.

The "rights revolution" that took place in the United States with the civil rights movement (see chapter 1) began a series of critical challenges to the prevailing moral climate through the courts. Canada came to participate in a similar phenomenon when it patriated the BNAA (British North America Act, Canada's original constitution) and rewrote it to contain a Charter of Rights and Freedoms in 1982. Now fundamental issues of rights were formally incorporated. Both countries could subsequently be described to have written documents that gave legitimacy to a set of dominant values. And it is these that we predict will be invoked to buttress new directions in morality policies.

The Charter of Rights and Freedoms has been used as justification for change in the direction of less punitive or restrictive policies applied to abortion, capital punishment, and same-sex relations. With the exception of marijuana and pornography, the Bill of Rights has been central to US Supreme Court rulings in all other issues. Such rulings extended rights to abortion and same-sex relations, including marriage, and imposed restrictions on capital punishment. The Second Amendment has been at the core of arguments on gun control, yet, because of the divergent interpretations it continues to evoke, without establishing a single, definitive position. Although pornography restrictions were eased through judicial rulings, pornography itself is not a protected right under either the Bill of Rights or the Charter of Rights and Freedom.

The policy changes we examine have proceeded without consistent support from what might otherwise be presumed to be an important indicator of values – those expressed in public opinion polls. This is true even after policy enactments, when public approval could be expected to rise. For example, public opinion did not coalesce in support of the abolition of capital punishment in Canada or of elective abortion in the United States. And, on the contrary side, gun control in the United States remains at odds with public opinion that favors more restrictions. Whatever the values found among the public at large, these do not appear to have been crucial to resolving moral conflicts.

Most important for establishing the legitimacy of new policy positions are judicial rulings that confirm the dominance of values incorporated into foundational statements about the nature of government and society. What is more significant to the final outcome, however, is whether judicial confirmation of dominant values is translated into legislative action (Schultz 1998). This is demonstrated in both countries by how marijuana has been treated. The Canadian Supreme Court held that reform must be enacted through legislation, given that criminalizing the simple possession of marijuana was not a violation of the Charter of Rights and Freedoms. The United States Supreme Court has upheld the reach of existing federal law in the Controlled Substances Act of 1970 to include even those states now permitting the medical use of marijuana.

Based on his analysis of abortion, school desegregation, and women's rights, Rosenberg (2008) argues that the high court cannot achieve social change in such complex and highly contested policy areas without the addition of legislation. We expand his argument by extrapolating from the judicial compliance literature, which argues that non-compliance is easier to recognize when there are specific, clear rulings rather than vague, unclear ones (Wasby 1970; Baum 1976; Songer and Sheehan 1990; Kapiszewski and Taylor 2013). By extension, one reason US Supreme Court edicts do not necessarily resolve moral conflict is that a ruling based on loosely constructed jurisprudence can invite policy variations among the states and provoke further litigation by opposition groups and movements. The difference between the death of prohibition after 1933 and continuing moral conflicts over gun control and abortion is that the former debate was resolved when an authoritative policy was adopted and opponents were left with no alternative policy venues to exploit. But just as fundamentally, the values invoked in ending prohibition had become the dominant ones. Abortion's reliance on the controversial woman's right to privacy and gun control's continuing entanglement with the Second Amendment both suggest more equivocal perspectives on dominant values.

Rosenberg's (2008) observations have application to Canada as well. For example, if we contrast the death of the abortion conflict after the final resolution of the *Morgentaler* case with the trajectory of controversy on abortion that followed *Roe v. Wade*, we note that the Canadian Supreme Court upheld clinic-based abortions in terms of healthcare, where there is a virtual consensus in support of universal health coverage, thus avoiding a more contentious extension of rights (Brodie 1994). In addition, the court appealed to another dominant value in deferring to parliamentary supremacy by inviting Parliament to re-codify a new law on abortion (Glendon 1989).

Overall, both countries are alike in the divided support they demonstrate for H_{P17}, that "resolution will be effective when it symbolizes commitment to inclusive and fundamental values." Supportive findings were similarly present for abortion and same-sex relations. Capital punishment confirmed expectations most clearly in Canada, but was more ambiguous in the United States. In the latter, the Supreme Court has imposed restrictions on capital punishment at the same time as it has upheld the death penalty as not violating the cruel and unusual clause of the Eighth Amendment. The remaining three issues were again similar in the two countries by their lack of support for the hypothesis.

Consensus across Parties

The history of prohibition revealed changing patterns of partisan involvement. Initially, the major parties in both countries were reluctant to become entangled in the controversy over alcohol use. But under pressure from social movements and with justification provided by wartime conditions, prohibition was enacted with considerable bipartisan support. Then, particularly in the United States, once prohibition was the law, it became the responsibility of the majority party. New pressures for repeal arose at a time of severe economic crisis. The latter produced sharp partisan divisions, which were carried over to repeal. Yet, in the end, there was considerable support for repeal from both parties in the United States as well as in Canada. That process leads us to anticipate that a final resolution of moral conflicts will be accompanied by the muting of party differences.

Unlike with prohibition, of the contemporary issues we consider, the role of partisanship in their resolution is also affected by whether or not parties are responding to prior judicial rulings. However, like the repeal of prohibition, resolution is also affected by whether or not a single party assumes leadership for its achievement (H_{P18}).

In Canada, the governing Liberal Party took the lead in legalizing abortion reform in 1969 and in abolishing capital punishment in 1976. The reluctance (more precisely, opposition) of Prime Minister Mulroney's Conservative government to reinstate capital punishment by means of a free vote in 1987, and its failure to recodify a law on abortion in 1988, effectively created a bipartisan accommodation on both those issues. Neither major party chose to reopen debate over abortion and both Liberal and Conservative platforms in 2008 pledged not to revisit this issue.

The Liberals under Prime Minister Chrétien enacted comprehensive gun control legislation in 1995, including the institution of a long-gun registry. The latter became a source of polarization between the major Canadian political parties. The contentiousness of the issue extended to significant sectors of the population (see chapter 7) and led to its repeal in 2012 by Stephen Harper's Conservative government. Widespread disagreement over the registry was then a factor in modifying the Liberals' views, expressed most recently by their leader, Justin Trudeau, who opposes renewing long-gun registration. The outcome is thus a resolution of the latest gun control controversy.

Although the Liberals tabled measures in 2002 and 2004 to decriminalize possession of small amounts of marijuana, legislation never passed before national elections brought to power a minority Conservative government that abandoned reform. But the 2015 election of a Liberal government has brought with it the call from Prime Minister Justin Trudeau for the legalization of marijuana. If bipartisan resistance to marijuana reform characterized Canada's post-war history (Fischer et al. 2003), today the Liberals and Conservatives may continue to remain polarized on the question of legalizing marijuana.

Political credit for codifying a more contemporary standard for adult pornography goes to the Conservatives following their victory in the 1957 elections, when Justice Minister E. Davie Fulton tabled Bill C-58 to amend the Criminal Code. Conflict over adult pornography then was relegated mainly to the judicial arena. When the policy debate shifted to child pornography, agreement on the need for restrictions cut across all the key Canadian parties. Legislation to combat child pornography was tabled in the House of Commons, first by the Conservatives and later by the Liberals, and, at various times, both major parties and the NDP had platform planks condemning child pornography.

Same-sex relations were legalized when the Liberal government revised the Criminal Code in 1969. But when the issue was reframed to emphasize same-sex marriage, parties were more averse to assuming leadership. Only judicial rulings forced the Liberal government in 2005 to codify the law on same-sex marriage, effectively removing the issue from partisan debate.

Evidence from the Canadian cases indicates that resolution of abortion, capital punishment, gun control, and same-sex relations was led primarily by Liberal governments. A Conservative government ensured initial reform in the legal contours of pornography, while child pornography quickly gained support for restrictions across all parties. The stability of those resolutions has been assured by a subsequent degree of consensus across party lines sufficient to remove them from the policy agenda, supporting H_{P18}. The only issue outstanding is the regulation of marijuana, where there also remains division between the two major parties.

Compared to Canadian parties, US ones have politicized moral conflicts much more than they have helped to resolve them. The most obvious case is abortion, where Republican and Democratic platforms have long staked out opposing positions (see appendix 2). This polarization helps explain why abortion persists as a volatile moral conflict in the United States.

On capital punishment and gun control, the Republicans have been straightforward in their policy stands: in favor of the former and opposed to the latter. Although the Democrats' sympathies appear to be in opposing directions, they have shied away from taking clear-cut policy positions. The result is to leave the Republicans as leaders of the anti-reform positions without creating a countervailing oppositional force strong enough to disrupt what functions as a kind of weak partisan consensus. But this kind of consensus does not support the hypothesized expectation since it did not contribute to resolution.

Although the "war on drugs" was inaugurated by President Nixon and reignited by Ronald Reagan, during the 1980s its intensity was fueled by a partisan competition over who could be tougher on drug enforcement (Jensen et al. 1991: 659–60). That competition could be used to support Meier's (1994) assessment that drug policy in the United States is one-sided, leading to a bipartisan consensus so powerful that marijuana reforms could not establish a foothold on the policy agenda of the national government. Yet we are inclined to see a lack of partisan agreement given the strength of arguments reframing marijuana that have made it a two-sided issue and the greater attachment of Democrats to reform of drug laws, even though that attachment has lacked clear party leadership.

From the period that begins our assessment of moral conflicts, Democrats were in favor of easing restrictions on pornography while Republicans were opposed. Evidence comes from the 1969 commission, appointed by President Lyndon Johnson, which advocated removal of constraints. Its recommendations were rejected by his Republican successor, Richard Nixon, while recommendations of the 1985 commission appointed by President Ronald Reagan were more restrictive. Although, today, pornography involving adults is no longer a contentious issue, its resolution was achieved through judicial intervention, not party involvement. New restrictions on child pornography, however, have resolved that conflict through bipartisan consensus.

Same-sex relations produced more mixed messages. In their earliest expression, it was the Democrats who were most overt in defending anti-discrimination rights while Republicans were largely silent. Opposition to gays and lesbians in the military garnered bipartisan support, as did the Defense of Marriage Act of 1996, both signed by Democratic president Bill Clinton. But polarization re-emerged with the struggle for same-sex marriage. It was opposed by the Republicans while supported in the Democratic platform in 2008 and 2012. (See appendix 2 and chapter 6.)

Partisan policies on moral conflicts play a major role in the latter's eventual resolution. In Canada, it has been mainly under the leadership of the Liberals that reforms have been enacted, stimulating, in turn, enough cross-party consensus to lead issues to exit the policy agenda. The Liberals did not provide decisive leadership on same-sex marriage, but assumed responsibility only after judicial rulings. At the time of writing, only marijuana remains unresolved, a result of what had been an absence of strong party leadership in advocating change and continuing partisan opposition to that change.

In contrast to Canada, where only marijuana remains unresolved and lacking in cross-party consensus, the United States has experienced resolution solely on the issue of child pornography, achieved through bipartisan consensus. The two US parties take different stands most sharply on abortion rights and, to a lesser degree, on same-sex marriage, but they also disagree on capital punishment, gun control, and earlier controversies over pornography. Sources of disagreement persist even as the Democrats support reform, where they are constrained by what they feel to be intractable barriers to change that reduce their willingness to play a leading role. (See chapter 6.) Along with the decriminalization and legalization of marijuana, capital punishment and gun control remain potent controversies because there is an implicit assessment that they are too hot for the Democrats to touch.

Resolution Is Difficult

Prominent divisions remain between the two countries over the fate of the six moral issues. Canada has been able to achieve resolution for all but one, and that is likely to be resolved relatively soon. Although abortion remains an issue without formal legislative support, and there are signs of continuing or even strengthening opposition to current practices, it is unlikely that any reopening of the issue will bring a return to old restrictions (Saurette and Gordon 2014). In the United States, however, all issues except for pornography remain mired in conflict.

National differences in outcomes are partially explained by the ways in which anticipated pathways to resolution played out. That does not mean, however, that lack of a perfect fit with expectations based on the experiences of prohibition can be attributed to the fact that prohibition had its own unique properties and arose in a particular historical period. Canada demonstrated, in support of H_{P16}, that the more recent perspectives on moral issues are the ones that have come to dominate in all cases but one. Those positions have been legitimated by their connection with foundational statements about the nature of both societies as predicted in H_{P17} for abortion, capital punishment, and same-sex relations.

When one of the major political parties takes the lead and passes legislation, resolution typically follows, anticipated in H_{P18}, but only in Canada. There, most policies were adopted under Liberal governments and then continued by Conservative ones. An exception was gun control, where Liberal efforts to impose a long-gun registry produced an ineffective policy that was then withdrawn, with the Liberals acquiescing to criticisms from their opponents. A second exception was marijuana, where the Liberals had been hesitant in their approach to changing policy, a position likely to alter under the latest administration.

In the United States, the major parties remain divided on all the issues analyzed, regardless of judicial rulings. Only pornography has left the policy agenda, first when access to adult pornography was de-regulated and liberalized by judicial actions and later when a bipartisan legislative consensus criminalized the use of child pornography. These findings from the two countries confirm the importance we attach to the role of political parties in achieving policy resolutions.

These differences in policy outcomes emphasize attributes of the two countries that serve to foster them. Canada shows evidence of support for the three hypothesized pathways to resolution affecting the six issues in fourteen of the possible eighteen instances, or 78 percent. But the United States was blocked from finding resolution in all but three instances (17 percent of possibilities).

Chapter 4 presented nine hypotheses accounting for why moral issues would have different national outcomes. Out of those, we found support for all but one. Supportive findings were associated with the following:

- Demographic characteristics will be associated with more contention in the United States (H_{C1}).
- There will be a greater role for the executive in Canada, whether in the person of the prime minister or the justice minister (H_{C3}).
- Congress will be the more prominent legislative body (H_{C4}).
- There will be greater partisan conflict in the United States (H_{C5}).
- Issues are more likely to be owned by one party in the United States (H_{C6}).
- Individual states are the more likely venue for continuing contention (H_{C7}).
- Canada provides more opportunities for nationalizing moral conflicts (H_{C8}).
- Courts remain more important actors in policy disputes in the United States (H_{C9}).

At least with respect to resolution, NGOs were no more important in the United States than they were in Canada. In other words, our findings provide powerful support for expectations that, despite their many similarities and despite their experience in facing similar moral conflicts, Canada and the United States remain distinct in their ability to resolve those conflicts.

What is still left to examine is a fuller understanding of why these variations exist. We turn in the final chapter to do this by seeing how the phases through which issues evolve work, in interaction with national differences, to further or impede their resolution.

REFERENCES

Adam, Barry. 1987. *The Rise of a Gay and Lesbian Movement*. Boston: Twayne Publishers.

Baum, Lawrence. 1976. "Implementation of Judicial Decisions." *American Politics Research* 4 (1): 86–114. https://doi.org/10.1177/1532673X7600400104.

Bean, Lydia. 2014. *The Politics of Evangelical Identity*. Princeton: Princeton University Press. https://doi.org/10.1515/9781400852611.

Brodie, Janine. 1994. "Health versus Rights: Comparative Perspectives on Abortion Policy in Canada and the United States." In *Power and Decision: The Social Control of Reproduction*, ed. Gita Sen and Rachel C. Snow, 123–46. Boston: Harvard School of Public Health.

Carmines, Edward G., and James A. Stimson. 1989. *Issue Evolution: Race and the Transformation of American Politics*. Princeton: Princeton University Press.

Carmines, Edward G., and Michael W. Wagner. 2006. "Political Issues and Party Alignments: Assessing the Issue Evolution Perspective." *Annual Review of Political Science* 9 (1): 67–81. https://doi.org/10.1146/annurev.polisci.9.091905.180706.

Fischer, Benedikt, Kari Ala-Leppilampi, Eric Single, and Amanda Robins. 2003. "Cannabis Law Reform in Canada: Is the 'Saga of Promise, Hesitation and Retreat' Coming to an End?" *Canadian Journal of Criminology and Criminal Justice* 45 (3): 265–98. https://doi.org/10.3138/cjccj.45.3.265.

Fleming, Anthony K. 2012. *Gun Policy in the United States and Canada*. New York: Continuum International Publishing Group.

Glendon, Mary Ann. 1989. "A beau mentir qui vient de loin: The 1988 Canadian Abortion Decision in Comparative Perspective." *Northwestern University Law Review* 83 (3): 569–91.

Goss, Kristin A. 2006. *Disarmed: The Missing Movement for Gun Control in America*. Princeton: Princeton University Press.

Haider-Markel, Donald P., and Jami Taylor. 2016. "Two Steps Forward, One Step Back: The Slow Forward Dance of LGBT Rights in America." In *After Marriage Equality: The Future of LGBT Rights*, ed. Carlos A. Ball,

42–72. New York: New York University Press. https://doi.org/10.18574/nyu/9781479883080.003.0003.

Hurka, Steffen, Christian Adam, and Christoph Knill. 2016. "Is Morality Policy Different? Testing Sectoral and Institutional Explanations of Policy Change." *Policy Studies Journal*, forthcoming (early view, https://doi.org/10.1111/psj.12153).

Jensen, Eric L., Jurg Gerber, and Ginna M. Babcock. 1991. "The New War on Drugs: Grass Roots Movement or Political Construction?" *Journal of Drug Issues* 21 (3): 651–67.

Kapiszewski, Diana, and Matthew M. Taylor. 2013. "Compliance: Conceptualizing, Measuring, and Explaining Adherence to Judicial Rulings." *Law & Social Inquiry* 38 (4): 803–35. https://doi.org/10.1111/j.1747-4469.2012.01320.x.

Marcus, Eric. 1992. *Making History: The Struggle for Gay and Lesbian Equal Rights*. New York: HarperCollins Publishers.

Meier, Kenneth J. 1994. *The Politics of Sin: Drugs, Alcohol, and Public Policy*. Armonk, NY: M.E. Sharpe.

Rosenberg, Gerald N. 2008. *The Hollow Hope: Can Courts Bring about Social Change?* 2nd ed. Chicago: University of Chicago Press. https://doi.org/10.7208/chicago/9780226726687.001.0001.

Saurette, Paul, and Kelly Gordon. 2014. "Bring on Canada's New Abortion Debate." *Toronto Star*, 20 May. https://www.thestar.com/opinion/commentary/2014/05/20/bring_on_canadas_new_abortion_debate.html.

Schultz, David A., ed. 1998. *Leveraging the Law: Using Courts to Achieve Social Change*. New York: Peter Lang.

Songer, Donald R., and Reginald S. Sheehan. 1990. "Supreme Court Impact on Compliance and Outcomes: Miranda and New York Times in the United States Courts of Appeals." *Western Political Quarterly* 43 (2): 297–316. https://doi.org/10.2307/448368.

Wasby, Stephen. 1970. *The Impact of the United States Supreme Court: Some Perspectives*. Homewood, IL: Dorsey Press.

Chapter Nine

The Phases of Moral Conflicts

Phases and Outcomes

We ended the previous chapter under the heading "Resolution is difficult." Of the six contemporary moral conflicts we consider, only pornography and, for the most part, same-sex relations have found a policy solution in the United States. In Canada, marijuana alone is unresolved. Chapter 8 emphasized how these national differences were tied to social, cultural, and political factors specific to each country, either impeding or fostering resolution. At the same time, even Canada still shows signs of underlying political contention. For example, the legalization of abortion remains unattached to legislation and the abolition of capital punishment coexists with the absence of support from a majority of the population. While we can conclude that there are powerful effects from the national setting in which moral conflicts take place, that does not take account of the history and development of the issues themselves. For that, we must go back to where we began, to our original focus on issue phases.

We adopted a focus on phases in order to uncover the processes through which issues evolve, not to write a history of specific issues but to discern commonalities in issue development. We built our phase model on the case of prohibition for the very reason that it had a history that had been resolved. In selecting prohibition as our starting point, we recognized that we would remain constrained by the possibly unique parameters of that particular issue as it occurred in a specific period of history. Yet convinced that there was still much to be learned from the history of prohibition, we moved on, deriving eighteen hypotheses from its experiences to predict the pathways of contemporary moral issues. A simple tally of whether those hypotheses were supported or not for all six contemporary issues found, out of a total of 108 possible effects, that 62 percent were supported in the United States and 73 percent in Canada. That is, in the majority of cases, the experiences of prohibition did anticipate the history of contemporary moral issues. But the results were not a perfect fit. A perfect fit between the trajectory of prohibition and that of another issue should mean that the latter followed the same steps to resolution. We know, however, that complete resolution is still elusive for many issues. That leads us to ask where, within every phase, at the level of each of the aspects hypothesized to affect issue outcomes, impediments to resolution occur. We are left to tease apart specific events and processes, fixed in historical time, from those constrained by unique national environments. Only then can we begin to suggest possible explanations for the remaining unanticipated relationships.

Emergence

Based on the experiences of prohibition, we began by anticipating that the emergence of two-sided moral conflicts would be stimulated by five factors: major environmental changes, triggering events, collective actors who respond to challenges by defending the original definition of the correct moral stance, the social status of those actors, and the organizational resources they can draw on. For all six issues in both countries, expectations were upheld for all but two processes – the existence of triggers and appearance of responders that challenge the status quo.

As we recall from chapter 2, triggers were not a factor in the emergence of prohibition. We therefore formulated H_{P2} in a relatively tentative way, acknowledging that, while triggers may occur, they are not essential to the emergence of moral conflicts. Underlying this formulation was the acknowledgment of two opposing positions. The public policy literature posits the importance of triggers to issue emergence; the social movement literature argues that the presence of a trigger has little subsequent impact on the fate of an issue unless it promotes the mobilization of sustained support or opposition. We found triggers only for capital punishment and gun control in Canada, both of which had a resolution. In the United States, triggering events were more frequent, affecting not only capital punishment and gun control but also abortion and same-sex relations, of which only the latter approaches

resolution. Of the opposing positions taken in the literature, our findings lean toward those taken by social movement scholars, that triggers,
in themselves, are weak predictors of eventual outcome. If the results in
the United States are to be taken seriously, triggers may, in fact, be an
impediment to resolution. That is not the case in Canada, however,
where the one issue still unresolved, that of marijuana, lacked a trigger,
and where a conclusion of low relevance would be more appropriate.

Activities by organized groups dedicated to the suppression of
alcohol use were critical to the emergence of prohibition and led us
to anticipate in H_{P3} that comparable groups would play similar roles
in defining issues' moral content. That was confirmed for all issues in
the United States, but not for marijuana and pornography in Canada.
In those two cases, the absence of organized pressure draws attention
to how Canada's civil society differs from that of the United States,
hypothesized in H_{C2} that "NGOs in the United States will have greater
impact on the life history of moral issues." We make the assumption
here that national differences can be even more powerful than those
arising from this particular phase.

Altogether, hypotheses that the emergence of moral conflicts is stimulated by major societal changes, the status of challengers to the status
quo, and the resources available to them are upheld regardless of issue
content or national setting. There is some potential for triggering events
to be an impediment to future resolution. Canada also alerts us to the
potentially special qualities of marijuana and pornography to affect
their outcomes, impeding resolution for the first and facilitating it for
the second.

Establishment

The establishment of prohibition on the political agenda took place
through five processes. Three of these – continued pressure by outside
groups (H_{P6}), prior legitimation of the issue's political relevance (H_{P7}),
and willingness of at least one political party to take a position (H_{P8}) –
were supported for all contemporary issues in both countries. We conclude that these processes define important pathways to establishment
that are generally relevant, regardless of the content of the issue or the
national setting.

H_{P9} anticipated that inside-access agenda setting available to authoritative leaders in any of the three branches of government would speed
the establishment of an issue. In Canada, political leaders played this

role for all issues except gun control. In the United States, it was the courts that led the way to establishment, but only for abortion and pornography. We may deduce from this finding not only that the performance of authoritative leadership is critical to eventual resolution but that actions specific to political leaders make the most difference.

Finally, the expectation that atypical means would be used to establish moral conflicts (H_{P10}) found no support in the United States, but did describe Canadian political behavior. Private member bills were tabled on abortion, capital punishment, pornography, and same-sex relations, and the Commons also relied on free votes (on abortion, capital punishment, and same-sex relations) unencumbered by firm adherence to party discipline – a deviation from normal parliamentary procedure. Loosening the link between moral issues and political parties then became a means for lowering the level of contention and easing the path to resolution. In the United States, paradoxically, the absence of tightly disciplined parties forecloses the ability to ease partisan divisions without, at the same time, setting up new bipartisan ones that could exacerbate the ability of moral issues to foster conflict.

We conclude that a principal long-term effect of the process of establishment stems from avenues used to achieve it, exemplified only in Canada. There, reliance on political leadership at this early phase of moral conflict as well as a willingness to selectively reduce the normal impact of partisanship opens pathways for subsequent resolution. The effectiveness of these moves extends across issues.

Decline

Once an issue becomes established on the policy agenda, it may still decline in salience. In Canada, we found evidence of decline for all issues except marijuana. In the United States, although there was declining or erratic attention from the media, all issues except pornography retained a place on party platforms. Given US resistance to decline, the hypotheses derived from the history of prohibition's decline are unlikely to have much application there.

We hypothesized that decline could occur under three circumstances. In the first, H_{P11}, decline comes about through a changing environment that makes one side of the issue less defensible. This was the case for all issues in Canada, but not for gun control, marijuana, and pornography in the United States. In that country, organized resistance to change kept those issues from losing salience, another illustration of H_{C1} that "the United States will display more conflict over moral issues than will Canada."

A second source of decline was associated with unacceptably high costs of policy enforcement, an important factor contributing to the eventual demise of prohibition and summarized in H_{P12}. Yet such costs have been relevant only to declining salience for marijuana in both countries, gun control in Canada, and same-sex relations in the United States. In chapter 1, we had been dubious about the relevance of costs to the fate of moral issues, since intrinsic to them were judgments of good and bad and right or wrong, judgments that seemed antithetical to mundane considerations of cost. But, in chapter 2, the experiences of prohibition persuaded us that costs, whether financial, social, or political, could be an important criterion in how politicians, interest groups, and the public evaluated moral issues and led us to offer cost as an expected factor affecting issue outcome. At the same time, Hurka et al. (2016) argue that factors of cost diminish the strictly moral quality of an issue, turning it into a latent rather than a manifest morality policy. They use drug policy as just such a latent issue. The consequences of latency are then expected to be an eased path to formulating morality policies, exactly the opposite of what we find in the case of marijuana. Even if cost was infrequently involved in why our issues declined in salience, it still remains relevant, although in opposing ways, facilitating the decline of gun control in Canada and same-sex relations in the United States but impeding the resolution of marijuana in both countries.

The final source of decline in prohibition was associated with the mobilization of countermovements, able to argue that their positions better represented the core values of the society, summarized in H_{P13}. However, we found no instances of countermovements contributing to the decline of contemporary issues. In Canada, decline was already underway as a result of the prior process of establishment, particularly in the form of authoritative leadership, making countermovement activities redundant. In the United States, in contrast, we are presented with the continuing potency of issues once established and their resistance to contrary pressures.

In summary, decline in issue salience, no matter how uneven, is an important step affecting the final outcome of moral conflict. However, in the United States, the force of old arguments about abortion, capital punishment, and same-sex relations held back decline but costs did move same-sex relations toward resolution. In both countries, costs had a prominent place in the decline of marijuana but without speeding its resolution. We admit, then, to not having come up with a full account of the dynamics of decline.

Resurgence

Although decline in salience presents a more modest phase in the life history of moral issues in the United States than it does in Canada, both countries experienced periods of resurgence. That resurgence is a factor in sustaining conflict and impeding resolution. As stated in H_{P14}, "Resurgence takes place when the problems initially addressed become more acute." We used the reframing of an issue as evidence of such resurgence, affecting abortion, gun control, marijuana, pornography, and same-sex relations in both countries. For the first three of these issues, reframing was presented as an affirmation that the underlying conditions had worsened, with basically no country differences. In the case of gun control and pornography, advocacy of greater control or restrictions on behavior dominated. Lessened restrictions were seen as the solution to the problems caused by current laws governing marijuana, while same-sex relations benefited from appeals to enhanced rights. Yet claims for the greater legitimacy of one side of the controversy do not seem to have had much impact in the case of marijuana or pornography in either country.

The resurgent phase leaves some puzzling gaps in explaining how it plays a part in any final resolution. We found both countries to be similar in whether issues were reframed as more acute and in which issues benefited from appeals to greater legitimacy. We also know that two issues had similar outcomes on both sides of the border: marijuana, which remains unresolved and pornography, which is resolved. This suggests that the content of an issue, at least in the resurgent phase, is what matters. Before examining that possibility, we look first at the final phase of resolution.

Resolution

After going through a turbulent history, moral conflicts may come to rest. We offered three hypotheses about the likely pathway for this to happen. The first, H_{P16}, predicted that the outcome would be in the direction of the newest conception of the issue. It was upheld for all issues that were resolved, that is, pornography and same-sex relations in the United States and all issues except marijuana in Canada.

H_{P17} predicted that resolution would be found in policies that affirmed more inclusive and dominant values. This has occurred for abortion, capital punishment, and same-sex relations in both countries. Although conflict over abortion and capital punishment are still not fully settled in the United States, the fact that newer policies can be represented as validation of basic societal values signals a positive sign for eventual resolution. The remaining three issues, of which all but marijuana are resolved in Canada and none in the United States, indicate barriers with differing degrees of openness to change in each country.

Finally, we predicted in H_{P18} that resolution would be enabled by partisan consensus. Lack of such consensus has held back change in policy only on marijuana in Canada. In the United States, bipartisan agreement allowed pornography to be resolved. Although we see signs of resolution over same-sex relations, that has still not brought US parties into agreement, although that likelihood appears possible. The importance we attach to partisanship in resolution was preceded by the role we assigned to parties in the establishment phase.

In this final phase, we identified the most direct links with resolution and the final hurdles to be overcome. Earlier impediments to resolution were found in the passage through all phases, made more difficult to overcome in the United States by interaction with its social and political character. This is not because Canadians are any less prone to moral transgressions or less inclined to rail against them, as historian Martel (2014) demonstrates from Canada's earliest beginnings. Nor is Canada any less likely than the United States to politicize moral issues. It is rather that the two neighboring countries began their search for nationhood under different circumstances that were then imprinted in their national narratives. Most critically, they began by adopting different institutions of governance that continue to shape how they respond to moral conflicts.

Insights from Two Issues

Two issues in both countries stand out for their contrasting outcomes – marijuana, which remains unsettled, and pornography, which was resolved. A closer examination of the phases through which these issues developed holds out the promise of adding further explanation as to why they arrived at their current status.

Comparing the initial establishment of opposition to restrictions on marijuana and pornography in chapter 5, we noted that both were similar in emerging without the help of triggering events in either country. Although we speculated earlier as to whether triggers could eventually impede resolution, the finding that the lack of trigger contributed to two opposing outcomes lends support to those who remain dismissive of the general relevance of triggers.

A second factor relevant to emergence involved the presence of challenging groups, found for all issues in the United States but not for marijuana or pornography in Canada. In other words, the actions of challengers in the United States did not differentiate between the two issues any more than did their absence in Canada. We are led to conclude that, at least with regard to emergence, we have not found why the issues had different outcomes.

Two of the five processes of establishment analyzed in chapter 6 differentiate pornography from marijuana. One, in the United States, relates to the initiatives of authoritative leaders. Pornography reform was established through inside-access, where authoritative actors – the courts in the United States and the government's introduction of legal measures in Canada – prevailed. However, efforts to impose such authoritative measures with regard to marijuana have been relatively ineffective, especially when compared to the greater role played by group pressures. The absence of such leadership in the case of marijuana and its presence for pornography is an important indicator of why the two issues remain different in their outcomes.

The second difference, in Canada, relates to the use of atypical means of establishment. Pornography reform was aided in its establishment through the introduction of private member bills which downplayed, to an extent, the contentiousness associated with partisan divisions. Unsuccessful efforts to decriminalize marijuana involved neither private members bills nor free votes in the House of Commons.

Chapter 7 provided evidence that both issues had gone through a phase of decline. Where they differed sharply was in the impact of arguments about the costliness of enforcing legal restrictions. Such arguments were of minor significance in the case of pornography, even taking account of the social costs of violence against women and children when used as the principal rationale for advocating revision of laws against child pornography. But costs of all kinds, from the financial ones related to enforcement to the social and political ones affecting young people and minorities, were prominent in making the case for decriminalizing marijuana. The contrasting use of arguments based on costs and their impact on resolution are quite different from what we would expect based on the case of prohibition, where cost promoted resolution.

Both issues entered the resurgent phase through reframing. Their reframing emphasized how the issues had become more acute, and did so without the help of movements legitimating the new positions. But this phase also reveals a paradox, in which the two issues with the greatest difference in outcomes were most alike as they went through resurgence.

The paradoxical finding about resurgence may have a bearing on the processes marijuana and pornography underwent in approaching or achieving resolution. In this final phase, marijuana stood apart from pornography solely with regard to the former's inability to achieve partisan agreement on how it should be resolved. Only now in Canada, under the Liberal government of Justin Trudeau, has there been willingness for that party to take a definitive stand. More generally, bipartisanship is a key to resolving moral conflicts in Canada. In the United States, only pornography has been able to achieve this degree of consensus, as it did in Canada, particularly once it was reframed into opposition to child pornography.

As this review of the contentious life history of marijuana and pornography has indicated, each phase through which an issue passes carries with it the potential for easing or impeding resolution. Those phases both operate independently of the national setting in which moral conflicts occur and interact with that setting. Nowhere are those interaction effects more prominent than in the relation between each nation's political institutions and the role played by political parties and authoritative actors. Those relations are the strongest predictors of the extent to which moral conflicts are resolved and then depart from the policy agenda. A less contentious partisan environment may be the key to less contentious moral conflicts.

If the path to the resolution of moral conflicts were straightforward and uncomplicated, this close examination of marijuana and pornography could have uncovered it. While it did contribute to our understanding, overall it confirmed that the phases through which moral issues go through produce a tortuous developmental history. The value of our accounting lies in the ways it has illuminated the multiple reasons for contentiousness that arise throughout each issue's history and for the consequent difficulty in achieving resolution. There are no simple solutions to ending moral conflicts.

REFERENCES

Hurka, Steffen, Christian Adam, and Christoph Knill. 2016. "Is Morality
    Policy Different? Testing Sectoral and Institutional Explanations of Policy
    Change." *Policy Studies Journal*, forthcoming (early view, https://doi.org/
    10.1111/psj.12153).
Martel, Marcel. 2014. *Canada the Good: A Short History of Vice since 1500*.
    Waterloo, ON: Wilfrid Laurier University Press.

Coding Media Coverage of Moral Conflicts

Canada

For the contemporary moral conflicts, the media citations for Canada were drawn from the *Canadian Periodical Index*, which included all the leading newspapers across Canada, but whose online access was limited to the most recent period of 1985–2010. For the earlier period 1950–84, we used the online access to the *Globe and Mail* (only). Whereas Soroka (2002: 133) coded the Canadian media agenda of his policy issues based only on the title of the article, the online version of the *CPI* as well as the *Globe and Mail* provides access to the entire document in all but a very few cases (e.g., roughly 99 percent of all the citations to the *CPI* during 1985–2010 offered full-text access to the articles), which allows for greater accuracy in coding each media citation for purposes of this analysis. This analysis of media coverage includes news stories, opinion pieces, and editorials but no letters to the editor. In terms of content, the article had to discuss the impact of the moral conflict on the domestic life of Canada, Canadian foreign relations (Canadian policy with respect to the United Nations), or Canadians who face extradition or deportation or who seek asylum in Canada because they face legal peril in another jurisdiction (e.g., facing the death penalty in the United States). All citations that focused on a particular moral conflict *in other countries* (e.g., the substantial coverage given to capital punishment in the United States) *were excluded* from this analysis since we are only concerned with the development of these moral conflicts within Canada.

For the search terms employed (see below), if they were highlighted in the title or subtitle of the article being cited in the *CPI* or the

Globe and Mail, that level of salience was sufficient to *include the article* in our universe of cases, without any further scrutiny of the article content. Here are some examples.

"Death Penalty for Child Killers," *Cambridge Times* (26 May 2009), *Canadian Periodical Index*.

"Death of Ottawa Policeman Rouses Basford to Call for Prompt Action on Gun Controls," *Globe and Mail* (13 July 1977), *Globe and Mail* Historical Newspapers ProQuest.

"Committee Backs Changes on Homosexuals," *Globe and Mail* (21 March 1969), *Globe and Mail* Historical Newspapers ProQuest.

"Jail for Marijuana Users on the Way Out," *Globe and Mail* (4 July 1972), *Globe and Mail* Historical Newspapers ProQuest.

"HIGH COURT BACKS A LEWD-BOOK BAN LIMITED TO YOUNG: New York Statute Upheld in First Pornography Ruling Covering Only Children; Adults' Ruling Stands; Decision Expected to Spur Other States to Approve Similar Restrictions; High Court Backs Pornography Ban," *New York Times* (23 April 1968), ProQuest Historical Newspapers: *New York Times* with Index.

But where the applicable search terms did not appear in the title or subtitles highlighted in the citation for an article in the *CPI* or the *Globe and Mail*, then the content of the article was scrutinized to determine whether "substantial" coverage was given to the issue in that particular article. By "substantial" we mean that the issue is given *some elaboration* in the article, not simply a quick reference, or its listing alongside various other issues, or a fleeting mention in an article devoted largely to other subject matters.

Prohibition. In Canada, for the historical case of Prohibition the precise phrase "National Prohibition" had relevance only for a brief two-year period at the close of the First World War. Therefore, we used the keyword "prohibition" to search the *Globe and Mail* (and its predecessor newspaper, *The Globe*, which merged with *The Mail and Empire* on 23 November 1936) for the entire period of 1880–1950. Of the total number (13,853) of citations retrieved, 5650 (or 41%) were included in our universe of cases to signify media coverage of the prohibition debate. However, a common term in Canadian news coverage during the late nineteenth century was Temperance, used with and without the term "prohibition" as such. There were voluminous newspaper references to Canadian temperance societies (Sons of Temperance; Women's

Christian Temperance Union; the Temperance Movement of Canada) as well as the fact that the Canada Temperance Act of 1864 (or the Dunkin Act) provided for "local option" prohibitory laws in Upper and Lower Canada and, after Confederation, the Scott Act (known also as the Canada Temperance Act of 1878) extended that local option regime through the Dominion of Canada. Another consideration is that pre-1900 digitalized copies of articles in *The Globe* too often were fragments of copy or other times opaque and difficult-to-read faded copies, so the prohibition issue is treated differently from the other contemporary issues discussed in this volume. That is, *any clue* from the title or article fragment that "prohibition" or Temperance was discussed (be it a meeting of temperance activists, or a temperance referendum, or a temperance law) is coded as media coverage of "prohibition" without any attempt to determine whether the coverage was a "substantial" component of the article or not.

Marijuana. The coding differentiates between "drug busts" (meaning police raids, arrests, seizures of grow operations, employment or professional suspensions for possession, judicial rulings, and also public awareness campaigns by the RCMP and other agencies). This "drug busts" category is defined in terms of law enforcement, whereas *all* other articles on marijuana are coded as "policy debate" since they often touched upon the public debate over the severity of punishments for minor drug offenses, arguments for decriminalization or legalization, or urging an exception for the medical use of marijuana, research on positive or negative effects of marijuana use, surveys of abuse and public attitudes, and parliamentary or provincial debates on such issues. The online search of the *CPI* for 1985–2010 using the keywords "marijuana" AND "Canada" yielded 3223 citations, of which 646 were excluded for lack of "substantial" coverage, leaving a universe of 1340 "policy debate" articles and 1238 "drug bust" articles. For the *Globe and Mail* over the period 1950–84, the search protocol included the term "marijuana" AND the filter NOT "United States" to exclude media coverage of marijuana in the United States. This search protocol resulted in 3190 citations in the *Globe and Mail*, of which 1411 (or 44%) were deemed to have "substantial" coverage of either "drug busts" (829 articles) or the "policy debate" (582 articles). Note: any article with "cannabis" (a more technical term for marijuana) in the title or subtitles was also automatically included in our data set without further scrutiny of the article content.

Pornography. The coding differentiated between "adult pornography" (where articles had no reference to "child pornography") and "child pornography" (where articles included coverage of that topic). The online search of the *CPI* for 1985–2010 using the keywords "pornography" AND "Canada" yielded 1229 citations, of which 298 were excluded, leaving a universe of 931 articles (76%), for which 232 had "substantial" coverage of "adult pornography" and 699 articles had "substantial" coverage of "child pornography." For the *Globe and Mail* during 1950–84, the search terms "pornography" AND the filter NOT "United States" yielded 967 citations for which 348 articles (or 36%) had "substantial" coverage. Of those, 318 articles had "substantial" coverage of adult pornography and 30 articles had "substantial" coverage of child pornography.

Capital punishment. The online search of the *CPI* for 1985–2010 using the keywords "capital punishment" OR "death penalty" AND "Canada" yielded 239 citations, of which 86 were excluded, leaving a universe of 153 cases (64%) with "substantial" coverage. For the *Globe and Mail* over the period 1950–84, the search protocol included the keywords "capital punishment" OR "death penalty" AND the filter NOT "United States" to exclude coverage of this issue in the United States. The search protocol yielded 2615 citations, but content scrutiny determined that only 780 articles (30%) had "substantial" coverage of capital punishment in Canada.

Gun control. The online search of the *CPI* for 1985–2010 using the key phrase "gun control" AND "Canada" yielded 1092 citations, of which 314 were excluded, leaving a universe of 778 cases (or 71%) for coding. For the *Globe and Mail* during the period 1950–84, the search protocol included the phrase "gun control" AND the filter NOT "United States" in an effort to exclude articles and editorials about gun control in the United States. That search protocol yielded 349 citations, but content scrutiny determined that only 155 articles (44%) had "substantial" coverage of the gun control issue in Canada.

Abortion. The online search of the *CPI* for 1985–2010 using the keywords "abortion" AND "Canada" yielded 3034 citations, of which 918 were excluded, leaving a universe of 2116 articles. For the *Globe and Mail*, the search protocol included the term "abortion" AND the filter NOT "United States" to eliminate articles or editorials about abortion in the United States. This protocol yielded 4336 citations for the period 1950–84, but their content scrutiny determined that only 1583 articles (37%) had "substantial" coverage on abortion and thus were included in this data set.

Homosexuality. Two separate online *CPI* searches for the period 1985–2010 were employed. The first used the search terms "homosexuals" OR "gay rights" AND "Canada" to yield 561 citations, of which 86 were excluded, leaving a universe of 475 articles (85%) with "substantial" coverage on homosexuals or gay rights. The second search used the key phrases "same-sex marriage" OR "gay marriage" AND "Canada" to yield 115 citations, of which 49 were excluded, leaving a universe of 66 articles (or 57%) with "substantial" coverage of the same-sex marriage issue in Canada. For the *Globe and Mail* during 1950–84, the search terms "homosexuals" OR "gay rights" AND the filter NOT "United States" yielded 1940 citations, but only 676 (or 35%) had "substantial" coverage of this issue in Canada. For the search using "same-sex marriage" OR "gay marriage" AND the filter NOT "United States" only seven articles were retrieved during the entire 1950–84 period.

United States

Since the historic online *New York Times* dates back to 1851, this one source will be used to track media coverage of all the moral conflicts in the United States. We limit all our searches to only "articles" and "editorials" and "front page/cover stories" for possible inclusion in our universe of cases.

Prohibition. Given that National Prohibition was enacted in 1920 and repealed in 1933, we need to include an extended period before and after that "Noble Experiment" but also a time period that parallels the Canadian experience, to allow for comparative analysis. Thus, we include all the years from 1880–1950. Because the debate in the United States was focused on enactment of "National Prohibition," unlike the situation in Canada, the precise search term "National Prohibition" was employed to access the historic online *New York Times* for each year during 1880–1950. It resulted in a total of 3519 citations, of which 2697 articles (or 77% of the total) were deemed to have "substantial" coverage of this issue.

Capital punishment. For all the other contemporary moral conflicts, the standard time period for tracking media coverage will be 1950–2010. Thus, the precise search phrase "capital punishment" yielded 6679 citations, of which 3253 articles (49%) were deemed to have "substantial" coverage of this issue and thus comprised the universe of cases for capital punishment. As previously stated, any article with "capital punishment" in its title or subtitles is automatically included in the database. But further note: since three other keywords are virtually synonymous with "capital punishment," any articles whose title or subtitles included "death penalty" or "death sentence" or "execution" were also automatically included in our data set.

Gun control. The precise search phrase "gun control" yielded 5548 citations, of which 2036 (or 37%) were deemed to have "substantive" coverage of the gun control issue.

Pornography. The search term "pornography" yielded 7973 citations, but each had to be scrutinized to determine whether the "substantive" coverage of the article focused on "adult pornography" or "child pornography" (to mean prohibiting access by children to pornographic materials and also the use of minors in pornographic materials). Only 2255 articles (28%) were deemed to have "substantial" coverage of either topic, with 1679 articles focused on "adult pornography" generally, while 576 made specific mention of "child pornography" in its content.

Media coverage of marijuana, gays, and abortion are an order of magnitude larger than any of the previous topics. The largest number of citations involved pornography (7973), but that number is dwarfed by the number of citations retrieved for marijuana, gays, and abortion, which totaled 62,672 citations. To hand-code all those citations would be a daunting task indeed. Thus, to make this coding task manageable, an abbreviated coding system was used instead of trying to scrutinize the content of every article identified. Here we follow the lead of Soroka (2002: 133), who explains: "All media time series are the product of title searches using the keywords listed below." Thus, we rely on the *title or subtitles* only that are highlighted in the citations by the *New York Times* index in order to code each article. In the universe of cases for these three issues, therefore, we only code the number of articles with "abortion" or "homosexuals"/"gay rights" or "marijuana" in their title or subtitles. Since this abbreviated coding strategy much reduces the frequency distribution, those three tables (3.1, 3.7, and 3.11) cannot be compared with the other tables in this series but can be compared among themselves. But more important for our analysis, the difference in frequency magnitudes over time would not necessarily skew the accuracy of the overall pattern of temporal change, especially the beginning and end points and any sharp fluctuations.

Abortion. The temporal pattern of coding "abortion" in the *New York Times* seems very plausible, and consistent with our overall theory, perhaps because of the specificity of that term and the absence of any other commonly used terminology to describe the termination of a pregnancy. During 1950–2010 the search term "abortion" yielded 28,955 citations, of which 4404 (or 15%) included that search term in the titles or subtitles of the articles.

Homosexuality. The specificity of abortion did not extend to the issue of homosexuals and gays. Here the problem is that no one common usage with respect to the gay community was standard from the 1950s through 2010. To attempt to capture the saliency of this issue, two key terms ("homosexuals" OR "gay rights") were employed for the entire period 1950–2010, which yielded 18,548 citations. Of that number, only 1221 (or 6.6%) had "homosexuals" or "gay rights" in the title or subtitles in the article. A further complication is that our perusal of articles during the 1950s showed, in fact, that "pervert" or especially "deviant" or "sexual deviant" were not infrequently used to describe homosexuals, so our restricting the search terms to "homosexuals" OR "gay rights" likely underestimates the salience (and negativity) of references to the gay subculture during those early years.

In contrast, a separate search was done using the phrases "same-sex marriage" or "gay marriage," with the result that 2700 citations were retrieved for the period 1950–2010 (but none before 1989). But of that number, only 343 (13%) had "same-sex marriage" OR "gay marriage" in the title or subtitles of the articles, though again the temporal pattern confirms the common understanding that this issue was last to surface on the systemic agenda since it culminated the decades-long struggle for gay rights. It was not until the mid-1990s, but especially during the first decade of the twenty-first century, that this issue gained saliency on the media agenda.

Marijuana. The search term "marijuana" retrieved 15,169 citations, but our scrutiny was limited to the 1496 articles with "marijuana" in the titles or subtitles of the articles (or 9.9% of the total). Of that number, 754 focused on "drug busts" over the period 1950–2010 and 742 focused on the "policy debate," though there was an obvious shift in emphasis from the earlier to the later period.

218   Appendix 1

Table A1 Media coverage of prohibition in Canada and the United States, 1880–1950

United States		Canada	
1880	3	1880	21
1881	4	1881	65
1882	5	1882	27
1883	2	1883	45
1884	20	1884	26
1885	5	1885	70
1886	7	1886	102
1887	11	1887	183
1888	29	1888	60
1889	5	1889	46
1890	7	1890	34
1891	10	1891	60
1892	13	1892	59
1893	7	1893	257
1894	3	1894	148
1895	7	1895	61
1896	9	1896	93
1897	1	1897	102
1898	1	1898	218
1899	1	1899	74
1900	5	1900	73
1901	0	1901	64
1902	1	1902	301
1903	1	1903	54
1904	2	1904	73
1905	1	1905	57
1906	1	1906	36
1907	0	1907	35
1908	6	1908	50
1909	3	1909	35
1910	0	1910	32
1911	3	1911	19
1912	4	1912	40
1913	5	1913	44
1914	22	1914	44
1915	16	1915	103
1916	22	1916	346
1917	43	1917	173
1918	43	1918	63
1919	125	1919	384
1920	73	1920	173
1921	57	1921	193
1922	79	1922	118
1923	149	1923	133
1924	65	1924	282
1925	68	1925	122
1926	183	1926	258

(Continued)

Table A1 Media coverage of prohibition in Canada and the United States, 1880–1950 (continued)

United States		Canada	
1927	85	1927	58
1928	81	1928	41
1929	137	1929	121
1930	322	1930	45
1931	209	1931	42
1932	371	1932	42
1933	253	1933	32
1934	24	1934	35
1935	18	1935	12
1936	12	1936	3
1937	3	1937	6
1938	5	1938	8
1939	9	1939	10
1940	4	1940	11
1941	1	1941	10
1942	10	1942	13
1943	4	1943	20
1944	8	1944	14
1945	0	1945	7
1946	1	1946	15
1947	2	1947	15
1948	6	1948	18
1949	1	1949	10
1950	4	1950	6

Source: *New York Times*, *Globe and Mail*.

Table A2 Media coverage of Canadian moral conflicts, 1950–2010, in *Globe and Mail* (1950–84) and *Canadian Periodical Index* (1985–2010)

Year	Abortion Total N	Gun control Total N	Capital punishment Total N	Marijuana Total N	Marijuana Busts	Marijuana Policy	Pornography Total N	Pornography Adult Porn	Pornography Child Porn	Homosexuality Total N	Homosexuality Gays	Homosexuality Marriage
1950	3	0	3	0	0	0	3	3	0	0	0	0
1951	8	0	2	2	2	0	0	0	0	0	0	0
1952	10	0	7	4	4	0	4	4	0	0	0	0
1953	7	0	13	1	1	0	0	0	0	0	0	0
1954	1	0	31	3	3	0	0	0	0	0	0	0
1955	6	0	11	1	1	0	1	1	0	1	1	0
1956	4	0	23	0	0	0	2	2	0	1	1	0
1957	7	0	4	2	2	0	1	1	0	0	0	0
1958	3	0	8	1	1	0	1	1	0	0	0	0
1959	8	0	8	9	9	0	2	2	0	0	0	0
1960	8	0	47	7	7	0	1	1	0	0	0	0
1961	28	0	28	10	10	0	4	4	0	2	2	0
1962	33	0	15	5	5	0	2	2	0	7	7	0
1963	22	0	6	11	9	2	2	2	0	4	4	0
1964	44	0	15	5	4	1	7	7	0	3	3	0
1965	23	0	48	24	23	1	9	9	0	4	4	0
1966	56	0	66	49	43	6	4	4	0	3	3	0
1967	85	0	31	83	63	21	5	5	0	18	18	0
1968	78	4	4	102	62	39	5	5	0	8	8	0
1969	52	2	13	128	63	66	5	5	0	18	18	0
1970	81	1	9	129	48	81	4	4	0	7	7	0
1971	91	0	13	92	31	61	4	4	0	9	8	1
1972	70	0	29	86	37	49	4	4	0	13	12	1
1973	65	2	68	71	51	20	6	6	0	6	6	0
1974	107	3	8	61	38	23	5	5	0	18	14	4
1975	133	42	72	50	24	26	6	6	0	31	30	1
1976	104	52	94	41	29	12	16	16	0	33	33	0
1977	37	17	6	72	44	28	24	21	3	64	64	0

Year												
1978	47	10	26	60	34	26	21	17	4	46	46	0
1979	41	12	5	58	31	27	18	18	0	123	123	0
1980	37	2	6	82	55	27	17	15	2	58	58	0
1981	36	4	3	52	34	18	16	13	3	115	115	0
1982	28	2	6	34	12	22	22	15	7	39	39	0
1983	135	1	7	25	15	10	37	34	3	23	23	0
1984	85	1	45	51	35	16	90	82	8	30	30	0
1985	198	1	16	86	17	69	38	36	2	15	15	0
1986	104	3	5	13	5	8	24	23	1	20	20	0
1987	97	1	54	30	22	8	25	24	1	24	24	0
1988	262	0	3	29	23	6	7	7	0	45	45	0
1989	274	6	1	22	17	5	5	5	0	14	14	0
1990	116	11	0	25	20	5	5	5	0	18	18	0
1991	42	28	5	21	15	6	10	9	1	19	19	0
1992	68	19	0	16	13	3	21	20	1	51	51	1
1993	45	10	1	25	8	17	28	10	18	36	35	0
1994	40	45	2	12	5	7	29	4	19	31	31	1
1995	71	96	7	20	10	10	20	6	16	22	21	0
1996	30	19	1	19	10	9	17	1	11	25	25	0
1997	2	0	2	4	0	4	1	1	0	2	2	0
1998	5	1	0	5	2	3	1	4	0	11	11	0
1999	2	1	0	3	0	3	10	2	6	3	3	0
2000	14	4	1	6	0	6	5	4	3	5	4	1
2001	4	0	2	16	0	16	13	0	9	3	3	0
2002	7	4	2	48	3	45	11	0	11	9	5	4
2003	5	3	0	41	3	38	4	1	4	17	7	0
2004	7	6	0	20	8	12	11	1	10	12	6	6
2005	10	5	0	29	7	22	20	0	19	26	12	14
2006	16	29	0	43	9	34	51	0	51	11	5	6
2007	24	26	11	105	51	54	78	12	66	23	16	7
2008	184	62	15	309	209	100	152	12	140	30	26	4
2009	41	83	9	328	186	142	207	18	189	14	10	4
2010	187	157	8	311	197	114	138	17	121	10	10	0

Table A3 New York Times coverage of US moral conflicts, 1950–2010

Year	Capital punishment Total N	Gun control Total N	Pornography			Abortion Total N	Marijuana			Homosexuality		
			Total N	Adult porn	Child porn		Total N	Busts	Debate	Total N	Gays	Marriage
1950	0	0	1	1	0	3	4	4	0	0	0	0
1951	5	0	0	0	0	4	38	36	2	0	0	0
1952	4	0	4	4	0	4	10	9	1	0	0	0
1953	5	0	3	3	0	2	7	7	0	0	0	0
1954	1	0	2	2	0	5	2	2	0	0	0	0
1955	4	0	8	8	0	9	4	4	0	0	0	0
1956	2	0	12	12	0	10	3	3	0	0	0	0
1957	7	0	9	9	0	2	1	1	0	0	0	0
1958	9	0	16	16	0	3	1	1	0	0	0	0
1959	22	0	38	38	0	4	4	4	0	1	1	0
1960	40	0	44	44	0	8	4	4	0	1	1	0
1961	18	0	26	26	0	1	4	4	0	1	1	0
1962	11	0	13	13	0	28	0	0	0	2	2	0
1963	10	0	29	26	3	5	7	7	0	4	4	0
1964	15	2	27	27	0	6	15	15	0	4	4	0
1965	51	6	28	27	1	19	9	9	0	2	2	0
1966	15	14	38	37	1	23	39	35	4	12	12	0
1967	24	43	36	36	0	86	71	45	26	19	19	0
1968	30	158	24	20	4	42	56	35	21	5	5	0
1969	22	44	59	59	0	67	68	31	37	5	5	0
1970	20	19	87	85	2	156	78	31	47	15	15	0
1971	30	21	64	64	0	91	62	20	42	21	21	0
1972	83	35	70	70	0	125	61	20	41	27	27	0
1973	78	18	109	108	1	112	72	40	32	39	39	0
1974	43	13	50	49	1	105	58	27	31	80	80	0
1975	44	68	42	41	1	88	45	21	24	34	34	0
1976	137	36	55	55	0	101	49	25	24	22	22	0
1977	129	10	162	139	23	129	78	33	45	67	67	0

Year												
1978	89	8	45	39	6	113	68	34	34	65	65	0
1979	86	8	35	31	4	106	43	21	22	56	56	0
1980	54	60	26	13	13	103	47	25	22	42	42	0
1981	60	59	29	20	9	100	26	21	5	19	19	0
1982	66	35	24	13	11	60	29	17	12	21	21	0
1983	123	14	19	16	3	40	16	9	7	33	33	0
1984	141	13	64	39	25	80	13	11	2	60	60	0
1985	96	19	38	36	2	108	19	17	2	44	44	0
1986	116	32	61	55	6	66	14	9	5	51	51	0
1987	90	22	19	16	3	57	14	5	9	39	39	0
1988	78	50	26	18	8	100	13	12	1	25	25	0
1989	101	53	29	26	3	256	9	6	3	27	26	1
1990	119	48	71	54	17	205	8	2	6	23	23	0
1991	97	76	21	17	4	162	13	5	8	30	29	1
1992	107	46	33	17	16	187	10	3	7	51	51	0
1993	101	95	35	17	18	150	7	2	5	72	71	1
1994	54	82	26	18	8	147	7	3	4	27	27	0
1995	83	44	56	21	35	118	9	4	5	31	29	2
1996	53	40	34	12	22	126	17	5	12	40	22	18
1997	51	52	38	11	27	101	29	4	25	15	14	1
1998	83	37	56	20	36	126	32	13	19	25	23	2
1999	64	186	32	14	18	92	17	8	9	19	14	5
2000	73	156	26	11	15	113	27	7	20	13	7	6
2001	68	34	31	13	18	52	19	6	13	5	5	0
2002	60	44	57	14	43	42	22	6	16	10	7	3
2003	63	28	44	15	29	50	16	2	14	20	6	14
2004	40	34	32	16	16	43	10	4	6	94	9	85
2005	43	21	32	17	15	62	13	4	9	35	12	23
2006	19	14	56	10	46	56	7	2	5	47	5	42
2007	57	47	42	17	25	47	9	1	8	23	8	15
2008	24	25	28	6	22	19	9	3	6	33	8	29
2009	18	35	17	7	10	52	19	5	14	76	8	68
2010	17	32	17	11	6	27	35	5	30	33	6	27

Morality Policy Planks in Major Party Platforms, Canada and the United States

Table A1 Canada: PC/Conservatives (PC/C), Liberals (Lib), New Democratic Party (NDP), Reform (Ref), and Canada Alliance (CA)

Election	Abortion	Capital punishment	Drugs	Gun control	Homosexuality	Pornography
1952						
1957						
1958						
1962		PC/C	PC/C			
1963		PC/C	PC/C			PC/C
1965						
1968						
1972	PC/C, NDP					
1974	PC/C					
1979	Lib	Lib	Lib	Lib		Lib[1]
1980						
1984	NDP		PC/C			PC/C, NDP
1988	NDP		Lib			
1993				PC/C, Lib	Lib, NDP	Lib
1997				PC/C, Ref	NDP	Ref[1]
2000	NDP		Lib, CA	PC/C, Lib, CA	NDP, CA	PC/C[1], CA[1]
2004	NDP		PC/C, Lib, NDP	PC/C, Lib, NDP	PC/C, NDP	PC/C[1], Lib[1]
2006			PC/C, Lib, NDP	PC/C, Lib, NDP	PC/C, Lib	PC/C[1], Lib[1]
2008	PC/C[1], Lib[1], NDP		PC/C	PC/C, Lib	NDP	NDP[1]
2011	NDP		PC/C	PC/C, Lib	NDP	PC/C[1]
2015	NDP		PC/C[1], Lib[1], NDP[1]	PC/C, Lib[1]	NDP	

Source: The Textual Data for Policy Analysis Project, under Coordinator François Pétry at Laval University, archives Canadian party manifestos 1949–2015. At http://www.poltext.org/en/part-1-electronic-political-texts/electronic-manifestos-canada.

A[1]: PC/C and Lib will not reopen the debate on abortion.

D[1]: Lib and NDP favor legalization of marijuana; PC/C opposed to legalization of marijuana.

G[1]: Liberals will not reinstitute the long-gun registry, which was abolished.

P[1]: focus only on child pornography; earlier anti-pornography planks did not mention child pornography except the 1979 Liberal plank, which also banned the use of children.

Table A2 United States: Republicans (Rep) and Democrats (Dem)

Election	Abortion	Capital punishment	Drugs	Gun control	Homosexuality	Pornography
1952						
1956						
1960						
1964						
1968		Dem	Rep[1], Dem	Rep[1] Dem[1]		
1972	Rep, Dem	Rep	Rep[1&2], Dem	Rep[1] Dem[1]		
1976	Rep[1] Dem[1]	Rep	Rep, Dem	Rep[1] Dem[1]		Rep
1980	Rep[1] Dem[1]	Rep	Rep, Dem	Rep[1] Dem[1]		
1984	Rep[1] Dem[1]	Rep	Rep[1], Dem[1]	Rep[1] Dem[1]	Dem[1]	Rep
1988	Rep[1] Dem[1]	Rep	Rep[2], Dem[2]	Rep[1] Dem[1]	Dem[1]	Rep
1992	Rep[1] Dem[1]	Rep	Rep[2], Dem	Rep[1] Dem[1]	Rep[2], Dem[1]	Rep
1996	Rep[1] Dem[1]	Rep, Dem	Rep[1&2], Dem	Rep[1] Dem[1]	Rep[2], Dem[1]	Rep[1], Dem[2]
2000	Rep[1] Dem[1]	Rep, Dem	Rep[1], Dem	Rep[1] Dem[1]	Rep[2], Dem[1]	Rep[1], Dem[2]
2004	Rep[1] Dem[1]	Rep	Rep, Dem	Rep[1] Dem[1]	Rep[2], Dem[1]	Rep[1]
2008	Rep[1] Dem[1]	Rep, Dem	Rep, Dem	Rep[1] Dem[1]	Rep[2], Dem[3]	Rep[1], Dem[2]
2012	Rep[1] Dem[1]	Rep, Dem	Rep, Dem	Rep[1] Dem[1]	Rep[2], Dem[3]	Rep[1]

Source: The American Presidency Project at University of California, Santa Barbara, archives US party platforms 1840–2012. At http://www.presidency.ucsb.edu/platforms.php.

A[1]: Republicans had pro-life planks, while Democrats had pro-choice planks.

D[1]: Also includes specific mention of "marijuana."

D[2]: Opposition to legalization or decriminalization of any illegal drug.

G[1]: Republicans usually emphasized gun rights (sometimes with support for modest gun controls), while Democrats favored specific gun controls (sometimes with a nod to gun rights).

P[1]: Exclusive or primary focus on shielding child access to pornography or child pornography.

P[2]: No explicit mention of pornography, but favors shielding children from media "violence" and parental use of V-chip.

H[1]: Includes "sexual orientation" in non-discrimination or non-prejudice plank.

H[2]: Opposition to same-sex marriage or defense of "traditional" marriage.

H[3]: Endorses same-sex marriage.

Index